# RESOLVED

## 13 Resolutions for LIFE

# ORRIN WOODWARD

### FOREWORD BY CHRIS BRADY

# RESOLVED

### 13 Resolutions for LIFE

## ORRIN WOODWARD

Second Edition, April 2012

Published by:
Obstaclés Press Inc.
4072 Market Place Dr.
Flint, MI 48507

*http://www.orrinwoodward.com*

*Cover design and layout by*
*Norm Williams - http://www.nwa-inc.com*

Printed in the United States of America

To those who RESOLVE to change the world
through changing themselves.

*The ancients who wished to manifest their clear character
to the world would first bring order to their states.*

*Those who wished to bring order to their states
would first regulate their families.*

*Those who wished to regulate their families
would first cultivate their personal lives.*

*Those who wished to cultivate their personal
lives would first rectify their minds.*

*Those who wished to rectify their minds
would first make their wills sincere.*

*Those who wished to make their wills sincere
would first extend their knowledge.*

*The extension of knowledge consists in the investigation of things.*

*When things are investigated, knowledge is extended.*

*When knowledge is extended, the will becomes sincere.*

*When the will is sincere, the mind is rectified.*

*When the mind is rectified, the personal life is cultivated.*

*When the personal life is cultivated, the family will be regulated.*

*When the family is regulated, the state will be in order.*

*When the state is in order, there will be
peace throughout the world.*

*From the Son of Heaven down to the common people,
all must regard cultivation of the personal
life as the root or foundation.*

*There is never a case when the root is in disorder
and yet the branches are in order.*

Confucius - The Great Learning

# Acknowledgements

Winston Churchill once said, "Writing a book is an adventure. To begin with, it is a toy and an amusement; then it becomes a mistress, and then it becomes a master, and then a tyrant. The last phase is that just as you are about to be reconciled to your servitude, you kill the monster and fling him out to the public." Although I thoroughly enjoyed the writing process, I can relate to Churchill's comments. Thankfully, I am now ready to fling this "toy to monster" book out to the public.

Writing a book is never a solo project. I am deeply indebted to many people whose expertise, wisdom, and encouragement kept me going long after the emotion of the moment was gone. My wife's and children's (Jordan, Christina, Lance, and Jeremy) encouragements and sacrifices made this book possible, and for that, I am forever thankful. On numerous occasions, in the middle of family time, ideas that would help improve this book would occur to me. Only a wife with the patience of Job could have patiently handled her husband's increasing obsession. Laurie Woodward is this kind of wife, and she is an immeasurable blessing in my life.

Furthermore, Chris Brady's belief in the concepts in this book helped me endure the setbacks and revisions in order to produce the book in its current form. All people need a balcony person like Chris in their lives to help them perform at their best. Additionally, much thanks goes to the Militellos (Kristine and Marc) for their endless hours of reading, editing, and thoughtful comments. Kristine's background as an English teacher was taxed to the limit by long-sufferingly editing the math-rich and English-poor writings of a former engineer.

Last, but not least, I would like to thank the Team office and LIFE field leaders for providing real-life examples of leadership on the front lines. It is their example of servant-based leadership that inspired me to write this book in the first place. The entire staff of Obstaclés Press Inc., particularly Bill Rousseau, Wendy Branson, Norm Williams, and Rob Hallstrand, worked around the clock to bring this book to fruition. I could not have asked for a better team to work with.

Finally, none of this would have been possible were it not for the saving grace of my precious Lord and Savior Jesus Christ. His patience in bringing a prodigal son back to Him surpasses all levels of comprehension. To Him be all the honor, glory, and praise.

# Table of Contents

Foreword ............................................................... 11
Introduction ...................................................... 13

## Private Achievements

Chapter 1    Purpose
Resolved: To Discover My God-Given Purpose .... 29
John Wooden .......................................... 43

Chapter 2    Character
Resolved: To Choose Character over Reputation
Any Time They Conflict ......................................... 49
Ludwig von Mises: Indomitable Character .......... 63

Chapter 3    Attitude
Resolved: To Have a Positive Attitude
in Al Situations ...................................................... 71
Roger Bannister: Attitude and the Quest for the
Four-Minute Mile .................................................. 84

Chapter 4    Vision
Resolved: To Align My Conscious (Ant)
with My Subconscious (Elephant) Mind
toward My Vision ................................................... 91
Will Smith ........................................................... 104

## Public Achievements

Chapter 5    Plan and Do
Resolved: To Develop and Implement a Game
Plan in Each Area of My Life .............................. 111
Lou Holtz: Planning and Doing ........................... 125

Chapter 6    Scoreboard
Resolved: To Keep Score in the Game of Life ..... 131
Sam Walton: Tracking the Scoreboard .............. 145

Chapter 7    Friendship
             Resolved: To Develop the Art and
             Science of Friendship ............................. 153
             C. S. Lewis and J. R. R. Tolkien: Friendship ...... 166

Chapter 8    Finance
             Resolved: To Develop Financial Intelligence ...... 173
             Ben Franklin: Financial Management -
             Money and Time .................................. 185

## Leadership Achievements

Chapter 9    Leadership
             Resolved: To Develop the Art and Science
             of Leadership ........................................ 193
             Sam Walton: Leadership Excellence .................. 207

Chapter 10   Conflict Resolution
             Resolved: To Develop the Art and Science of
             Conflict Resolution ............................... 215
             Lewis and Tolkien: Lost Friends ........................ 228

Chapter 11   Systems
             Resolved: To Develop Systems Thinking............. 235
             Ray Kroc and McDonald's .................................. 249

Chapter 12   Adversity Quotient (AQ)
             Resolved: To Develop Adversity Quotient ........... 257
             Billy Durant: Adversity Quotient ....................... 269

Chapter 13   Legacy
             Resolved: To Reverse the Current of Decline
             in My Field of Mastery ....................................... 277
             Colonial New England Fiat Money ..................... 290

Appendix A   George Washington's Rules of Civility and Decent
             Behavior in Company and Conversation ........... 297

Appendix B   George Washington's Partial List of Maxims ..... 305

Appendix C   Ben Franklin's Thirteen Virtues ......................... 309

Appendix D   Jonathan Edwards's Seventy Resolutions .......... 311

Bibliography ......................................................... 319

# Foreword

It has been said that everyone wants to change the world, but only a few feel the need to change themselves. Even just a basic study of history, however, would show that those who first focus on self-improvement usually end up doing the most good in the world. Why should this be so? Perhaps it stems from the fact that excellence doesn't occur by accident, but rather, from intentional effort correctly applied over time. Subsequently, a person's example of excellence increases his ability to influence others. The much-touted "ripple effect" then takes hold, and change resonates outward in ever-widening circles from the genesis of a lone individual who cares to change his or her own life first.

I have been in a unique position to observe for nearly two decades a real-life example of the above-mentioned type of person. At age eighteen, I struck up an acquaintance with a young man roughly my age as we were entering an engineering co-op program together with a handful of other equally bright but naïve students. Orrin Woodward came from humble origins, having a sometimes-stressful home life, extremely tight finances, and no connections whatsoever. With nothing but hope and ambition, he worked his way through college until he landed in an engineering position, where he thrived and was quickly recognized as a dedicated worker and a creative problem solver. He soon won several accolades and promotions, including four U.S. patents and a national benchmarking award. Then he decided to try his hand at being an entrepreneur, and our paths once again crossed. I had heard of his corporate success and had seen his achievements from a distance, and when he chose to invite me into his business endeavors, I at once got a front-row seat to witness what would become a true Horatio Alger story.

Orrin Woodward began his business journey by immediately working on himself. A voracious reader, he devoured books on people skills, sales techniques, relationship building, success, leadership, and attitude. Over time, his self-directed education went deeper, from the surface-level genres of skills to the heart-level categories of principles. He also broadened his education, taking economics, history, theology, literature, philosophy, and even art. As he applied his aggressive learning to his entrepreneurial activities, his business began to thrive. Today, Orrin Woodward is widely recognized as a top leader in several business categories and is a sought-after expert on leadership—having recently been named one of the World's Top 10 Leadership Gurus. Today, his success (which, in addition to his professional achievements, includes a healthy and productive family life, a marriage of twenty years, a worshipful faith, and a worldwide network of friends and supporters) and lifestyle are diametrically opposite to his beginnings. A larger contrast between origins and accomplishments would be hard to imagine.

The kind of success obtained by Orrin Woodward is admirable and desirable—worthy of study and emulation. It is for this reason that I have been encouraging him to endure the hardships and hard work of crafting this book. Although we collaborated on a number of books before—and Orrin already enjoys best seller status—this project is different. It is his answer to the question: "How did you do it?" It is, therefore, extremely personal (although he doesn't wish it to be about himself) and laborious. It is full of historical research and illuminating examples, which required much study and fact checking. And, quite frankly, with the depth of its content and the width of its application, it is stunning. Anyone who reads this book will be immediately struck by the scholarship of its author. It is so much more than a well-researched tome, however; it is a road map. In a world full of formulas for success and quick fixes, *RESOLVED: 13 Resolutions for Life* goes all the way to the core. It reaches into the heart, stimulates the mind, and motivates the will.

In my book *Rascal: Making a Difference by Becoming an Original Character*, I attempted to depict the type of person who musters the courage to go against the grain and boldly pursue a God-given direction, regardless of who follows or fights against such a move. If, indeed, that book succeeded in showing how to step out of the crowd, this book shows what to do after having done so. Through thirteen profound resolutions, readily applicable to daily life, Orrin Woodward gives us a window on the reasons undergirding his monumental success and a very specific ladder of success for us to climb for our own success. More importantly, he shows us how we can maximize our potentials and, yes, perhaps even change the world by first working to become the best that we can be. In these pages, it becomes clear that success is no accident and significance is ever more the result of strenuous intentionality. I believe the overall effect of this book on the reader will be a life transformed, and that, I surmise, would be Orrin's greatest wish.

Chris Brady
Apex, North Carolina
September 2011

# Introduction

In the early eighteenth century, three young Colonial Americans resolved to build lives of virtue by studying and applying daily resolutions. Each of them made his life count, creating a legacy of selfless thoughts, words, and deeds. The first, through tireless sacrificial leadership and against indescribable odds, defeated the mighty British Empire with his ragtag group of colonial volunteers. The second—through his growing international fame, sterling character, and endless tact—became America's leading diplomat, forming international alliances that secured war funding, without which, the colonials' cause would have been doomed. The third, through his overwhelming intellectual and spiritual gifts, became Colonial America's greatest minister, who, by preaching and writing, fanned the flames of the Great Awakening—a spiritual renewal in Colonial America—which further led to political and economic freedoms after the American Revolution. These men—George Washington, Benjamin Franklin, and Jonathan Edwards—transformed themselves by diligently studying and applying their resolutions, thus creating an enduring legacy, not just through what they did, but more importantly, through who they were. George Washington transformed into a man of character whose love of principles surpassed his love of power; Ben Franklin transformed into a man of tact whose desire for influence surpassed his need for recognition; and Jonathan Edwards transformed into a spiritual giant whose humility surpassed his need for human advancement. All three developed wisdom by overcoming "self." By developing, studying, and consistently applying their resolutions, these men changed not only themselves but also the world.

If three of the greatest Americans utilized resolutions to develop wisdom and virtue, why isn't this practice taught in every family, school, and church around the world? Stephen Covey suggests an answer: "As my study took me back through 200 years of writing about success, I noticed a startling pattern emerging in the content of literature. . . . I began to feel more and more that much of the success literature of the past 50 years was superficial. It was filled with social image consciousness, techniques and quick fixes—with social band-aids and aspirin that addressed acute problems and sometimes appeared to solve them temporarily, but left the underlying chronic problems untouched to fester and resurface time and again." Society, it seems, values image over integrity, commercialism over character, and fame over foundations—and what a high price has been paid for these errors. In his book *The Revolt of the Masses*, José Ortega y Gasset describes this dichotomy: "The most radical division that is possible to make of humanity is that which splits it into two classes of creatures: those who make great demands on themselves, piling up difficulties and duties; and those who demand nothing special of themselves, but for whom to live is to be every moment what they already are, without imposing upon themselves any effort towards perfection—mere buoys that float on the waves."

Washington, Franklin, and Edwards achieved lasting greatness not by floating as buoys but by swimming against the current. Resolved to be different, they nurtured themselves on principles, not on personalities, seeking the true greatness of character, not the false friendship of fame. Author Jim Black wrote, "For most of our history, Americans placed greater stock in a man's character than in his possessions. The American Dream held that, by hard work and self-discipline, we could achieve success. And success was not measured in material possessions alone. . . . The common wisdom of the day taught that greed, luxury, and self-indulgence were the passions of weak character. And the frugal nature of the pioneers taught that the treasures to be valued most were the virtues of honesty, good character, and moral strength." Covey similarly describes America's founding success literature: "The first 150 years or so focused on what could be called the Character Ethic as the foundation of success—things like integrity, humility, fidelity, temperance, courage, justice, patience, industry, simplicity, modesty, and the Golden Rule." Without character, in other words, one can never be truly successful because the foundation of all long-term successes isn't what a person owns but who he is. Regretfully, society seems to have forgotten this commonsense principle, probably because common sense isn't so common today.

## A Natural Nobility

Life's enduring principles have fallen victim to today's microwave-age thinking. Everyone wants success, but most settle for planting "personality ethic" tomatoes when true success requires nurturing "character ethic" oak trees in the field of achievement. It's time to get out of the tomato patch and return to the foundation forest of character development, the forest that fed mighty oaks like Washington, Franklin, and Edwards. True character-based leadership requires endless hours of self-examination, which is a process of comparing one's actions to stated resolutions and making needed changes in order to grow in character. People who take shortcuts in character development only end up shortening themselves. Economist William Roepke describes this process:

> Only a few from every stratum of society can ascend into this thin layer of natural nobility. The way to it is an exemplary and slowly maturing life of dedicated endeavor on behalf of all, unimpeachable integrity, constant restraint of our common greed, proved soundness of judgment, a spotless private life, indomitable courage in standing up for truth and law, and generally the highest example. This is how the few, carried upward by the trust of the people, gradually attain to a position above the classes, interests, passions, wickedness, and foolishness of men and finally become the nation's conscience. To belong to this group of moral aristocrats should be the highest and most desirable aim, next to which all the other triumphs of life are pale and insipid . . . The continued existence of our free world will ultimately depend on whether our age can produce a sufficient number of such aristocrats of public spirit.

The best way to become a moral aristocrat is to build trust in others by building trust in oneself. Following one's own deeply held principles by using resolutions, therefore, is the path to building both personal and public trusts. Simply put, any person who cannot trust himself to follow his convictions shouldn't be shocked when others refuse to trust his convictions as well. This isn't the work of a day, a week, a month or even a year. Trust is literally built over a lifetime since character is molded through a person's consistent study and application of his principles (resolutions) in his life. Sadly, if one had to ask a thousand randomly selected people, he probably wouldn't find anyone who has developed, written, studied, and applied specific resolutions in his life.

In the Western world, character development through written resolutions is a lost art; along with this loss is the subsequent loss of significance, meaning, and morality. The West is fatally wounded, having suicidally stabbed itself in the heart.

## Resolved—Definitions

Resolutions are written resolves that are studied daily to help guide a person's behavior while he is forming his fundamental character. Dictionary.com has several definitions of the term *resolve*, some of which are relevant when discussing life resolutions:

1. to come to a definite or earnest decision about; determine (to do something): I have resolved that I shall live to the full.
2. to deal with (a question, a matter of uncertainty, etc.) conclusively; settle; solve: to resolve the question before the board.
3. music to cause (a voice part or the harmony as a whole) to progress from a dissonance to a consonance.

It is the intention of this book that when a person learns to apply resolutions in his life, he will see all three of these definitions fulfilled. Written resolutions should encompass the whole person; they are a plan that is devised to develop his character and thinking, from who he is to whom he desires to be. When a person writes and studies his resolutions, he resolves to live internally what he proclaims externally. He cannot influence others until he has influenced himself. As Mahatma Gandhi said, "Be the change you want to see in the world." By beginning with himself, forging the resolutions into his being, a person becomes a living model of his principles and a change agent for others by successfully changing himself.

## George Washington—Resolved to Develop Character

When he was young, Washington had a fiery temper, but he developed an iron-willed discipline in order to check its excesses. Richard Norton Smith, in his book *Patriarch*, said, "The adolescent Washington examined Seneca's dialogues and laboriously copied from a London magazine one hundred and ten 'rules of civility' intended to buff a rude country boy into at least the first draft of a gentleman." The French Jesuits had developed these 110 rules as principles to live by, and Washington's methodical writing process helped him adopt many of these maxims as his resolutions in life. As Richard Brookhiser, author of *Founding Father*, wrote, "His manner and his morals kept his temperament under control. His commitment to ideas gave him guidance. Washington's relation to ideas has been underestimated by almost everyone who wrote of him or knew him, and modern education has encouraged this neglect. . . . His attention to courtesy and correct behavior anticipated his political philosophy. He was influenced by Roman notions of nobility, but he was even more deeply influenced by a list of table manners and rules for conversation by Jesuits." Character and self-mastery were his goals, which he endeavored to reach by living his guiding ideals of fortitude, justice, moderation, and dignity inherent in every human being.

For Washington, life became a series of resolutions to live by. He wrote and studied many maxims throughout his life. Here are two examples (see appendix for more):

1.  With me it has always been a maxim rather to let my designs appear from my works rather than by my expressions.
2.  Happiness and moral duty are inseparably connected.

Washington developed and studied his maxims repeatedly, becoming convinced of the correctness of the maxims, teaching virtue over happiness and duty over rights and resolving to live based on the principles implied in them. In the book *George Washington's Character*, Katherine Kersten asked:

> What would Washington have accomplished if happiness, rather than integrity and service, had been his life-goal? Instead of suffering with his men through the snows of Valley Forge, he might have followed the example of Benedict Arnold, another Revolutionary War general. Though brave and talented, Arnold valued his own well-being and prosperity above all else. Out of self-interest, he plotted to betray West Point to the British, and died a traitor to his nation. What can we learn from Washington and his contemporaries about character-building? They teach us, most importantly, that "the soul can be schooled." Exercising reason and will, we can mold ourselves into beings far nobler than nature made us.

The end of the quotation summarizes character-based training beautifully: "the soul can be schooled." Washington attended this class daily as he went on his way developing the nobility of character that he needed in order to unite the American colonies. General Henry Knox spoke truthfully when he shared that it was the strength of Washington's character—not the laws of the new Constitution—that held the young republic together. In a tribute to his friend, Congressman Henry "Light-Horse Harry" Lee eulogized Washington: "First in war, first in peace, and first in the hearts of his countrymen, he was second to none in humble and enduring scenes of private life. Pious, just, humane, temperate, and sincere; uniform, dignified, and commanding; his example was as edifying to all around him as were the effects of that example lasting....Correct throughout, vice shuddered in his presence and virtue always felt his fostering hand. The purity of his private character gave effulgence to his public virtues....Such was the man for whom our nation mourns."

Lee's tribute testifies to Washington's faithful application of his resolutions in his life, living his maxims both privately and publicly.

## Ben Franklin—Resolved to Develop Wisdom

When he was young, Ben Franklin didn't always behave in a sensible manner. In fact, he offended many leading citizens of Philadelphia with his self-assumed air of importance. In the book *Launching a Leadership Revolution*, Chris Brady and I share a story about young Franklin: "A confidant took him aside one day and was both bold and kind enough to share the truth with Franklin that people didn't like him. Although amazingly brilliant, nobody cared. They couldn't stand to be around him. He was too argumentative and opinionated. His informer even told him that people would see Franklin approaching on the street and cross the road so as to avoid any contact with him. Franklin was devastated. But his reaction to the cold, hard truth was perhaps one of the most important components of his meteoric success." At twenty years of age, Franklin chose to move in a new direction, launching a self-improvement project he called "moral perfection." He started with four resolutions: "He resolved to become more frugal so that he could save enough money to repay what he owed to others. He decided that he would be very honest and sincere 'in every word and action.' He promised himself to be industrious 'to whatever business [he took] in hand.' Lastly he vowed 'to speak ill of no man whatever, not even in a manner of truth' and to 'speak all the good I know of everybody.'" From these four resolutions, he created his world-renowned list of thirteen virtues (see appendix for complete list) and developed a plan to study one virtue every week during the fifty-two weeks of the year. Here are two of his virtues:

2. *Silence.* Speak not but what may benefit others or yourself; avoid trifling conversation.
8. *Justice.* Wrong none by doing injuries, or omitting the benefits that are your duty.

Franklin's methodical approach to character and wisdom development allowed for each virtue to be studied four weeks every year, and he evaluated his performance weekly against the standard of moral perfection. In Franklin's autobiography, he discusses his plan to check his performance by comparing it to the aspired virtues: "I made a little book, in which I allotted a page for each of the virtues . . . I might mark, by a little black spot, every fault I found upon examination to have been committed respecting that virtue upon that day." After some time, Franklin's personal improvement plan helped him become one of the most respected citizens of Philadelphia, routinely requested to serve various volunteer organizations. In *Time* magazine, Walter Isaacson explains Franklin's belief that increased personal virtue leads to increased public responsibilities as follows:

> That led him to make the link between private virtue and civic virtue and to suspect, based on the meager evidence he could muster about God's will, that these earthly virtues were linked to heavenly ones as well. As he put it in the motto for the library he founded, "To pour forth benefits for the common good is divine." It is useful for us to engage anew with Franklin, for in doing so we are grappling with a fundamental issue: How does one live a life that is useful, virtuous, worthy, moral, and spiritually meaningful?

By studying a different virtue every week, Franklin made great gains throughout the course of his long life. Although he didn't achieve perfection, his growth in wisdom led to him becoming one of the most influential diplomats in history. Indeed, many historians believe he (even more than Washington) was the indispensable man of the 1787 Constitutional Convention, tempering the rhetorics of both the Federalists and the anti-Federalists. Historian William MacDonald writes, "Franklin's voice was always in favor of the more generous provision, the ampler liberty; was always earnestly opposed to whatever might tend to make governmental oppression at some future time possible....Some of his finest utterances were in maintenance of that plea; and it is a symptom of the noble feeling with which Franklin was regarded by the noblest men, that Hamilton would give his support to Franklin's recommendations, though they were essentially moral criticisms of the policy which he himself thought best for the country." Franklin's principle-centered diplomacy influenced not only the people who were of the same turn of mind as he was but also his political opponents—a true testament to his character and honor.

## Jonathan Edwards—Resolved to Serve with Humility

Jonathan Edwards was a preacher, a theologian, and a missionary to Native Americans. Shortly before his death, he assumed the presidency at the College of New Jersey (Princeton University). He "is widely acknowledged to be America's most important and original philosophical theologian." Furthermore, Author George Marsden writes, "Edwards was extraordinary. By many estimates, he was the most acute early American philosopher and the most brilliant of all American theologians. At least three of his many works—*Religious Affections*, *Freedom of the Will*, and *The Nature of True Virtue*—stand as masterpieces in the larger history of Christian literature."

Edwards began his ministry with little advanced billing. His first pastoral position at nineteen years of age in 1722 in New York City, then a thriving metropolis of ten thousand people, was far away from his Connecticut hometown. Dr. Stephen Nichols, author of *The Resolutions of Jonathan Edwards*, writes of the young pastor, "Amidst all of this uncertainty and flux, this young man Jonathan Edwards needed both a place to stand and a compass for some direction. So he took to writing. He kept a diary and he penned some guidelines, which he came to call his 'Resolutions.' These resolutions would supply both that place for him to stand and a compass to guide him as he made his way." A. C. McGiffert described Edward's method of resolutions: "Deliberately he set about to temper his character into steel." Tempering is a process that "toughens" metals, just as written resolutions "toughen" the internal person through study and course corrections. This tempering process takes time, but the internal fortitude and self-mastery gained living one's convictions, not one's preferences, are worth paying any price.

Jonathan Edwards dutifully wrote seventy resolutions (see appendix) between 1722 and 1723. He committed to read these seventy resolutions once every week for the rest of his life. He fulfilled that commitment, reading the resolutions more than one thousand eight hundred times over the next thirty-five years of his life. Here are two of his resolutions:

1.  Resolved, that I will do whatsoever I think to be most to God's glory, and my own good, profit and pleasure, in the whole of my duration, without any consideration of the time, whether now, or never so many myriads of ages hence. Resolved to do whatever I think to be my duty and most for the good and advantage of mankind in general. Resolved to do this, whatever difficulties I meet with, how many and how great soever.

31. Resolved, never to say anything at all against anybody, but when it is perfectly agreeable to the highest degree of Christian honor, and of love to mankind, agreeable to the lowest humility, and sense of my own faults and failings, and agreeable to the golden rule; often, when I have said anything against anyone, to bring it to, and try it strictly by the test of this resolution.

Edwards would have many occasions to apply his resolutions. After his pastoral service in New York, on February 15, 1727, he joined the congregation of his grandfather Solomon Stoddard in Northampton, Massachusetts. In 1729, Stoddard died, leaving Edwards the sole minister in charge of one of the largest, wealthiest, and proudest congregations in the colony. Stoddard, in his later years, had introduced several doctrinal changes not founded upon the Scriptures. Since he was new in the congregation, Edwards continued the innovations when he assumed pastoral leadership. But in 1749, after years of successful ministry and intensive biblical study, Edwards's conscience balked at the doctrinal errors, which precipitated angry responses from church members. The controversy concluded with Edwards's dismissal by a margin of one vote. Many would have railed against this injustice; but Edwards, dignified as always, preached his farewell sermon with truth, love, and grace, exiting Northampton without rancor or bitterness. Edwards was, as Randall Stewart wrote, "not only the greatest of all American theologians and philosophers but the greatest of our pre-nineteenth century writers as well," making his gracious humble spirit even more impressive. He didn't fight for his rights; instead, he accepted the congregation's ruling, stating it was God's will, and took a position as missionary to the frontier Indians. He consistently displayed a grace-filled spirit of forgiveness to his many detractors, some of whom, years later, apologized for their involvement in the spread of misinformation. Can anyone imagine the infamy of being associated with the congregation that dismissed one of the best theologians and philosophers in American history?

Edwards, in his final years, never missed a beat, writing several Christian literature classics and leaving an enduring testament to the power of character-based resolutions to transform a person from the inside out. He faithfully lived his principles externally because that was who he had become internally. Specifically, he didn't just give lip service to his resolutions; he lived them.

## Mind, Heart, and Will

If success was as simple as writing a few resolutions and studying them daily, wouldn't more people apply this method so that they would become successful? Dr. Martyn Lloyd-Jones explains why only a few achieve lasting success: "Man is a wonderful creature; he is mind, he is heart, and he is will. Those are the three main constituents of man. God has given him a mind; He has given him a heart; He has given him a will whereby he can act." Transforming one's life, then, requires the whole person to be involved—his mind, his heart, and his will must be engaged in the process. True change isn't just a mental (mind) assent, isn't just an emotional (heart) experience, and is more than just regimented (will) learning. For some will read the resolutions and make a mental nod of approval but won't involve the heart or will. Even though they claim to have knowledge on how to succeed in life, they never seem to achieve anything. To know but not to do is not really to know since if one knew how satisfying authentic success would be, he wouldn't delay in striving for it. Resolutions must engage the mind and go beyond it, tapping into the heart and will to produce lasting real change.

Without uniting the mind, the heart, and the will together, people will not achieve their desired results. For example, many who attend a seminar have their hearts touched by the seminar's message but don't seem to comprehend mentally (mind) or follow through physically (will) with a plan for success. These people jump from one achievement fad to another and gain emotional (heart) releases but accomplish little that is of real substance. Life has been hard on them, so they attend another fad seminar, seeking not real change but a cathartic release of tension. Other people study their resolutions and attempt to transform themselves through sheer willpower, but unless their minds and hearts are engaged, their efforts will not last. They attempt to take up the resolutions rather than be taken up by them. The will can withstand motions; but without the heart and the mind, or the passion and the understanding, the process of transformation lacks zeal. As the old saying goes, "A man convinced against his will is of the same opinion still." A methodical, passionless, robotlike study of the resolutions will not get the job done.

It's only with a mind that understands, a heart that generates passion, and a disciplined will to follow through that change inside a person is generated. Sadly, most success seekers' journeys end in disappointment after they have made the common mistake of compartmentalizing the parts of their personhood rather than allowing them to work together. The good news, though, is that anyone can develop his ability to work on the mind, heart, and will simultaneously. The process is simple, but certainly not easy, and requires immense discipline to marry the three constituent parts together in the pursuit of excellence in any area that a person has resolved to change. By seriously thinking about where to focus, writing clear resolutions, resolving to read, and applying them on a consistent basis, anybody can—like Washington, Franklin, and Edwards—resolve to change. Moreover, when a person changes himself, he begins a process that ultimately transforms the world around him.

## Living the Thirteen Resolutions

Throughout my life, I have studied the greatest men and women in history. Learning from their examples, I developed and applied thirteen resolutions in my life so that I could move from "purpose detected" to "vision fulfilled." Peter Senge shared that purpose, vision, and core principles (resolutions) are three key concepts, writing, "These governing ideas answer three critical questions: 'What?' 'Why?' and 'How?'...Taken as a unit, all three governing ideas answer the question, 'What do we believe in?'" A person who believes in his life's mission, then, should know that the resolutions are the how, the purpose is the why, and the vision is the what. When he knows why he is living, what he is supposed to do, and how he plans on achieving his purpose, his date with destiny is set. First, he detects his purpose; second, he studies and applies the thirteen resolutions with his mind, heart, and will; and third, he journeys toward his God-given personal vision. Lamentably, only a few get all three parts correctly. And just as it takes three legs to stabilize a stool, it takes all three "governing ideas" to fulfill a person's destiny since his destiny is fulfilling the what, why, and how of his life.

Vision is tomorrow's reality expressed as an idea today. The ladder that connects a person's vision with his purpose is his resolutions. The thirteen resolutions are the ladder's rungs that help a person climb from where he is to where he desires to be. Philosopher Ortega y Gasset wrote, "Destiny does not consist in what we feel we should like to do; rather it is recognized in its clear features in the consciousness that we must do what we do not feel like doing." In the same way, climbing the resolution ladder of success isn't easy, but when a person knows why he started, what he desires to accomplish, and how he plans on getting there, his personal preferences pale in comparison to the fulfillment of his destiny. The thirteen resolutions will demand endless hours of effort in "schooling the soul" in order for a person to climb the rungs of the ladder up to his vision. Heraclitus conveyed a message that would last for ages, emphasizing the importance of character to finish what one has started, when he said, "Character is destiny." Anyone desiring a noble destiny must first develop a noble character. Living the thirteen resolutions will develop a person's character, transforming him from the inside out, helping him climb the ladder from "purpose detected" to "vision accomplished," thus realizing his God-given destiny.

The following are the thirteen resolutions placed in the weekly order in which they should be studied. By studying one resolution for a week and applying the principles as needed, a person will be able to examine each resolution four times a year. The resolutions are broken into three sections—private achievements, public achievements, and leadership achievements. The order in which these sections are mentioned represents a natural progression since private victories must precede public ones; and when these two types of victories are combined, they create the character and the competence that produce leadership influence. Leaders have followers, known as communities, according to John Maxwell. If you call yourself a leader but no one is following you, then you are only out for a walk. The thirteen resolutions take you through the entire process, from private to public to leadership success; and the goal is to learn how to apply the right principles at the right time, leading to the formation of wisdom. Indeed, the ultimate goal for any person learning and applying the thirteen resolutions is to develop wisdom for *life*.

## Private Achievements

1. *Resolved: To Discover My God-Given Purpose.* I know that when my potential, passions, and profits intersect, my purpose is revealed.
2. *Resolved: To Choose Character over Reputation Any Time They Conflict.* I know that my character is who I am, and my reputation is only what others say that I am.
3. *Resolved: To Have a Positive Attitude in All Situations.* I know that by listening to my *positive voice* and turning down my *negative voice*, I will own a positive attitude.
4. *Resolved: To Align My Conscious (Ant) with My Subconscious (Elephant) Mind toward My Vision.* I know that ending the civil war between the two is crucial for all achievements.

## Public Achievements

5. *Resolved: To Develop and Implement a Game Plan in Each Area of My Life.* I know that planning and doing are essential parts of the success process.
6. *Resolved: To Keep Score in the Game of Life.* I know that the scoreboard forces me to check and confront the results and make needed adjustments in order to win.
7. *Resolved: To Develop the Art and Science of Friendship.* I know that everyone needs a true friend to lighten the load when life gets heavy.

8. *Resolved: To Develop Financial Intelligence.* I know that, over time, my wealth is compounded when income is higher than expenses.

## Leadership Achievements

9. *Resolved: To Develop the Art and Science of Leadership.* I know that everything rises and falls based on the leadership culture created in my community.
10. *Resolved: To Develop the Art and Science of Conflict Resolution.* I know that relationship bombs and unresolved conflicts destroy a community's unity and growth.
11. *Resolved: To Develop Systems Thinking.* I know that by viewing life as interconnected patterns rather than isolated events, I improve my leverage.
12. *Resolved: To Develop Adversity Quotient.* I know that AQ leads to perseverance in overcoming obstacles and setbacks.
13. *Resolved: To Reverse the Current of Decline in My Field of Mastery.* I know that a true legacy leaves the world a better place than I found it.

Imagine each of these resolutions as an instrument in an orchestra. Each plays beautiful music, but when they work together, they produce an orchestral masterpiece, a living symphony of success. This book provides the instruments to play life's symphonic masterpiece. Since I started implementing the thirteen resolutions in my life, every challenge, to date, has been resolved as much as humanly possible by applying the right resolution, or resolutions, at the right time. Many will browse this book; some will read it; but only a few will read, study, and apply the resolutions in their lives. This book was written for the few: the few who yearn to be champions, the few who search for purpose, the few who desire to reach their potentials, and lastly, the few who hunger to fulfill their destinies.

On a bishop's tomb in Westminster Abbey is written:

When I was young and free and my imagination had no limits, I dreamed of changing the world. As I grew older and wiser, I discovered the world would not change, so I shortened my sights somewhat and decided to change only my country. But it, too, seemed immovable. As I grew into my twilight years, in one last desperate attempt, I settled for changing only my family, those closest to me, but alas, they would have none of it. And now as I lie on my death-bed, I suddenly realize: If I had only changed myself first, then by example I would have changed my family. From their inspiration and encouragement, I would then have been able to better my country and, who knows, I may have even changed the world.

Resolve to master the principles of this book, to apply the thirteen resolutions to your life, and to climb the ladder from "purpose detected" to "vision fulfilled." Resolve to be transformed by the wisdom gained from your journey. Resolve that, through your journey, you are going to, first, transform yourself and, then, transform your community, and that your transformed community will provide the means to change the world. These are bold words, indeed, but they are true, nonetheless. Opportunity is knocking. Don't knock it. Don't fear it. Instead, seize it by opening your door and claiming your destiny.

CHAPTER 1

# PURPOSE
## Resolved: To Discover My God-Given Purpose

*I know that when my potential, passions, and profits intersect, my purpose is revealed.*

## Living on Purpose

Viktor Frankl, a Nazi death camp survivor, learned the importance of having a purpose for living during his struggle to survive the brutal treatment inflicted on him by his captors. In the process, he developed a philosophy of purpose called "logotherapy." Stephen Covey's masterpiece, *The 7 Habits of Highly Effective People*, describes Frankl's theory: "Many so-called mental and emotional illnesses are really symptoms of an underlying sense of meaninglessness or emptiness. Logotherapy eliminates that emptiness by helping the individual to detect his unique meaning, his mission in life." Author Charles Perkhurst, observing the same principle, stated, "Purpose is what gives a life meaning." Sadly, many will live their entire lives without purpose, allowing life to lead them rather than leading their lives.

A purposeless life is similar to a hoopless basketball game—one can hurriedly dribble up and down the court; however, nothing of any consequence seems to get accomplished. Doesn't this describe the majority of people in the game of life? They are running frantically back and forth in no particular direction, having no purpose, meaning, or significance. But when hoops are placed on life's backboards, the objective of the game becomes clear, thus creating meaning for people to run up and down the court in order

29

to achieve the purpose of scoring points. What previously seemed like a waste of energy is now an activity with the specific intent of accomplishing purposeful objectives. This is what purpose does in a person's life. Dr. Myles Monroe wrote, "The poor man, the rich man, the black man, the white man—every person has a dream in his heart. Your vision may already be clear to you, or it may still be buried somewhere deep in your heart, waiting to be discovered. Fulfilling this dream is what gives purpose and meaning to life.... When you die, you're meant to leave this earth not on a pension but on a purpose." Purpose provides direction to a person's life, making every task, even seemingly mundane ones, filled with significance.

The modern man is suffering the debilitating effects of his self-imposed loss of purpose and meaning. When Friedrich Nietzsche wrote, "God is dead. God remains dead. And we have killed him," he understood that by rejecting God, he had killed meaning and purpose. Philosopher Bertrand Russell agreed to Nietzsche's statement and commented, "Unless you assume a God, the question of life's purpose is meaningless." Furthermore, Russell confronted the utter hopelessness of his atheistic philosophy:

> That man is the product of causes which had no prevision of the end they were achieving; that his origin, his growth, his hopes and fears, his loves and his beliefs, are but the outcome of accidental collocations of atoms; that no fire, no heroism, no intensity of thought and feeling, can preserve an individual life beyond the grave; that all the labors of the ages, all the devotion, all the inspiration, all the noonday brightness of human genius, are destined to extinction in the vast death of the solar system, and that the whole temple of Man's achievement must inevitably be buried beneath the debris of a universe in ruins—all these things, if not quite beyond dispute, are yet so nearly certain, that no philosophy which rejects them can hope to stand. Only within the scaffolding of these truths, only on the firm foundation of unyielding despair, can the soul's habitation henceforth be safely built.

Russell's philosophy is a dismal belief system, indeed, and one that has infected millions of people, leaving them without hoops in the game of life. Woody Allen surmised, "More than any other time in history, mankind faces a crossroad: One path leads to despair and hopelessness, and the other to total extinction. Let us pray we have the wisdom to choose correctly." The legacy of this acidic belief, poured directly on the roots of purpose, destroyed the fruits of hope, meaning, and significance, leaving only the bitter fruits of paralysis and cynicism to fill the void in the poisoned soil.

Thankfully, one doesn't have to drink the modern man's toxic brew of beliefs. In fact, many are rejecting these fatalistic views of godless philosophers, yearning instead for meaning, purpose, and a sense of destiny. Indicative of this trend is the smashing success of Rick Warren's *The Purpose Driven Life*. With over thirty million copies sold since 2002, Warren's book is reaching many people with a message of forgiveness, hope, and purpose. In the book introduction, Warren wrote, "You cannot arrive at your life's purpose by starting with a focus on yourself. You must begin with God, your Creator. You exist only because God wills that you exist. You were made by God and for God—and until you understand that, life will never make sense. It is only in God that we discover our origin, our identity, our meaning, our purpose, our significance,

> No one can choose the day he was born, but everyone can choose responsibility for discovering why he was born.

and our destiny. Every other path leads to a dead end." As author Carl Townsend said, "They say there are two important days in your life: the day you were born and the day you find out why you were born." No one can choose the day he was born, but everyone can choose responsibility for discovering why he was born.

Why are people created? What is the purpose of one's life? Author Daniel Pink identifies three elements that are included in a purposeful life:

1. Autonomy: the urge to direct our own lives
2. Mastery: the desire to get better at something that matters
3. Purpose: the yearning to do what we do in the service of something larger than ourselves

To achieve one's purpose, autonomy, mastery, and character must combine together. For without autonomy, a person isn't directing his life and, therefore, is accomplishing not his purpose but someone else's. Furthermore, without mastery, he is not improving in something that matters; and if what he is doing doesn't matter, then it certainly isn't his purpose. Lastly, only a person of character desires to be of service to something larger than himself, contributing to others to make a difference and leaving his mark in the world, transcending all selfish motives and actions. In order to fulfill his purpose, then, a person must have or build all three prerequisites. He must build character, hunger for autonomy, and develop mastery in his profession by living purposefully for excellence.

## Purpose HedgeHog

In his book *Good to Great*, Jim Collins discussed the hedgehog concept as a way to understand how a company or an individual can become exceptional. Similarly, once a person understands Collins's hedgehog circles, he will begin to understand that these circles can help define his purpose. Collins explained, "More precisely, a Hedgehog Concept is a simple, crystalline concept that flows from deep understanding about the intersection of the following three circles:

1. What can you be the best in the world at (and, equally important, what you cannot be the best in the world at)?
2. What drives your economic engine?
3. What are you deeply passionate about?"

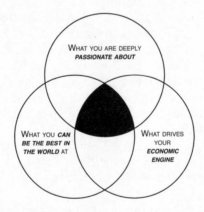

Collins further explained the hedgehog concept through an example:

> To quickly grasp the three circles, consider the following personal analogy. Suppose you were able to construct a work life that meets the following three tests. First, you are doing work for which you have a genetic or God-given talent. ("I feel that I was just born to be doing this.") Second, you are well paid for what you do. ("I get paid to do

this? Am I dreaming?") Third, you are doing work you are passionate about and absolutely love to do, enjoying the actual process for its own sake. ("I look forward to getting up and throwing myself into my daily work, and I really believe in what I'm doing.") The intersection of these three circles is the Hedgehog Concept.

Collins explained that it's essential to have all three circles intersecting to determine a person's hedgehog concept. For example, if a person makes a copious amount of money but cannot be the best in his field, then he is only good, not great. Similarly, if he becomes the best at something but isn't passionate about it, then he will not maintain his greatness, as others who are more committed will surpass him. Finally, a person can be as passionate as anyone can be about something, but if he isn't the best at it or it is not economically viable, then he has a fun hobby, not a productive business enterprise. Collins's book teaches that only when all three circles intersect can a company unlock its potential and move from good to great.

In a similar fashion, what would happen if, using the hedgehog concept as a model, a person developed the three circles for his hedgehog purpose? By slightly changing the three circles, we can create the purpose hedgehog.

1. Passion
2. Potential
3. Profits

Purpose, in this instance, is the intersection of a person's passion (motivation), potential (one's God-given talents), and profits (economic engine). It's only when a person makes all three circles intersect that he will ultimately fulfill his destiny by living a purposeful life.

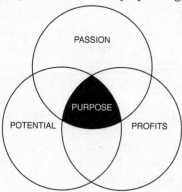

## Passion

Passion, the first attribute of purpose, is a mixture of what a person loves and what he hates, creating his motivation to change something in his current reality. What would someone do with his life if he could do anything? Sometimes it's a love of something that drives the passion to change the world, but at other times, it's what angers or disappoints him about the world that leads to his purposeful assignment to change it. All great achievements must be maintained through passion; otherwise, criticisms, setbacks, and pressures will eventually wear achievers down. According to Jay Elliot, author of *Steve Jobs Way*, when people would ask Jobs about entrepreneurship, he would answer, "What's your idea?" Typically, the potential entrepreneur would say, "I don't know yet." Jobs would answer, "I think you should go get a job as a busboy or something until you find something you're really passionate about." Jobs believed that what separates the successful entrepreneurs from the nonsuccessful is perseverance (which is part of adversity quotient discussed in Resolution 12). He said, "You put so much of your life into this thing. There are such rough moments that I think most people give up....You have to be burning with an idea, or a problem, or a wrong that you want to right." Without passion, you will never stick it out when the going gets tough. Passion is nonnegotiable. It's passion that keeps one going in the face of seemingly insurmountable odds, and it is the same passion that keeps him refusing to quit no matter how painful the journey to the top is.

> **All great achievements must be maintained through passion.**

## Potential

The second part of purpose is discovering one's potential: What are his unique gifts and skills? Everyone is born unique. What abilities can a person bring to the table that can benefit the world? Author Marianne Williamson emphasized the nearly unlimited potential of every human being when she wrote:

> Our deepest fear is not that we are inadequate. Our deepest fear is that we are powerful beyond measure. It is our light, not our darkness that most frightens us. We ask ourselves, "Who am I to be brilliant, gorgeous, talented and fabulous?" Actually, who are you NOT to be? You are a

child of God. Your playing small does NOT serve the world. There is nothing enlightened about shrinking so that other people won't feel insecure around you. We were born to manifest the glory that is within us. And as we let our light shine we unconsciously give other people permission to do the same. As we are liberated from our own fear, our presence automatically liberates others.

The greatest treasures on earth can be found in the numerous cemeteries across the world. For in these cemeteries lie the buried potentials of the multitude who played it safe throughout life. Why is everyone playing it safe all the way to the grave? Doesn't daring to reach for greatness make sense—since no one is making it out alive anyway? Playing it safe only ensures that a person never reaches his potential, thus never fulfilling his purpose.

## Profits

The third aspect of purpose is profits—turning one's potential and passion into a fruitful calling. Some may be thinking that profits shouldn't be included in a person's purpose, but without a viable economic engine, he cannot pursue his calling because little details like eating, drinking, and housing accommodations keep interfering. In a free society, people will only reward others financially when they are satisfied with the products or services that are offered. By pursing his passion and potential and ensuring that a customer need is filled, a person can thrive in today's flat world. The corporate cradle-to-grave jobs are dead, but serving customers' needs will never go out of style. If anything, serving customers' needs has never been more important since competition in today's market comes from all over the globe. Shoddy products and services will not be tolerated, making it imperative that passion and potential be merged with profitable markets in order to prosper.

Wally Amos, an air force veteran who worked as a talent agent with the William Morris Agency, loved chocolate chip cookies. His aunt Della raised him and taught him a tasty cookie recipe when he was a child. He would send home-baked chocolate chip cookies to celebrities to entice them to meet with him and maybe sign a deal to be represented by the William Morris Company. (By using this method of selling, he discovered Simon & Garfunkel.) Although he was a good agent, his passion was cookies. On March 10, 1975, Amos, taking the advice and encouragement of his friends, opened a cookie store in Los Angeles, California, and called it Famous

Amos. In his first year of operation, he sold $300,000 worth of cookies, and in the second year, he brought in more than $1,000,000 in sales. He eventually sold his company and has become a multimillionaire. Today, his brand is still one of the most recognized names in the field of cookies. His meteoric success was achieved by aligning his passion, potential, and profits with his life's purpose, making Famous Amos cookies a worldwide phenomenon.

## What, Why, and How

Whatever a person is doing, he should do it with all his might, and eventually, doors will be opened, revealing his purpose. For when a person discovers his purpose, he conceives his vision, a picture of what his fulfilled purpose looks like (to be discussed further in Resolution 4). However, in order to turn this vision into reality, he must also develop and live by the principles needed to accomplish it. Senge described these principles by asking a question: "How do we act, consistent with our mission along the path toward achieving our vision?...[this will] describe how the company [or individual] wants life to be on a day-to-day basis, while pursuing the vision." The thirteen resolutions are the principles by which a person should live in order to achieve his vision, fulfilling the purpose of his life. Regardless of the field in which people choose to apply these principles, they will find all thirteen resolutions relevant since they are based on the natural laws of life—applicable in any field, at any time, and under all circumstances. When a person detects his purpose, he lifts the fog off his vision, driving him to form a team of people who would help him make his vision a reality. All businesses are first created metaphysically (as visions) in the entrepreneur's mind and then created physically in the material world by the community. This follows Ralph Waldo Emerson's statement: "An institution is the lengthened shadow of one man." But this isn't quite right, for when a person detects his mission, others surround him not only to complete the mission but also to improve it. Moreover, the more the team buys into the vision, the clearer the picture of the future becomes, enhanced by the ideas and the abilities of the team. Senge described this phenomena, writing, "They now have partners, 'co-creators'; the vision no longer rests

> Whatever a person is doing, he should do it with all his might, and eventually, doors will be opened, revealing his purpose.

on their shoulders alone. Early on, when they are nurturing an individual vision, people may say it is 'my vision.' But as the shared vision develops, it becomes both 'my vision' and 'our vision.'" When the purpose, vision, and principles align, a disciplined culture develops; it is this culture that propels businesses forward.

## Steve Jobs—Hedgehog Purpose

Steve Jobs, founder and CEO of Apple, showed the results of living one's purpose personally and professionally. Chris Brady, a co-author of *Launching a Leadership Revolution* and an Apple connoisseur, defined Apple's hedgehog concept this way: "To deliver incredibly creative and 'cool' technology that is intuitively useful and reliable for any class of user—particularly the user who doesn't care to know about the intricacies of a hammer in order to make productive use of one. (In other words, to make the technology invisible and the usability and dependability dominant.)" Jobs wanted not only an intuitive product but also one that created an experience of satisfaction so that a customer would feel emotionally attached to the product and share his experience with others. Jobs might have had the firmest grasp of a CEO on consumer preferences, intuitively understanding customers' love of simplicity, elegance of design, and the "cool" factor. Moreover, his obsession, according to Elliot, was "a passion for the product . . . a passion for product perfection." Jobs's personal hedgehog purpose and Apple's hedgehog concept closely resembled each other since both emerged out of the intersection of Jobs's passions, potential, and profits, validating Emerson's belief that great companies are shadows of great leaders.

With Jobs's passion aligning beautifully with his potential, the last piece of the puzzle for him was to determine how to make money.

Jobs's company, Apple, although not the top seller of computers, was and is the most profitable. Apple's offerings of unique products, like iPod, iPad, and iPhone, in a market of Windows' software clones, have revolutionized the high-tech field. Jobs, through both Apple and Pixar, aligned his passion and his potential to create profits, thus fulfilling his purpose.

Because of Jobs's powerful vision, he created a culture around his passion that attracted, as Senge said, "co-creators." Jobs's purpose was the driving force, helping attract many talented people to Apple's culture. The assembled team of these talented people can then fulfill the company's purpose by living its principles and completing its vision. Mac engineer Trip Hawkins described Jobs as having "a power of vision that [was] almost frightening. When Steve [believed] in something, the power of that vision [could] literally sweep aside any objections, problems or whatever. They just [ceased] to exist." Elliot agreed, writing, "The Mac and every product since then are more than 'just products.' They are a representation of Steve Jobs's intense commitment. Visionaries are able to create great art or great products because their work isn't nine-to-five. What Steve was doing represented him; it was intuitive but inspired." Purposeful people like Jobs infect their entire community, bringing a community's passion, potential, and profits to the forefront. Needless to say, purpose in an organization's culture positively affects the company's culture, thus its bottom line. Elliot explained, "When you believe in your product and people as totally as Steve [did], your people stick with you. Apple has one of the highest retention rates in Silicon Valley," mainly because Jobs's purpose, vision, and principles united the Apple community with a highly effective culture. Jobs, speaking at the Stanford commencement ceremonies, shared his belief in purpose: "Again, you can't connect the dots looking forward; you can only connect them looking backwards. So you have to trust that the dots will somehow connect in your future. You have to trust in something—your gut, destiny, life, karma, whatever. This approach has never let me down, and it has made all the difference in my life."

## Big Rocks First

In order to live a life of purpose, a person must learn to focus his time on purpose. Time is the stuff that life is made of, making time management a crucial skill. But for one to develop effective time management without directing it toward his purpose is to efficiently manage wasting his life. For even with good time management, the majority of his time will be dribbled away on unimportant activities unless it is purpose and vision directed. Hyrum Smith, in his book *The 10 Natural Laws of Successful Time and Life Management*, wrote, "Time is just like money. When you decide to spend one hour watching TV, you have also decided not to spend the time on what? Everything else. You would be very upset if someone gained access to your bank account and stole all your money. Most people, though, don't blink an eye when all sorts of culprits sneak into their lives and steal their time."

Nearly all executives would agree that reading will help one grow as a leader when what he reads is properly applied, but few seem to read as often as they should. Smith asked a group of executives why, if they felt reading was so important, they weren't reading more. After an uncomfortably long silence, a guy in the back row finally offered, "Books don't ring." What a profound response! Books don't hop up and say, "Hey, I'm a really good book. Why don't you read me?" Instead, they passively wait for hungry leaders to read them. Reading is a purposeful activity but not an urgent one. Covey, in his book *First Things First*, described the importance of prioritization:

> In the middle of the lecture the presenter pulled out a wide-mouth jar and placed it on the table, aside to some fist-sized rocks.
>
> After filling the jar to the top with rocks, he asked, "Is the jar full?" People could see that no more rocks would fit, so they replied, "Yes!"
>
> "Not so fast," he cautioned. He then got some gravel from under the table and added it to the jar, filling the spaces between the rocks. Again, he asked, "Is the jar full?"
>
> This time the students replied, "Probably not."
>
> The presenter then reached for a bucket of sand below the table, and dumped it on the jar, filling the spaces between the rocks and the gravel. Once again he asked, "Is the jar full?"
>
> "No!" the students shouted. Finally, he grabbed a pitcher of water and filled the jar completely, asking the public what they could learn from that illustration.
>
> One of the participants answered, "If you work at it, you can always fit more into your life."
>
> "No," said the presenter. "The point is, if you don't put the big rocks in first...would you never have gotten any of them in?"

For a person living a life of purpose, the big rocks are the activities that move him closer to the fulfillment of his purpose and vision. He must learn to say no to the good so that he has time to say yes to the great. When he says that he doesn't have time, that isn't true. What is true is that he doesn't prioritize his time for a certain activity. Indeed, both the wealthiest man and the poorest man in America have twenty-four hours in a day, but what they do with their twenty-four hours makes all the difference. Mastery of any activity, according to Malcolm Gladwell, requires ten thousand hours—meaning, a person can be a master in nearly any field by applying himself. However, he cannot be a master in all fields simply because there isn't enough ten-thousand-hour segments to go around. Laserlike focus—the ability to narrow options to the essential few—is crucial for all successful people. Covey described his thoughts on the difference between urgent and important:

> Urgent matters are usually visible. They press on us; they insist on action. They're often popular with others. They're usually right in front of us. And often they are pleasant, easy and fun to do. But so often unimportant! Importance, on the other hand, has to do with results. If something is important, it contributes to your mission, your values, your high priority goals.

Urgent matters should be attended to right away, but high-priority items, although important, are typically not urgent and require the discipline of planning in order to schedule and apply the time needed to complete them. Learning to delegate any task that others can do nearly as well as you can is an important attribute of all leaders. Busyness is not the goal—productivity is. If someone in the community can perform a task nearly as well as you, if not even better, then why should you continue doing it? Delegating tasks is an essential skill for all productive purpose-centered leaders. In order to fulfill one's purpose, it is imperative that he invest time and effort on assignments that he is uniquely qualified to perform.

## Purpose-Oriented Time Management

Time management doesn't have to be overcomplicated. In fact, in the early twentieth century, Ivy Lee, considered by many as corporate America's first public relations man, discussed a simple but effective time management technique with Charles Schwab, one of Andrew Carnegie's business partners:

> One day a management consultant, Ivy Lee, called on Schwab of the Bethlehem Steel Company. Lee briefly outlined his firm's services, ending with the statement: "With our service, you'll know how to manage better."
> The indignant Schwab said, "I'm not managing as well now as I know how. What we need around here is not more 'knowing' but more doing; not 'knowledge', but action; if you can give us something to pep us up to do the things we

ALREADY KNOW we ought to do, I'll gladly listen to you and pay you anything you ask."

"Fine," said Lee. "I can give you something in twenty minutes that will step up your action and doing at least fifty percent."

"Okay," said Schwab. "I have just about that much time before I must leave to catch a train. What's your idea?"

Lee pulled a blank 3 x 5 note sheet out of his pocket, handed it to Schwab and said: "Write on this sheet the five most important tasks you have to do tomorrow." That took about three minutes.

"Now," said Lee, "Number them in the order of their importance." Five more minutes passed.

"Now," said Lee, "Put this sheet in your pocket and the first thing tomorrow morning, look at item one and start working on it. Pull the sheet out of your pocket every fifteen minutes and look at item one until it is finished. Then tackle item two in the same way, then item three. Do this until quitting time. Don't be concerned if you only finished two or three, or even if you only finish one item. You'll be working on the important ones. The others can wait. If you can't finish them all by this method, you couldn't with another method either, and without some system you'd probably not even decide which are most important."

He went on, "Spend the last five minutes of every working day making out a 'must do' list for the next day's tasks. After you've convinced yourself of the worth of this system, have your people try it. Try it out as long as you wish and then send me a check for what YOU think it's worth."

The whole interview lasted about twenty-five minutes. In two weeks, Schwab sent Lee a check for $25,000—$1,000 a minute. He added a note saying the lesson was the most profitable he had ever learned. Did it work? In five years, it turned the unknown Bethlehem Steel Company into the biggest independent steel producer in the world and made Schwab a hundred-million-dollar fortune and the best known steel man alive at that time.

Time management is one of the most powerful multipliers of results known to mankind. When a person begins to work on his purposeful important items first, prioritizing from most important to least important (big rocks to small rocks), he ensures that key issues (tasks moving a person toward his purpose and vision) are addressed first, leaving less time for nonproductive tasks or time

wasters. The productivity of an entire leadership team will multiply as the important replaces the ur-
gent in people's schedules, aligning everyone toward the purpose and vision of
the company. Remember, if a person
cannot manage his time, then he cannot
lead his life.

> **Remember, if a person cannot manage his time, then he cannot lead his life.**

The crucial lesson to learn is that
a person cannot manage time properly
until he has identified what he is called to do, why he is doing it,
and how is he supposed to accomplish it. Only when he has identified them will he ensure that every move he makes moves him
closer to fulfilling his life's calling. Living a life of purpose isn't
easy, but fulfilling one's calling satisfies much more than comfort
or convenience. As E. N. Gray, author of *The Common Denominator of Success*, wrote, "The successful person has the habit of doing
the things failures don't like to do. They don't like doing them either necessarily. But their dislike is subordinated to the strength
of their purpose."

In summary, people follow people who know their purpose.
Accomplishing private achievements leads to external public
achievements. With enough public achievements, a person builds
a following or a community, allowing him to develop his leadership achievements by creating a culture around his core principles
(resolutions). A person must move up his ladder in order from private achievements to public achievements to leadership achievements with a specific objective if he intends to leave a legacy for
the next generation. Indeed, purpose is the cornerstone of all true
successes, for without it, people will not resolve to climb the ladder.
This is the reason purpose is the first of the thirteen resolutions.

### John Wooden

On October 14, 1910, in Hall, Indiana, John Robert Wooden was born to a Dutch-Irish family. The farmhouse where he grew up had a few of the modern-day conveniences, like running water and electricity, but young John was given something much greater by his parents: a belief that he could fulfill his purpose through hard work. Wooden lived his purpose because his passion, potential, and profits aligned in coaching. In his book *Wooden on Leadership*, he described his purpose by saying, "What occurred in the practices is what gave me joy and satisfaction—teaching others how to bring forth the best of which they are capable. Ultimately, I believe that's what leadership is about: helping others to achieve their own greatness by helping the organization to succeed." Wooden might not have won every contest he entered, but he never surrendered because he knew his reason. His legendary sense of purpose, one of the cornerstones of his success, led a farm boy from the fields of Indiana to UCLA, which ultimately led to ten NCAA titles in his last twelve years, including a record seven in a row. There are many qualities that can be learned from John Wooden, but central to his philosophy of life was that everything happens for a purpose.

Wooden was not blessed physically with a Michael Jordan frame, with a height of only 5'10" and a weight of 175 pounds; but he maximized what he was given—quickness and speed—through sheer determination when he was a player at Purdue University. In fact, Piggy Lambert, Purdue's coach for twenty-nine years, said that Johnny was the best-conditioned athlete that he ever coached in any sport. In the book *Wooden*, written with Steve Jamison, John revealed the secret to his superhuman work ethic:

> My dad, Joshua, had great influence on my own personal definition of success. . . . One of the things that he tried to get across to me was that I should never try to be better than someone else. Then he always added, 'But Johnny, never cease trying to be the best you can be. That is under your control. The other isn't....' The concept that success is mine when I work my hardest to become my best, and that I alone determine whether I do so, became central to my life and

affected me in a most profound manner.

Wooden's legendary focus led Purdue to the 1932 Helms Foundation unofficial national championship. It also led him to the college's Hall of Fame. But to him, the fame of winning was only secondary to the inner peace he got from knowing that he had done his personal best. He defined success as "the peace of mind that is a direct result of self-satisfaction in knowing you did your best to become the best you are capable of becoming." In other words, one may lose but still be a champion if he did his personal best. On the other hand, one may win but still not be a winner if he didn't do his personal best. This philosophy imbued all of his teams with an unquenchable drive for excellence, night in and night out, fulfilling their potentials with purpose. Wooden believed that the external scoreboard was secondary to the internal scoreboard, where players competed more against themselves than against other teams to reach their potentials. He explained it this way: "Championships were never the cake; they were the icing. Doing our best was the cake."

Wooden coached high school basketball for eleven years before moving to the NCAA by accepting the head coaching position at Indiana State. After two years there, leading his Indiana State team to the NAIB finals, he accepted the head coaching position at UCLA in 1948. He was led to believe that UCLA would soon have a state-of-the-art basketball facility to support his efforts. However, the promise wasn't fulfilled until nearly seventeen years later, forcing his UCLA teams to practice under less-than-desirable conditions.

To say that the UCLA facilities were outdated would be an understatement, with many modern high schools having better training facilities. It's hard to imagine, but Wooden's future UCLA dynasty practiced basketball on the third floor of the old Men's Gymnasium, the same floor that both the gymnastic and wrestling programs used for their practices, many times simultaneously. In fact, the place was infamously labeled the BO barn because of its lack of ventilation and the smells emanating from hardworking athletes. Wooden recalled:

> For sixteen years, I helped our managers sweep and mop the floor every day before practice because of the dust stirred up from the other activities. These

were hardship conditions, not only for the basketball team....You could have written a long list of excuses why UCLA shouldn't have been able to develop a good basketball team there. Nevertheless, the B.O. barn was where we built teams that won national championships in 1964 and 1965. You must take what is available and make the very most of it.

If a person were to study Wooden, he would see the recurring theme that whatever the situation was, by knowing his purpose, Wooden endured and overcame. Instead of waiting for conditions to improve, his purpose drove his team to improve, which eventually led to improved conditions.

Only a few remember that it took Wooden sixteen years to put all the puzzle pieces together to launch his dynasty in 1964 with UCLA's first NCAA title. In contrast, most people today are too impatient with the success process, applying hard work for a day, a week, or maybe even a year, expecting to be a champion regardless of whether they have invested the full ten thousand hours needed for mastery. On the other hand, how many people enjoy investing sixteen years without winning championships and yet remain as committed, if not more so, at the start of the seventeenth year? Only a person who knows and is living his purpose behaves in this bizarre fashion. Wooden believed his teams were champions long before their 1964 NCAA title confirmed it because they strived to reach their full potential daily, living their purpose. Wooden described his philosophy by saying:

> There is a standard higher than merely winning the race: Effort is the ultimate measure of success.... When it's over, I want your heads up. And there's only one way your heads can be up—that's to give it your best out there, everything you have....To my way of thinking, when you give your total effort—everything you have—the score can never make you a loser. And when you do less, it can't somehow magically turn you into a winner.

For most champions, it's that extra effort when everyone else has run out of gas that makes the difference between victory and defeat.

Over and over, a person discovers that a purpose-centered work creates its own luck. For example, look at the chain of events that led to Lew Alcindor (now Kareem Abdul-Jabbar), one of the most recruited collegiate athletes ever, choosing to attend UCLA. Because Wooden instilled pride in his teams, expecting a superior work ethic regardless of the practice conditions at the BO barn, UCLA endured their hardships and won two consecutive championships. Moreover, because they reached the finals, the games were aired nationally on TV. One of the many fans who watched the games was a young athlete named Lew Alcindor. He became intrigued with Wooden and UCLA. Alcindor's interest in UCLA led to a commitment from the athletic director, J. D. Morgan, to finish building the Pauley Pavilion by the fall of 1965, just in time for the basketball season. This isn't just coincidence, but rather, another example of a person who, by fulfilling his purpose, created his own LUCK—"laboring under correct knowledge."

With the entrance of Lew Alcindor, UCLA launched a nearly unbeatable dynasty. However, even after Alcindor's exit to the pros, Bill Walton and the "Walton gang" continued the winning streak, not missing a beat. In fact, UCLA's impressive list of records and accomplishments borders on the unbelievable. Wooden's UCLA teams won a record seven consecutive championships and an amazing eighty-eight consecutive games in a row!

Much has been written about UCLA's ten championships in twelve years, but UCLA's competitive greatness was formed much earlier. UCLA's winning ways began sixteen years earlier when a young coach created a purposeful culture founded on a simple concept: hard work applied to reaching one's potential made a person a winner regardless of the external scoreboard. By creating a culture of superior work ethic at UCLA, Wooden, despite the poor practice facilities, competed consistently against universities with better fundings and talents. His teams' finest hours were the endless years sweating it out in the BO barn using their ten thousand hours to master the game of basketball. If it wasn't for this superhuman commitment when no one was watching, there wouldn't be the winning teams that everyone acclaims today. Former heavyweight champion Joe Frazier highlighted a similar principle, citing the hundreds of miles he ran before his title fights: "If I cheat when the lights are out, I will be found out under the big lights." Although Wooden's teams didn't win NCAA titles during their first fifteen years, they never cheated the process needed to achieve mastery. In truth, they achieved something infinitely more important than championships: the self-respect engendered by giving their personal bests to fulfill their purpose. It's commonly called the "mirror test." Can a person look in the mirror, win or lose, and know that he gave his personal best? If he can answer positively, then competitive greatness is formed. However, if he cannot answer affirmatively, then no amount of trophies, recognitions, or awards can erase the fact that he flunked the "mirror test" cheating himself out of his personal self-respect. Wooden passed the mirror test daily, coaching for forty years, refining his craft, winning internal victories in front of his mirror, before the rest of the world witnessed his external victories on national TV.

To the sports community, Wooden's teams seemed to appear out of nowhere, lighting up the NCAA tournament regularly after 1964, but to the few in the know—those who witnessed firsthand the rest of the story—his last twelve years of public achievements were simply the fruits of his first twenty-seven years of internal achievements—purpose, character, attitude, and mental alignment. Champions, by discovering their purpose, invest ten thousand hours plus, typically in anonymity, until mastery is reached. At that point, they splash onto the world scene in a way that is best captured by Henry Wadsworth Longfellow's words: "The heights by great men reached and kept / Were not attained by sudden flight, / But they, while their companions slept, / Were toiling upward in the night."

Many athletes and coaches today, so focused on getting in the win column, shortcut the success process, thus skipping the internal achievements, starting with the purpose resolution. Instead, they attempt to advance directly to the public achievements through gimmicks, drugs, or other immoral methods, hoping to bypass purposeful hard effort, but it would be a losing foolish endeavor. Wooden would calmly explain to them that winning is an internal, not an external, event, teaching that the moment they cut corners, they only cheat themselves, robbing themselves of purpose in order to gain cheap wins. Dave Meyers, the captain of Wooden's last championship team, shared a story that pointed out the difference between society's definition and Wooden's definition of success:

> As a pro, absolutely nothing else mattered but

winning. If you missed a shot or made a mistake, you were made to feel so bad about it because all eyes were on the scoreboard. Winning was all that mattered and all anybody talked about: "We've gotta win this game," or "We shoulda won that game," or "How can we win the next game?" Win. Win. Win.

Coach Wooden didn't talk about winning—ever. His message was to give the game the best you've got. "That's the goal," he would tell us. "Do that and you should be happy. If enough of you do it, our team will be a success." He teaches this, he believes it, and he taught me to believe it.

Everyone who knew Wooden learned the lesson of his purpose: if one handles the inner scoreboard, the outer scoreboard takes care of itself. Imagine the impact that could be made in society if this philosophy of purpose were adopted by the top leaders in every field. Leaders, instead of emphasizing the outer scoreboard of life, would teach people to achieve their purpose by fulfilling their potentials, thus helping people pass the inner "mirror test." When enough people in an organization or a team pass their "mirror tests," the external scoreboard is nearly assured. Champions are created when teams focus more on the internal scoreboard than on the external one. Doing this ensures that no matter how many victories are piled up, there are always areas of dissatisfaction that can be further improved by tireless effort.

John Robert Wooden passed away on June 4, 2010, after ninety-nine years of achievement, passing along his success legacy to the world. Wooden's life exemplifies legendary sportswriter Grantland Rice's words: "For when the One Great Scorer comes to mark against your name, He writes—not that you won or lost—but how you played the game." Wooden knew how to play the game of life, modeling character, honor, passion, hard work, and fidelity to all who knew him. He leaves a powerful legacy, passing the baton of excellence to the next generation of leaders.

Wooden wrote these prophetic words in his book *Coach Wooden's Pyramid of Success*: "I am ready to meet Him [the Lord] and I am eager to see my wife, Nellie." Wooden is with his Lord and wife today, having fulfilled his life's purpose and having heard the words, "Well done, thy good and faithful servant."

## CHAPTER 2

# CHARACTER
## Resolved: To Choose Character over Reputation Any Time They Conflict

*I know that my character is who I am, and my reputation is only what others say that I am.*

*To sin by silence when they should protest makes cowards of men.*

—Abraham Lincoln

In a person's life, he will have many opportunities to choose between character and reputation. In order to make the right choice, he must understand the separate virtues that, when combined, create an immovable character.

### Integrity

To be a leader, a person's integrity should be nonnegotiable; for without it, no one will follow him for long. Integrity is ensuring that a person does not intentionally do wrong. Leaders with integrity still receive criticism, but they know that people with integrity expect to be believed; and when they're not, they let time prove them right. Author Mark Sanborn believes integrity is essential. He wrote, "When integrity ceases to be a leader's top priority, when a compromise of ethics is rationalized away as necessary for the 'greater good,' when achieving results becomes more important than the means to their achievement—that is the moment when a leader steps onto the slippery slope of failure. It is imperative to your leadership that you constantly subject your life and work to the highest scrutiny." Words like *honorable*, *honest*, *trustworthy*, *dutiful*, and *faithful* describe a person with integrity.

The history of the West is filled with men and women whose personal integrity was founded on moral precepts. In America, at the turn of the twentieth century, one could go to nearly any town and quickly discover communities nurtured on moral absolutes. One example is in a small Indiana town where a dad named Joshua Wooden, a farmer, taught his young family, including his son John, the meaning of integrity.

## John Wooden's Three Principles

1. Never lie.
2. Never cheat.
3. Never steal.

Imagine how simple life would be if everyone followed these principles, which are essential for becoming a man or woman of integrity and building trust. A person must compare his actions to these three absolutes. As C. S. Lewis remarked, "A man does not call a line crooked unless he has some idea of a straight line." Simply stated, no one will willingly follow a leader who violates these three principles of integrity since people follow leaders only as far as they trust them.

## Never Lie

The first principle "Never lie" means a person's worth is his word. This requires that a person's statements can be trusted as truth. When he states the facts as he knows them to be, instead of as he wants them to be, would like them to be, or exaggerates them to be, then he is being truthful. Many people fall into the habit of lying because they want to impress others with their "amazing" accomplishments. It may be hard to speak honestly when one wants to impress others, especially, when he knows that the truth isn't that impressive, but that is what truthfulness is. Sadly, many people, fearful of looking bad and more concerned with their reputation than with their integrity, will choose the perceived easier

> The first principle, "Never lie," means a person's worth is his word.

50

way by exaggerating, therefore lying, choosing to appear good rather than be honest. What a perverse perspective!

Jack Canfield discussed integrity, writing, "In reality, lying is the product of low self-esteem—the belief that you and your abilities are not good enough to get what you want . . . the false belief that you cannot handle the consequences of people knowing the truth about you—which is simply another way of saying, I am not good enough." Lies warp a person's character over time, literally confusing truth with fiction in the liar's mind. The Judeo-Christian belief system teaches that lying comes from the author of all lies, Satan. When a person opens the door to lying, his conscience becomes hardened to such an extent that he falls into his own web of deceit. Were it not for God's grace, it would be nearly impossible for him to unwind his mass of fabrications. As Walter Scott wrote many years ago, "Oh what a tangled web we weave, when at first, we practice to deceive." Tell the truth, the whole truth, and nothing but the truth when speaking with others. Indeed, the only exception to this rule is when the truth will damage another person's reputation through gossip. In this instance, unless a person is sharing with someone who is in a position to resolve a conflict, it's best not to share what he knows, remaining silent instead. Not sharing what he knows will cause damage to others (since gossip kills a person's reputation through loose lips) enables one to protect others while ensuring that he does not lie.

People of integrity protect others' reputations while examining their own hearts for any hypocrisy. Martin Luther, a great reformer, wrote, "Unless a man is always humble, distrustful of himself, always fearing his own understanding and passions, he will be unable to stand for long without offense. Truth will pass him by." A person must be on guard, always remaining vigilant, because he will not consistently speak truth to others if he is constantly lying to himself. C. S. Lewis observed the principle, writing, "When a man is getting better he understands more clearly the evil that is still left in him . . . A moderately bad man knows he is not very good, a thoroughly bad man thinks he is all right." Do not be deceived; internal lies always lead to external ones.

## Never Cheat

The second principle "Never cheat" helps a person maintain integrity, building trust with others. When a person is cheated, trust is thrown out the window, rarely to return. Ironically, people who cheat end up cheating themselves in the long run since no one will trust or follow a leader who is a cheater. Remember, if a person is bragging to someone about how he cheated others, he most likely will, if given the opportunity, cheat that person as well. Since there is no honor among thieves, it's best not to associate with liars, cheaters, or stealers, as their bad habits might rub off on others.

Cheating may seem to be a shortcut to success, but in reality, it's a dead end. Don't be fooled because dishonest leaders cannot build or maintain trust for long, which will force an unscrupulous person to do much more work for much less results compared to a person with old-fashioned integrity. Great businesses are built by men and women of principles who follow through on their word, fulfilling their commitments, without the need for multiple contracts or threatening lawyers to coerce others. In *Gorgias*, Socrates said, "If it were necessary to do or to suffer injustice, I would choose rather to suffer than to do injustice." Suffering injustice may hurt materially for a season, but doing injustice hurts a person's soul eternally. Remember, the person who is cheated the most is the cheater himself since he cheats himself out of integrity.

Tennis professional Andy Roddick understood this principle and displayed integrity and honor in a 2005 Italia Masters tournament in Rome. It was match point for the tennis player, meaning, one more point and he would win. Fernando Verdasco hit his second serve, and it was called "out" by the line judge. In a move as rare as it is noble, Roddick refused to accept the point. Instead, he explained to the line judge that the serve was actually "in," pointing to a faint indentation on the clay court directly on the white line. Verdasco, having conceded defeat, had already moved to the net, believing the match was over, but Roddick didn't "cheat" his way to victory. He believed his integrity was worth more than a win he hadn't earned. The line judge, impressed by Roddick's honesty, overruled his own call, and the game resumed. Verdasco came from behind and eventually won the tennis match, but Roddick won an even bigger victory: a victory of personal integrity. Roddick's legendary integrity is now part of ethics history. Stephen M. R. Covey has called it "Roddick's choice," the ability to demonstrate integrity even when it's costly to do so. The line judge might have called the serve "out," but Roddick knew the truth, refusing to accept the bad call because he knew he would have cheated Verdasco, himself, and the fans. Maintaining his integrity and self-respect was more important to him than maintaining his win-loss percentage, a standard of ethics worthy of emulation.

## Never Steal

The third principle "Never steal" is essential for building leadership. If a person steals, he forfeits any trust built in his team, leaving his leadership influence practically void. One of the biggest reasons for the decline in the productivity of the West is the epidemic of stealing in our culture today. In fact, the Robert Half Personnel Agencies has calculated that time theft alone is costing the American economy approximately $70 billion a year, which is equivalent to the annual revenues of conglomerates the size of Boeing, Walgreens, and Apple, to name just a few. Time theft is the deliberate actions of employees to misuse or waste time while on the company clock, which causes permanent damage in productivity. Many who wouldn't consider stealing directly from their employers' wallets or purses have no qualms about indirectly stealing time and their corresponding hourly wage from their employers. Why this huge difference in thinking? Perhaps it's because one is easy to get away with, while the other is riskier because a person could lose his job. But if his only reason for not stealing is the fear of getting caught, then his integrity is in serious need of repair. From the perspective of productivity, these three principles are required; but when the worth of character is added, these three become priceless. A person who steals may gain materially in the short run, but he robs from his own character, ultimately leading to bad consequences in the short run, in the long run, and most importantly, for eternity. This isn't a fair trade on any terms.

Commit now to never lie, to never cheat, and to never steal. No matter what someone does, don't go down to his level, as two wrongs will never make a right. Chuck Colson, founder of Prison Fellowship, criticized the Harvard Business School for its situational ethics, claiming that its commitment to philosophical relativism has

> **Commit now to never lie, to never cheat, and to never steal.**

ruined the foundation for real world ethics. Harvard asked Colson to come speak to the MBAs, which he did, titling his talk "Why Harvard Can't Teach Ethics." Colson, writing for *Christianity Today*, described the event thus:

> I expected a riot after my 45-minute talk in a packed lecture hall. But the students were docile; I didn't hear a single good question. Were the students so unfamiliar with moral philosophy they didn't know enough to challenge

me?

I left Harvard worried. What would happen to these students when they became leaders of American business? One of the students at Harvard during that period was Jeffrey Skilling, the now-discredited former Enron CEO.

Enron's collapse exposes the glaring failure of the academy. Ethics historically rests on absolute truth, which these institutions have systematically assaulted for four decades.

Wooden's three principles aren't relativistic suggestions but absolute principles responsible for feeding the Western civilization's moral foundations since the Old Testament era.

## Character

Integrity is a crucial attribute, but a person can have unimpeachable integrity and still not have character. Character moves beyond integrity and requires courage to fulfill its high calling.

Integrity is not doing wrong, while character is doing what is right. For example, John, an older boy, bullied young Billy at school. Tom watched the incident happen but didn't participate. Tom displayed integrity by not joining in the bullying, but not character. For Tom to have character, he must move beyond integrity and have the courage to defend young Billy, willing to risk his personal peace and safety for the sake of justice. Although integrity (refusing to do wrong) is good, character (expecting people to have the courage to do what is right) is even better. If Tom had helped Billy, he would have moved from integrity to character through his courageous actions.

A person moves from integrity to character when he holds on to his principles even when a conflict with others who violate these principles arises. Conversely, a person who has integrity can still lack character by choosing comfort over convictions when a conflict arises. Moreover, a person who fears conflict more than hypocrisy will protect himself by surrendering his principles for the sake of peace. A leader quickly learns that anytime he chooses to stand on his convictions, he naturally upsets others who choose to sit on their conveniences. However, leaders of character refuse to surrender their principles no matter what, understanding that character is more important than comfort or reputation. As Wooden said, "Be more concerned with your character than your reputation, because your character is what you really are, while your reputation is merely what others think you are."

Character is a special quality inside a person that enhances all other virtues, making him appear larger than life. In truth, without character, none of the other resolutions matter since living without character is like building a house on quicksand. Character is more than just what a person says or does; it's who a person is.

## Developing Character

Even after identifying that character is more important than reputation, one might wonder how to develop character. The simple, but not easy, formula for character is this: character = integrity × courage. This formula helps a person see the relationship between each of the virtuous attributes. Author C. S. Lewis highlighted the importance of courage when he wrote, "Courage is not simply one of the virtues, but the form of every virtue at the testing point." Therefore, a person of integrity who is without courage fails the test and lacks the character to stand his ground when his highest principles are challenged. It's only at the testing point, when his integrity and core principles are challenged, that his level of character can be determined.

Character demands courageous actions, and courage is the virtue most lacking in today's culture. Most people would rather have peace and affluence, minding their own business, than stand against oppression, especially if the oppression is not directed at them. People of character, however, respond differently, knowing that by refusing to check injustice, they are subtly supporting it. Reverend Martin Niemoeller, a Nazi prison camp survivor, explained, "First they arrested the Communists—but I was not a Communist, so I did nothing. Then they came for the Social Democrats—but I was not a Social Democrat, so I did nothing. Then they arrested the trade unionists—and I did nothing because I was not one. And then they came for the Jews and then the Catholics, but I was neither a Jew nor a Catholic and I did nothing. At last they came and arrested me—and there was no one left to do anything about it." Character demands action to end injustice.

When a person has the courage to get involved, how does he know what the correct principles to follow for character are? Each person must develop a moral grid to live by. Without moral absolutes, a compass to discern right from wrong, anything becomes permissible. Who says that stealing is wrong? What if 51 percent of the people voted in favor of stealing, does that make it right? Moral absolutes then are not based on votes but on the moral order inherent in the world. The Western world was built on the Judeo-Christian principles from the Bible. With this moral foundation, the West produced freedom with order, wealth with morality, and charity with love, leading to progress in many fields. These principles weren't perfectly applied, but even with notable moments of hypocrisy, the West has advanced the cause of truth in the physical, mental, and spiritual realms. However, over the past one hundred years, the Western moral order has been declining; and along with this decline is the subsequent decline of freedom, order, wealth, morality, charity, and love. Is mankind secure when the West has become a technological giant but, simultaneously, a moral midget? In order to restore character then, leaders must restore their courage.

## Courage Isn't Pragmatism

Courage is a person's choice to get involved in defending his highest principles, even when his own personal interest isn't what is at stake. Courage isn't pragmatism, a determination to get involved only if it enhances his position, power, or wealth; rather, as Gus Lee, author of *Courage*, wrote, "courage doesn't depend on practical outcomes, risk versus gains analysis, or collateral impact on others—that's pragmatism. Pragmatism is the application of practicality, utility and consequences to decision making." Courage is principle-based, driving leaders with courage to sacrifice personal benefits in order to uphold the greater principle at stake. Winston Churchill, the legendary English prime minster, emphasized, "Courage is rightly esteemed the first of human qualities.... because it is the quality which guarantees all others." Lee further wrote, "Courage is addressing wrongs in the face of fear, regardless of consequences, of risk to self, or of potential practical gains. That's why everyone practices pragmatism and risk balancing.... Courageous leadership is about utilizing all of our brains, character and spirit to advocate principles regardless of the odds, heedless of fear, apart from collateral impact, and independent of personal career needs." How rarely does one see leadership of this caliber today? Les Csorba, in his book *Trust*, described the debilitating effects of pragmatism: "When we follow leaders without a moral compass interested in only results, get ready for the ditch. The ditch into which modern leadership has fallen is the pit of pragmatism." Many confuse compromise and pragmatism, and Stephen L. Carter, a Yale Law School professor, succinctly described their difference: "Compromises that advance high principles are acceptable; those that do not advance high principles are not."

Pragmatism, then, is compromising one's highest principles for short-term personal advancements. Courage, on the other hand, accepts only noble compromises, willingly sacrificing personal gains to advance one's highest principles. Robert Morrisette explained, "I have heard it said that courage is not the absence of fear, but the perception that there is something far more important at stake. Having such a 'something' gives us the ability to resist giving in to fear and to eventually rise above it. It is only in the presence of fear that true courage can be exercised, but without this 'something,' how can we see beyond those things we're afraid of?" If a leader's objectives aren't important enough for him to face his fears, then he isn't going to experience much success in leadership. Imagine, if David hadn't had the courage to face Goliath, he would have simply compromised his faith for a false peace. He would have remained an unknown shepherd boy instead of becoming the king of Israel. In the same way, people without the courage to confront their Goliaths will not achieve leadership mastery because they refuse to confront and learn from their challenges. Courage, in today's pragmatic world, is a lost virtue that must be rebirthed in order for character-based leadership to thrive again.

> The greatest crisis in America is a crisis of leadership and the greatest crisis of leadership is a crisis of character.
> —Howard Hendricks

Professor Howard Hendricks said, "The greatest crisis in America is a crisis of leadership and the greatest crisis of leadership is a crisis of character." Leadership is character in motion; without character, there cannot be leadership. Furthermore, one cannot develop character by just reading, thinking, and speaking (although these help), because character must be forged in the theater of leadership. Character isn't a binary switch; it doesn't divide people into two groups, one with character and the other without character. Instead, think of character less like an on/off switch and more like a dimmer switch. A few people have no character at all, a few others have sterling character that cannot be bought, and the masses fall into a gradient dial, spread across from a little to a lot of character. The more character a person displays, the less he will exploit others for his gain.

## Exploiters versus Producers

There are only two distinct paths a person can take in life. He can either choose to produce results through performance or search for ways to exploit other people's production. The question is: At what price does he switch from being a producer to being an exploiter? This is the price at which one sells out his character. People of character refuse to sell out at any price, but people without character pragmatically look for opportunities to sell to the highest bidder, sacrificing character for personal profits. Producers create value by serving other people's needs, while exploiters plunder from producers to serve their own needs. If producers do not satisfy their customers, either directly in the service industries or indirectly by creating products that are desired, they will fail in business.

**Producers create value by serving other people's needs, while exploiters plunder from producers to serve their own needs.**

Since producers do not look for handouts, only hand-ups, they must have character in order to build trust with their customers. For without character, the customers' trust will be broken, driving customers to competitors who have been proven trustworthy. Producers focus on building long-term relationships through character, serving customers in a win-win fashion, developing repeat business.

Exploiters, on the other hand, produce nothing or next to nothing, relying on privileged positions gained through their political maneuverings, rewarded through other people's labors. Lord Acton said, "Power corrupts; absolute power corrupts absolutely." In reality, absolute power doesn't corrupt; it just reveals a person's character. His willingness to exploit is always present, lying dormant until his increased power places him in a position to reveal his lack of character by exploiting others. Exploiters love to live parasitically off producers, fattening themselves from fruits produced in others' gardens. Exploiters flock to professions where performance is difficult to measure; positions in government, bureaucratic corporations, and even large religious or charitable organizations all fit the bill. These fields are ripe for exploiters because, here, they can more easily hide from the real customers, advancing through office politics, not customer service. Any field protected from marketplace realities will see exploiters increase and producers decrease. The higher a person's character is, the harder it is to buy him, for he resists all offers or threats intended to bend his character to an exploiter's will. However, most people do have a price, selling out their character for the rewards offered, surrendering their alleged principles for their pocketbooks or peace.

## Exploitation and Plunder

Frédéric Bastiat, a great nineteenth-century French economist and statesman, wrote:

> Now since man is naturally inclined to avoid pain—and since labor is pain in itself—it follows that men will resort to plunder whenever plunder is easier than work. History shows this quite clearly. And under these conditions, neither religion nor morality can stop it. When, then, does plunder stop? It stops when it becomes more painful and more dangerous than labor. It is evident, then, that the proper purpose of law is to use the power of its collective force to stop this fatal tendency to plunder instead of to work. All the measures of the law should protect property and punish plunder.

Absolute power opens an avenue for plunder, creating opportunities for exploitation, allowing the few to make money without serving the many. Since there aren't any free lunches in life, somebody is paying for this. Indeed, when a person, through force and coercion, exploits a metaphorical free lunch, he has stolen from another individual his time, effort, and reward. Just because someone has the power to exploit doesn't make it right. As Horace Greeley explained, "The darkest hour in any man's life is when he sits down to plan how to get money without earning it."

It takes people with impeccable personal character to withstand the temptation to exploit, choosing principles over profits by refusing to personally gain at the expense of others. In the annals of history, there are only a few recorded instances of people, like Cincinattus or George Washington, willingly surrendering power for the sake of justice. The courageous few stand for their principles, withstanding unjust criticisms and dishonest gains to defend their character. No matter what happens, these people refuse to give up their character. This is what is lacking in today's leaders of the West.

## Freedom and Consumer Power

By reviewing how character, or lack of it, affects the economy, one can learn why today's lack of character is creating havoc in Western society. In a true free enterprise system, power is in the hands of the consumers as the system allows the customers to have sovereignty over their personal wishes. If someone else has sovereignty over the customers' choices, then the customers have lost their ability to choose, thus losing their economic freedom. Without the ability to choose, freedom is just an illusion. This is one of the biggest lessons to learn about liberty: Without economic freedom, true liberty doesn't exist.

In a free-enterprise system, if a customer isn't happy, he votes with his feet and finds someone who will serve him properly. Furthermore, freedom ensures that when money changes hands, it does so through service to customers, not through control over them. Character is essential for *free enterprise* because when consumers are given the power of choice, entrepreneurs must earn their trust to obtain and maintain their businesses. Free enterprise refuses to allow the *state* or *big business* to lord itself over consumers who have no other options.

By studying the trends of the West over the last one hundred plus years, a person can quickly see that free enterprise has morphed into Corporatism, Fascism, and Statism—systems of state and corporate controls over consumers. This transfers power from the consumers to the hands of a few government and business bureaucrats, who, through a lack of character, exploit consumers for their personal benefit. Any economic system that denies the consumer his right to choose promotes someone else to be the final arbiter of his wishes, mocking the free enterprise system. When a person comprehends this, it doesn't take him long to connect the dots, understanding why exploiters passionately dislike free enterprise. For if every business remained free from government special deals, exploiters would be forced to compete against other companies by serving customers rather than by coercing them.

Governments provide the largest fields for exploitation since they have no competitors because they own the monopoly of force in society. For this reason, it is crucial to keep government involvement in the economy to a bare minimum. Free enterprise, by making the customer king, ensures that all businesses are created to serve customers, not customers created to serve businesses.

## Socialism and State Power

Much that is written on the alleged benefits of socialism, a sad economic system debunked in theory and practice, has been written by exploiters seeking a place to hide from their personal and professional scoreboards. Why would an exploiter write anything factual about a free system that would surely condemn in principle and deny in practice his privileged and unearned position? Instead, exploiters blather on about equality and fairness without clearly defining these terms, keeping the customers confused as to their sovereignty over their own economic choices.

A famous quote, sometimes attributed to Winston Churchill, states, "If you aren't socialist before twenty-five, you have no heart; if you are socialist after twenty-five, you have no brain." Sadly, in our society, many are losing their brains, with producers being attacked by a growing legion of exploiters, demanding more of the fruits of producers' labors by marking unequal results. But how can people demand equal results when the efforts are so unequal? Socialism is an acid, decaying the roots of our freedoms, feeding the worst aspects of human nature, and giving pride, greed, and envy free rein to destroy everything in its poisonous path. Leaders must choose the harder right than the easier wrong since America, like every country, stands or falls based on the number of producers compared to the number of exploiters in society. The more exploitation is rewarded, the more difficult it becomes to be a producer. History records that when a society develops more exploiters than producers, its decline and fall approaches. Leaders of character must be developed, stemming the advancing tide of exploitation flowing across the Western world. Just because it is easier to become a member of the thriving exploiters' community known as the "Something for Nothing Club" (SFNC) doesn't mean one should join it.

## Character plus Competence Equals Trust

Even if a person has the character not to join the SFNC, he must do more to become a leader, adding competence in his chosen field with character to produce trust. In his book *The Speed of Trust*, Stephen M. R. Covey wrote, "Trust is a function of two things: character and competence. Character includes integrity, your motive, your intent with people. Competence includes your capabilities, your skills, your results, your track record. Both are vital." It takes a competent character-based leader, therefore, to propose plans that move his company forward. Covey described how trust creates speed in an organization by people not needing every i dotted and every t crossed. Since the followers trust the leader, they know that details will be worked out properly, creating business at the speed of trust. When enough people with character and competence join together, they create trusting communities, changing the world, one person and one team at a time. In order to create a team that creates change, one must build or find leaders who influence their teams with the principles found in the thirteen resolutions. Csorba wrote, "In Reflections on the French Revolution, Edmund Burke called those low-profile leaders members of the 'little platoons.' And today it is Chuck Colson, the founder of one of those not-so-little platoons anymore (Prison Fellowship) who suggests that it is the small society of little platoons led by ordinary people who rejuvenate civic duty." History records many examples of a brave minority, who, tired of the state of decline in their societies, built leadership platoons of change through the trust formed by the convergence of character and competence, creating a tipping point for change, literally altering the course of history through their leadership. Without jumping too far ahead in the resolutions, it's safe to say that positive change cannot happen without a moral foundation of character. A person of character, standing on his principles, influences more people than a thousand who have surrendered their character to the SFNC. Be a producer in life. Refuse to make decisions based on your conveniences; instead, make decisions based on your character.

> **Be a producer in life.**

J. R. R. Tolkien, in his novel *The Lord of the Rings: The Two Towers*, provided a wonderful example of courageous leadership against all odds:

FRODO. I can't do this, Sam.

SAM. I know. It's all wrong. By rights we shouldn't even be here. But we are. It's like in the great stories, Mr. Frodo. The ones that really mattered. Full of darkness and danger they were. And sometimes you didn't want to know the end. Because how could the end be happy? . . . But I think, Mr. Frodo, I do understand. I know now. Folk in those stories had lots of chances of turning back, only they didn't because they were holding on to something.

FRODO. What were they holding on to, Sam?

SAM. That there's some good in this world, Mr. Frodo, and it's worth fighting for.

## Ludwig von Mises: Indomitable Character

Ludwig Von Mises, an Austrian economist, stood for truth against the economic trends of his day. He defended free enterprise and classic liberalism when nearly all were stumbling over one another to receive perks and preferment offered by governments looking for professors to teach the joys of government intervention and economic controls. Many economists conceptually understood the errors in the Keynesian policies, knowing that government spending sprees would only lead to massive debt and unemployment. By choosing preferment over principles, the Keynesian economists surrendered their convictions for conveniences, riding the Keynesian wave to career advancement.

Mises, steeled by his character and resolve, was, at first, a lone voice crying in the wilderness, refusing to go along with the deceit, repeatedly pointing out the logical fallacies inherent in the Keynesian economic policies. This wasn't a popular stand in the first half of the twentieth century. In fact, Ludwig and his wife, Margit, barely made it out of Europe ahead of the Nazi blitzkrieg. Jörg Hülsmann, author of *Mises: The Last Knight of Liberalism*, wrote:

Mises was two months shy of his fifty-ninth birthday. He was on the invaders' list of wanted men. Two years earlier, they had ransacked his Vienna apartment, confiscating his records and freezing his assets. Mises then hoped to be safe in Geneva. Now nowhere in Europe seemed safe. Not only was he a prominent intellectual of Jewish descent; he was widely known to be an arch-enemy of National Socialism and of every other form of socialism. Some called him "the last knight of liberalism."

He had personally steered Austria away from Bolshevism, saved his country from the level of hyperinflation that destroyed inter-war Germany, and convinced a generation of young socialist intellectuals to embrace the market. Now he was a political refugee headed for a foreign continent.

The couple arrived in the United States with barely any money and no prospects for income. Mises's former students and disciples had found prestigious positions in British and American universities (often with his help), but Mises himself was considered an anachronism. In an age of growing government and central planning, he was a defender of private property and an opponent of all government intervention in the economy. Perhaps worst of all, he was a proponent of verbal logic and realism in the beginning heyday of positivism and mathematical modeling. No university would have him. Margit began to train as a secretary.

Over the next decade, husband and wife would slowly rebuild their lives in America, with Mises finding new allies in his fight for truth. In the midst of these challenges, he published his most important book *Human Action*. It would earn him a following whose admiration and devotion were beyond anything he had known in Europe.

With his courage and logic, Mises identified the long-term consequences of socialist and fascist errors, strengthening the growing intellectual resistance to Statism. Mises was a man of character, a man without a price, living his life according to Virgil's Roman motto, "Tu ne cede malis sed contra audentior ito," which translates, "Do not give in to evil, but proceed ever more boldly against it." Mises proceeded to do just that. The late dean of the Austrian School Murray Rothbard, one of the greatest economic minds and good friend of Mises, wrote:

> Holding these views, and hewing to truth indomitably in the face of a century increasingly devoted to statism and collectivism, Mises became famous for his "intransigence" in insisting on a non-inflationary gold standard and on laissez-faire.
>
> Effectively barred from any paid university post in Austria and later in the United States, Mises pursued his course gallantly. As the chief economic adviser to the Austrian government in the 1920s, Mises was single-handedly able to slow down Austrian inflation; and he developed his own "private seminar" which attracted the outstanding young economists, social sci-

entists, and philosophers throughout Europe. As the founder of the "neo-Austrian School" of economics, Mises's business cycle theory, which blamed inflation and depressions on inflationary bank credit encouraged by Central Banks, was adopted by most younger economists in England in the early 1930s as the best explanation of the Great Depression.

At a time when the crowd was streaming toward Statism in the form of Nazism, Fascism, Socialism, Communism, New Deal, Fair Deal, etc., Mises rejected the blatant errors in each of these forms, overcoming the tides of time by deeply thinking of their underlying principles. Regardless of the personal and professional cost, he refused to teach what he knew wasn't true, even though opportunities abounded had he gone with the economic flow. He could not do it and still maintain his intellectual integrity, for he knew in his heart that Keynesianism was wrong. Rothbard shared:

> For Mises was able to demonstrate (a) that the expansion of free markets, the division of labor, and private capital investment is the only possible path to the prosperity and flourishing of the human race; (b) that socialism would be disastrous for a modern economy because the absence of private ownership of land and capital goods prevents any sort of rational pricing, or estimate of costs, and (c) that government intervention, in addition to hampering and crippling the market, would prove counter-productive and cumulative, leading inevitably to socialism unless the entire tissue of interventions was repealed.

Today, Mises looks prophetic, having predicted the severe economic disruptions in the economy by the wholesale swallowing of Keynesian errors. With the West's economic malaise in full bloom, gutted through years of inflationary spending and soaring debt loads, nearly everyone now recognizes that Mises was right all along.

Only a few will ever comprehend the level of courage that Mises required to sustain the personal and professional abuses he received. Yet somehow, he never wavered in his belief that time would eventually prove him right, even if that meant he would be in his grave already by then. Intellectual truth meant more to Mises than anything else because he believed that a person of character understands that following the truth is more important than rewards, recognition, or professional perks. Robert Heilbroner, a famous economist of the Keynesian school, recognized Mises's courageous stand. After Communism's surprising worldwide collapse (at least surprising to the Keynesians), Heilbroner admitted Keynesians' intellectual defeat at the hands of Mises and the Austrian School. In the book *The World After Communism*, Heilbroner concluded:

> But what spokesman of the present generation has anticipated the demise of socialism or the "triumph of capitalism"? *Not a* single *writer in the Marxian tradition!* Are there any in the left centrist group? None I can think of, including myself. As for the center it-self—the Samuelsons, Solows, Glazers, Lipsets, Bells, and so on—I believe that many have expected capitalism to experience serious and mounting, if not fatal, problems and have anticipated some form of socialism to be the organizing force of the twenty-first century.
>
> Here is the part hard to swallow. It has been the Friedmans, Hayeks, von Miseses, *e tutti quanti* who have maintained that capitalism would flourish and that socialism would develop incurable ailments. Mises called socialism "impossible" because it has no means of establishing a rational pricing system; Hayek added additional reasons of a sociological kind ("the worst rise on top"). All three have regarded capitalism as the "natural" system of free men; all have maintained that left to its own devices capitalism would achieve material growth more successfully than any other system.

Heilbroner deserves applause because he confronted the socialistic demise in the late 1980s, not by diverting people's attention, not by making excuses, but by honestly reviewing the data, concluding that Mises and his followers had accurately predicted Keynesianism's economic collapse decades before. Heilbroner openly discussed the "elephant in the room" avoided by today's Statist-oriented economists—the lack of results wherever Keynesianism or Socialism or Communism has been attempted. The Socialist or Statist economists and politicians were wrong, and even if a million of them called untruth truth, it still wouldn't make it so. Mises and his small group, although deprived of honors and recognition in their lifetimes (with the notable exception of Hayek, who, a year after Mises's death, received the Nobel Prize, most likely in recognition of the Austrian School's recently deceased leader), stood for economic truth.

With one of the top Keynesian economists conceding defeat, time has certainly proven Mises right. Government intervention, far from being a modern-day elixir, has damaged economies and markets wherever its poison has been imbibed. Sadly though, once economic error sinks into the mind of the body politic, rooting it out takes time and effort, but it must be done. As Mises stated in *Human Action*, "Economics deals with society's fundamental problems; it concerns everyone and belongs to all. It is the main and proper study of every citizen." All citizens should study the history of political, economic, and spiritual freedoms, the very freedoms that undergird the liberties enjoyed today in the West.

If Mises pointed out the fallacies of inflationist and socialist policies in the 1920s, then why did the West proceed for nearly a century on a spending and borrowing binge, resulting in near bankruptcy for most governments of the West? The answer revolves around character, or more pointedly, lack of character. "Follow the money" (FTM) is the motive behind most politicians' questionable behaviors. FTM and its brother "something for nothing" (SFN) combine to make a powerful force in overcoming principles and character wherever they are allowed to prosper unchecked. Since most people have a price, educators and politicians FTM into supporting Keynesian policies and are rewarded for selling out their character and for supporting faulty economics, rationalizing their sellout by the pots of gold offered to them at the end of the rainbow. This behavior created the current that Mises opposed in his battle for truth against errors.

Politicians sell out their character for inflation because

they are always short of two things in modern democracies: money to buy votes and votes to obtain further money. In the past, a politician could not spend government money unless he raised revenues through increased taxes. Since tax hikes were highly unpopular, he feared losing his elected position; therefore, he restrained his appetite for spending in order to remain popular with his voters. Today, however, through the "joys" of Keynesian economics, this check on poor behavior is gone. Politicians can now spend more money than taxes raise indefinitely, without having to even suggest increasing taxes. How do they do this? They do it by inflating the money supply through printing fiat paper money (monopoly money) and calling it legal tender. Keynesian policies have given Western governments an unlimited money supply to buy more votes without raising taxes, thus avoiding the ire of the fooled electorate. The inflated money loses its monetary value as it's diluted within the economy, but Keynesian politicians don't seem to mind. They are willing to sacrifice the citizens' wealth through inflation for their personal benefits in money and votes. What makes an inflationary policy so devious is that it isn't easily understood by the people. Politicians hide behind their Keynesian sound bites while in office, and then leave bankrupt governments as their legacy, long after they are retired. Indeed, Keynesian economics provides an amenable worldview for current politicians because it condones their SFN inflationary money policies (a secret tax on citizens' money) without having to risk an election day disaster. Keynesians can even proclaim to their voters that they didn't raise taxes, yet secretly, they inflated the money supply taxing everyone, hurting most those who live on a fixed income and cannot afford the higher prices that inflation produces.

Most politicians, however, are not concerned with the citizens' long-term wealth; instead, they are focused on their short-term need of money and votes to get reelected. A politician's mind-set is, why worry about the country's long-term viability when he will be out of office and not responsible for the crash. Politicians quickly learn the game—pandering to the needs of the current voters and even promising more benefits to them but ignoring the long-term consequences of their irresponsible behavior. Their concern for being elected today trumps damage to the country years, if not decades, hence. Nonetheless, John Maynard Keynes, understood the long-term consequences of his policies, but when confronted, he answered, "In the long run, we are all dead." That is a humorous quip, perhaps, but it avoids the underlying issue.

Any system that provides current politicians access to future tax dollars in order to buy an election today is immoral. Indeed, the parties become bidders of other people's money, promising gifts to current constituents to be paid for by future tax payers, many not yet even born. When a person comprehends this point, he will understand why Mises was persecuted so vehemently: He pointed out the illicit nature of the alliance between the state and the Keynesian economics professors and refused to go along with the inflationary charade at the taxpayers' expense.

The economists sell out their character for comfort, money, and power gained by supporting popular Keynesian policies. Individuals, in their pursuit of gains, can advance by writing, teaching, and supporting Keynesian theories of government intervention. But why do most universities support government intervention in the economy? Can you say FTM? Who is funding nearly every university in America and the Western world? Is it the same Western governments who benefit from the universities teaching the flawed Keynesian economics? The same government that partners with educators, convincing the masses of the benefits of Keynesian inflationary policies, then rewarding the educators with money grants, prestigious university posts, and government advisory roles in the Statist governments. All these professors have to do is promote the popular Keynesian policies to move ahead. If a person were to FTM, the process flows something like this in a simple rendition: Government prints paper money, stealing value from all Americans, taking some of the money to reward the economic educators (doctrinaires), who write mighty tomes (propaganda) in support of said governments, creating a virtuous cycle of advancement for exploiters in both the political and the educational fields. And all of these benefits are paid for by the masses, who, ignorant of the scheme, merely wonder why it becomes tougher every year to make a living. Politicians win by spending money that doesn't belong to them; economists win by receiving advancements for teaching flawed doctrine; and the citizens lose by declining in wealth and opportunities, surrendering "we the people" to become "we the exploited." Mises pointed out the scheme, refused to participate, and paid the price for his character-based stand, being blackballed from every major university teaching post even though he was recognized as one of the greatest economists of all time.

Young and impressionable students, not trained to recognize the fallacies of Keynesianism, become susceptible to propaganda, despite the fact that after five thousand years of recorded history, Statist policies have never worked anywhere. Even the kings of propaganda, Hitler and Lenin, would be proud of the level of deceit here. Hitler taught, "Make the lie big, make it simple, keep saying it, and eventually, they will believe it." He also said, "How fortunate for leaders that men do not think." Not to be outdone, Lenin espoused, "A lie told often enough becomes truth." If economists are rewarded for following the company line, and the companies, in this case, are funded by the government, then it doesn't take a grand conspiracy theory, but merely an understanding of FTM and SFN, to see why our present economic policies support further government interventions regardless of whether they are bankrupting the Western nations or not. What other valid explanation could explain the United States' multitrillion-dollar national debt? It's hard for anyone to make a character-based stand in the workplace when the boss rewards bad behavior and punishes good behavior. People are left in a moral quandary, pitting their money against their morals. Millions of people surrender their morals for money, engulfing the world in darkness; but when one person sets his soul on fire with the truth, his light radiates a path out of the darkness. This is exactly what Ludwig Von Mises did: he lit a path out of the darkness for others to follow. Where is the next generation of men and women willing to set their souls on fire for the truth? Where are the courageous citizens who cannot tolerate falsehoods any longer, who bravely choose to live by Virgil's quote, "Do not give in to evil, but proceed ever more boldly against it"?

## CHAPTER 3

# ATTITUDE
## Resolved: To Have a Positive Attitude in All Situations

*I know that by listening to my* positive voice *and turning down my* negative voice, *I will own a positive attitude.*

It's amazing how much a person can learn about another's attitude by listening. People who say that they have a positive attitude but think negatively reveal their true state when they start speaking. For example, when mentoring, I like to start with, "Tell me the good, the bad, and the ugly. The good we will celebrate, the bad we will make adjustments for, and the ugly we will pray about." This is sure to get people talking, helping me identify not just what happened but what people think about what happened. A person's thinking is more important than the actual event since the event happens only once, but what he thinks about it remains in his heart and mind and is shared over and over with himself and others. Painful experiences are common to both achievers and nonachievers, but whether this empowers or disempowers depends on the story created from the experience. Ironically, failure in life isn't from outside events but from the inside stories a person tells himself.

### Positive and Negative Voice Tellers

Inside a person's head are two voices. The first, the positive voice, speaks all the good about each situation, seeing the world through a positive perspective. The second, the negative voice, speaks all the bad about each situation, seeing the world from a negative perspective. One cannot eliminate either the negative voice or the positive voice entirely, but he can learn to turn up and down each of them. Winners consistently turn up the positive voice and turn down the negative voice, leading to a healthy positive attitude on life. Others, on the other hand, those who struggle with their attitudes, reverse this process, turning up the negative voice and turning down the positive voice. In fact, most people struggle with attitudes because they are wired with the negative voice shouting and the positive voice whispering at them. In a similar way, Zig Ziglar compares the voices within a person's head to visiting a bank with a positive and negative bank teller:

> In your mind bank, there are two tellers—both of whom are obedient to your every command. One teller is positive and handles positive deposits and positive withdrawals. The other teller is negative and will accept all negative deposits and provide you with negative feedback.
>
> As the owner of your mind, you have complete control over all withdrawals and most deposits. The deposits represent your total experiences in life. The withdrawals determine your success and happiness. Obviously, you can't withdraw anything that hasn't been deposited. (That's true in the cash bank too, isn't it?)
>
> Each transaction involves a choice of which teller to use. Confront the negative teller with a problem, and he will remind you of how poorly you performed in the past. He will predict failure with your current problem. Confront your positive teller, and he will enthusiastically tell you how you successfully dealt with far more difficult problems in the past. He will give you examples of your skill and genius and assure you that you can easily solve this problem. Both tellers are right because: whether you think you can or you think you can't—you are right.

The difference between a positive person and a negative person then isn't determined by his experiences, but by which bank teller voice he consistently chooses to visit. Here is a humorous example explaining the difference:

> An avid positive-oriented duck hunter was in the market for a new bird dog. His search ended when he found a dog that could actually walk on water to retrieve a duck. Shocked by his find, he was sure that his negative-oriented friend would never believe him. He decided to try to break

the news to his most pessimistic friend by inviting him on a duck hunt to witness his amazing dog firsthand. As they waited by the shore, a flock of ducks flew by. They fired, and a duck fell. The dog responded and jumped into the water. The dog, however, did not sink but instead walked across the water to retrieve the bird, never getting more than his paws wet. The friend saw everything but did not say a single word.

On the drive home, the hunter asked his friend, "Did you notice anything unusual about my new dog?"

"I sure did," responded his friend. "He can't swim."

No matter what information or results a person provides to his negative voice, the voice will always find a creative way to criticize it. The positive and negative voice hunters received the same information but developed completely different stories, based on which voice they were listening to. Winners and nonwinners receive the same stimuli but choose to interpret and respond to events differently.

## Reframing

But how does listening to a voice make any difference in a situation? In truth, the voice doesn't change the facts; however, it can radically change how a person responds to them. Author Stewart Robertson describes two ways to change how a person views a situation through what he calls reframing. A person can change either the content or the context of a situation by reframing how he thinks about it. Robertson said, "Content reframing is changing the meaning of a behavior to help you see the good side and appreciate the otherwise unlovely character. Context reframing is finding a way to make an event or behavior to be represented in such a way that it would have value no matter how negative you think it might be."

> **A person can change either the content or the context of a situation by reframing how he thinks about it.**

The positive voice reframes potential negative events into empowering positive viewpoints, while the negative voice frames everything into disempowering viewpoints. In *Creators Syndicate*, author Mary Hunt shared a powerful example of reframing:

Years ago, my husband and I decided not to replace

my car once the lease was up. The plan was that because we work together, we would share his car until we could pay cash for a second car. We figured that would take six months or so.

I won't say this new arrangement was enjoyable. Actually, I hated it. I felt as if I'd lost my freedom. My wings were clipped; no more spontaneity for me. If I wasn't being "chaperoned" as a passenger in my husband's car, I was having to ask permission to borrow it. Let me just put it this way: I was not the most pleasant passenger.

We'd been commuting together for about three months when I realized that it wasn't the situation that was intolerable. It was me. I was making myself miserable, not recognizing that the nicest guy in the world was willing to take me anywhere I wanted to go, anytime I wanted to get there. I was ungrateful and horribly self-centered. I needed an attitude change, and I needed it quickly.

I decided I had to reframe my thinking because the situation wasn't going to change anytime soon. I decided that rather than a pathetic dependent child, I would see myself as a woman of privilege. I have a driver!

Every day, I am driven back and forth to work, during which time I am free to chat, read, write, think, knit or nap. I never have to wash a car. I don't have to pump gas into it, insure it, register it, or have it "smogged" (a California thing)—all because my driver is also my maintenance man. Several times a year when I need to go in a different direction, I get a rental car, which allows me to try out some brand-new fancy cars and get my fix behind the wheel. See? A different way of looking at the same situation.

When Hunt listened to her negative voice, she framed the events negatively in content ("I am a pathetic dependent child.") and in context ("My husband is too cheap to give me my own car."). It was only after she disciplined her thinking, turning down the volume of the negative voice and turning up her positive voice, that she framed the events positively in content ("I have my own personal driver.") and context ("I get more time with my husband while saving time and money."). It may be easier to listen to the negative voice, but it's much harder to live with the results of doing it. It takes practice to habitually turn down the negative voice, seeking instead the teller with the positive voice, but it must be done in order to develop a positive mind-set. Leaders are perpetual reframers of events for themselves and their organizations. A person's life can be fundamentally changed, experiencing joy instead of misery through the power of reframing, for the joy or misery experienced isn't in the event itself but in the mind-set chosen to define it.

Another great example of reframing an event occurred during the 1984 presidential campaign. Many were concerned about Ronald Reagan's age, fearful that a man in his mid-seventies would not be able to handle the pressures of the presidency. When age was brought up by Mondale during one of their debates, Reagan said, "I will not make age an issue of this campaign. I am not going to exploit, for political purposes, my opponent's youth and inexperience." Not surprisingly, Reagan's age issue wasn't discussed again for the duration of the campaign.

The key is to tune in to the positive voice teller immediately, reframing any event through a positive perspective in real time. However, there will be moments when a person listens to his negative voice inadvertently. How does one root out the negative thinking planted by the negative voice?

## Pulling Negative Weeds

When a person listens to his negative voice or another person's negative voice, he develops negative thinking, which germinates in his mind similarly to weeds growing in a garden. Weeds are negative viewpoints, attaching themselves to a person's thinking, blocking good ideas from taking root. They (negative thoughts) can sneak into his mental garden, and they must be pulled immediately. If allowed to grow, they become stronger, developing root systems in his thinking patterns, making eradication difficult. They create "stinking thinking," producing negative attitudes and selfish behaviors, which prohibit the growth of fruits in his life. Don't provide fertile soil in the mind for weeds; don't allow weeds to seed into the heart; and whatever you do, you should not allow negative seeds to spread out of your mouth, becoming a carrier of negativity that further infects yourself and others. Simply put, if weeds are constantly growing in a person's thinking, then he knows that he is tuning into his negative voice. Positive attitudes are an inside job, just as weed-free gardens are a gardener's job.

> **Winners don't make the rules in the game of life; nonetheless, they must learn to apply the rules in their favor in order to win.**

75

Remember, what happens to a person in life does not matter nearly as much as how he responds to what happens to him. No one can plant weeds in a garden without the owner's permission, but sadly, most people neglect the tending of their gardens. The typical person, before learning of his mental gardening responsibilities, has allowed seeds to be scattered anywhere in his garden. From the radio, television, friends, coworkers, and family, he is constantly bombarded with seeds, many of them destructive. Most people have no idea of the damaging effects that negative ideas have on positive attitudes. Indeed, people allow others to plant any seeds available, producing more weeds than fruit in their mental gardens. Sadly, this surrenders a person's results in life to his surroundings, rather than to his choices. But if attitudes in life determine the altitudes of life, then when a person decides to move on, he must assume the responsibility of tending his garden, pulling the weeds daily, while nurturing fruit-producing ideas. Why is it easier to have "stinking thinking" than positive thinking? This is a question similar to asking why it's easier to have weeds growing in a garden than it is to have fruits. Winners don't make the rules in the game of life; nonetheless, they must learn to apply the rules in their favor in order to win. Choose to respond like a winner, focusing on solving challenges, not whining about problems. Problems are a given, but solutions exist in a leader's choices. Pull the weeds—guard the mind and protect the heart—for out of the abundance of the heart, the mouth speaks.

## Long-Term versus Short-Term Perspectives

Why let negativity seep into our hearts especially when we don't know the long-term results of current events? Why do so many people get worked up, assuming everything is going against them, when actually, obstacles are blessings in disguise? Since human beings cannot know the beginning from the end, wisdom dictates that they reframe the events of life with a positive mind-set, empowering themselves to see the opportunities in every challenge rather than just the challenges in every opportunity. The following fable teaches this lesson well:

A farmer had only one horse. One day, his horse ran away. All the neighbors came by, saying, "I'm so sorry. This is such bad news. You must be so upset."

The man just said, "We'll see."

A few days later, his horse came back with twenty wild

horses. The man and his son corralled all twenty-one horses. All the neighbors came by, saying, "Congratulations!
This is such good news. You must be so happy!"

The man just said, "We'll see."

One of the wild horses kicked the man's only son,
breaking both his legs. All the neighbors came by, saying,
"I'm so sorry. This is such bad news. You must be so upset."

The man just said, "We'll see."

The country went to war, and every able-bodied young
man was drafted to fight. The war was terrible and killed
every young man, but the farmer's son was spared since his
broken legs prevented him from being drafted.

All the neighbors came by, saying, "Congratulations!
This is such good news. You must be so happy!"

The man just said, "We'll see."

A person's attitude helps him maintain hope in the plan, even
when current events seem to be turning against him. People who
listen to their negative voice attract other negative voice people; on
the other hand, people who listen to the positive voice attract other
positive voice people. In fact, it's not the events in a person's life
that make the biggest difference; rather, it's the people he attracts
to himself that ultimately tip the scale in his favor between success
and failure. Simply put, achievement-oriented people will not associate for long with a negative voice, be it their own or another's.
Unless he is seeking to hang out with negative voices, he must
turn down his negative voice because when he does so, he no longer
attracts others who are listening to their negative voice. Charles
Swindoll made an emphatic statement:

> The longer I live, the more I realize the impact of at-
> titude on life. Attitude, to me, is more important than facts.
> It is more important than the past, than education, than
> money, than circumstances, than failures, than successes,
> than what other people think or say or do. It is more im-
> portant than appearance, giftedness, or skill. It will make
> or break a company....a church....a home. The remarkable
> thing is we have a choice every day regarding the attitude
> we will embrace for that day. We cannot change our past.
> We cannot change the fact that people will act in a certain
> way. We cannot change the inevitable. The only thing we
> can do is play on the one string we have, and that is our
> attitude....I am convinced that life is 10 percent what hap-

pens to me, and 90 percent how I react to it. And so it is with you....we are in charge of our attitudes.

## Wooden's Second Set on Attitudes

Former UCLA coach John Wooden taught his teams a second set of three principles, which are related to attitude:

1. Never whine.
2. Never complain.
3. Never make excuses.

These three principles help a person evaluate whether or not he has tuned in to his negative voice. The negative voice is responsible for scattering weeds in the mental garden, eventually producing the bad fruits of whining, complaining, and excuse making. In fact, the level of damage done to a person listening to his negative voice advances from whining, moving farther down the path of negativity to complaining, and then to completing the damage by entering into full-fledged victim status when he makes excuses. These three principles will help a person identify how many weeds are growing in his mind from listening to his negative voice. The good news is that, at any time, the gardener can assume responsibility for pulling the weeds growing in his mental garden and start listening to his positive voice. The bad news is that the longer the negative voice has a person's ear, the more work he has ahead of him to weed out his garden, just as ignoring a garden for a month isn't as difficult to clean up as ignoring a garden for several years. Nonetheless, if a person has fallen into whining, complaining, and excuse making, there is no better time than today to start the weed eradication project. By studying these three principles, a person can determine the current status of growth in his garden.

## Never Whine

Winners don't whine and whiners don't win. When a person responds to any situation by whining, it is a sure sign that the negative voice was consulted. Whining, a high-pitched or nasal-sounding appeal for sympathy, may get him some temporary attention, but it certainly hinders his ability to lead. Whining asks the question, "Why is this happening to me?" And when he asks a bad question, he consults his negative voice for an answer. Learn instead to ask, "What can I learn from this?" Thankfully, only the positive voice can answer that question. Leaders don't search for sympathy from the negative voice; rather, they search for solutions from the positive voice. True, there are times when solutions aren't readily available, but even in such situations, there is no reason to turn to the negative voice, whining like a child. Instead, strap the helmet on a little tighter and work harder. When milk is spilled on the ground, whining about who spilled it isn't going to help, but cleaning it up will.

When the going gets tough, the tough become winners while the rest become whiners. If a leader does get knocked down, temporarily hearing his negative voice, he quickly works to pull the weed, refusing to be a spreader of his negativity. If the weed is extra difficult, he can seek out mentors who have more experience with all the variations of mental weeds. Predictably, if a person doesn't kill his own weeds, he will become a carrier of negativity to others, forfeiting his leadership by contaminating others with his poisonous mixture of weeds and whining. Leadership is the ability to create confidence and trust in people; therefore, if a person listens repeatedly to his negative voice, his attitude will be unstable at best. This disqualifies him from leadership until he learns to habitually listen to his positive voice and pull the weed seeds. Attitude simply isn't optional for leaders. Wooden placed whining first on his list because it is the beginning sign that someone is tapping into the wrong voice. Anyone plugged into a steady diet of his negative voice eventually reveals this fact by verbalizing the whining that previously formed in his mind, entered his heart, and finally flowed out of his mouth.

**Attitude simply isn't optional for leaders.**

## Never Complain

The second principle "Never complain" is a deeper infection of negativity. If whining is the common cold variety of negative attitudes, then complaining is the pneumonia of negative attitudes. A complainer points his finger at others and away from himself by saying, "Why did they do it this way and make it so tough for me?" By complaining about others, a person feels less responsible to fix his own problems. Negative attitudes eventually turn into false beliefs, similar to seeds eventually growing into large weeds that infect the whole garden. An example of the negative voice turning a negative thought into a false belief is when negatively thinking, "I am not talented enough," becomes a full-grown weed, "Since success is only for the talented, and I am not talented, why should I put forth the effort?" When a limiting belief is adopted, people will soon defend it, as Richard Bach, author of *Jonathan Livingston Seagull* wrote, "Argue for your limitations, and sure enough, they are yours." By listening to one's negative voice, failure becomes a self-fulfilling prophecy, leading to a life of complaining about bad luck. One has wrongly concluded that since he doesn't have extraordinary talent, he isn't part of a special group of elite achievers. People, fearing the pain of change, or more specifically, the pain of pulling their own weeds, run to self-deception in an effort to defend their fragile egos. They subconsciously know that if they were to ever admit that they have what it takes to win, then the weed seed would be exposed as a lie wrapped in an excuse. It's a person's lack of attitude, not his lack of talent, that is the main reason for failure. If a person complains, one knows that he is consulting with his negative voice, sliding down the slope of negativity from whining to complaining. He is sick with a poisonous attitude and is now a carrier of negativity into other people's lives.

Leaders address issues head-on, seeking to resolve, not worsen, the matter. They know that if they start complaining, they will

> **Leaders address issues head-on, seeking to resolve, not worsen, the matter.**

surrender leadership by listening to their negative voice. Has complaining about something ever produced real change? Henry Ford II said, "Never complain, never explain," emphasizing the worthlessness of complaining about circumstances or explaining them away through excuses. Mentally complaining may release a person from feeling responsible, but by passing the buck, he has also passed on leadership since a leader accepts responsibility. Bitter or better, those are the two choices people have in life. Complaining leads to bitterness and resentment, while changing leads to joy and thankfulness. Everyone plays a part in resolving challenges, even if it's just encouraging others rather than complaining to or about them. One of the best ways identified to turn down the negative voice is to simply ignore it. Stop listening to the negative voice; instead, replace it with positive books, positive audios, and positive associations.

## Never Make Excuses

This leads us to the third principle in Wooden's set of three, avoiding the death knell of all leadership: making excuses. People who make excuses no longer ask questions; instead, they make self-deceived statements like, "It's not my fault; others are fully responsible for my failures." When a potential leader falls prey to this intoxicating brew of negativity spewing from his negative voice, he takes the full slide ride from whining to complaining, fulfilling the negative trifecta with excuses. Leaders find reasons to win; others find excuses to lose. In business and in life, you can either make a million dollars or a million excuses, but you cannot make both at the same time. Winners have an attitude that "they will until," accepting no excuses from themselves. Why is it so easy to make excuses for lack of results in any activity? It's so easy because excuses provide people with perceived justifications for remaining unchanged. This may provide temporary relief from the pain; however, it's the pain that creates the leverage to drive real change. Most people quickly develop coping mechanisms like blaming, excuse making, and finger pointing to avoid not only the pain of defeat but also the responsibility to grow and change.

People with a positive attitude know that temporary defeats are only lessons on the path to success. Thomas Edison was once asked how it felt to fail hundreds of times on the way to developing the incandescent light-bulb. He replied that he hadn't failed **Failure is an event, not a person.** hundreds of times, but actually had successfully identified hundreds of ways that wouldn't work. Edison proves that failure isn't final for a person with a good attitude. All winners discipline their thinking to ensure setbacks in life are merely stepping stones for advances. Failure is an event, not a person. But without a winner's thought processes, people will label themselves failures instead of learning from a failed event. Whether a person ultimately succeeds or fails has more to do with his attitude than his circumstances. Winston Churchill said, "Success is going from one failure to another with no loss in enthusiasm." Study any of the top performers in any field, and one will find that they refused to make excuses, literally seeking for ways to be responsible in any situation. A leader must perform checkups from the neck up, asking himself if he has fallen prey to whining, or worse, complaining, or the deadliest one of all, becoming a full-fledged victim by making excuses. If one finds any of these three negative principles at work within, it's time for him to restore his mental garden.

## Develop a Thankful Spirit

Probably the simplest way to start the restoration of one's mental garden is to focus on one's blessings. It's hard to have a negative attitude when a person views his life through the lens of thankfulness. Conversely, it's hard to have a positive attitude when a person views life through the lens of unthankfulness. Remember the story of a man who was complaining because he had no shoes? He stopped complaining when he saw someone with no feet. Thankfulness is reframing one's perspective, choosing to listen to the positive voice. At times, a person must deal with negativity, but one doesn't need to swim in it. Instead, he should handle it as though it is garbage: gather it up and throw it out. Whatever he does, he should refuse to fall into bitterness and resentment. He should choose to find the blessings in life, which are always present, even in the darkest of times.

This ninety-two-year-old lady beautifully models the fact that attitude is a choice:

> She is fully dressed each morning by eight o'clock, with her hair fashionably coiffed and her makeup perfectly applied, in spite of the fact that she is legally blind. Today, she has moved to a nursing home. Her husband of seventy years recently passed away, making this move necessary. After many hours of waiting patiently in the lobby of the nursing home, where I am employed, she smiled sweetly when told her room was ready. As she maneuvered her walker to the elevator, I provided a visual description of her tiny room, including the eyelet curtains that had been hung on her window. "I love it," she stated with the enthusiasm of an eight-year-old having just been presented with a new puppy. "Mrs. Jones, you haven't seen the room.... just wait," I said. Then she spoke these words that I will never forget. "That does not have anything to do with it," she gently replied. "Happiness is something you decide on ahead of time. Whether I like the room or not does not depend on how the furniture is arranged. It is how I arrange my mind. I have already decided to love it. It is a decision I make every morning when I wake up. I have a choice. I can spend the day in bed recounting the difficulty I have with the parts of my body that no longer work, or I can get out of bed and be thankful for the ones that do work. Each day is a gift, and as long as my eyes open, I will focus on the new

day and all of the happy memories I have stored away . . . just for this time in my life."

This ninety-two-year-old lady encapsulates everything on attitude: listening to the positive voice while turning down the negative voice; reframing both the content and the context of her situation; and having a thankful, joyful spirit. When a person chooses to have a thankful spirit, turning habitually to his positive voice, he draws upon a wellspring of options, helping him to overcome the challenges that he is sure to meet on his life's journey. The voice that a person chooses to listen to determines the fruit that he produces in life. Choose wisely.

## Roger Bannister: Attitude and the Quest for the Four-Minute Mile

For over three-thousand years of recorded history, beginning in the eighth century BC with the ancient Greek Olympics, human beings have dreamed of breaking the four-minute mile. The ancient Greeks loved their athletic competitions, believing that they developed the martial spirit in the people necessary to succeed in war. The Greek city-states seemed to live for war but loved their sports events even more, calling temporary truces, if necessary, in order to enjoy their athletic events. Each city-state brought its best athletes to the competitions, with the largest, most honored of competitions held every four years in Olympia, in an event called the Olympics.

The Greeks sought after an ideal called *paideia*. It stood for perfection, the goal to be preeminent in a specific field of achievement. For the Olympic mile race, the *paideia* was identified as four minutes flat, a perfect sixty seconds per quarter mile.

The Greek runners' training and conditioning regimens were impressive. For example, Pheidippides, an Athenian herald, once ran 150 miles from Athens to Sparta in less than two days, an amazing feat even by today's ironman standards. For over a thousand years, Greek runners trained intently, dreaming of being the first to achieve the mythical *paideia*. In fact, Greek folklore recounts amusing training methods in an attempt to reach the target—one consisting of unleashing lions to chase the runners—a bizarre attempt to motivate the runners. The dream of the four-minute mile had captured the Greek mind, but the *paideia*, the perfection, was never achieved. The last of the ancient Olympics was held near the end of the fourth century AD; the over-one-thousand-year quest for the perfect mile closed without anyone breaking through the barrier.

The beginning of the twentieth century witnessed a new level of worldwide sporting competitions, especially with the advent of the modern Olympics in 1896. The best of the best now met every four years, creating the competitive excellence that helped many athletes shatter previous world records. This competitive reawakening rebirthed the original Greek quest, the *paideia*, for the four-minute mile. Runners from across the globe dreamed again to be the first one to break through the mythical ideal, running a sub-four-minute mile.

In 1915, the mile record stood at 4:12.6, still over twelve seconds off the target set by the ancient Greeks. For the next thirty years, runners from all over the world continued to inch the mile time closer to four minutes. On July 17, 1945, Gunder "the Wonder" Hägg, ran a mile in 4:01.3. He was so close to the coveted prize, a mere 1.3 seconds away, yet he never broke the barrier. Hägg's world record stood for nearly nine more years, the longest duration of time for any mile record to stand for the entire twentieth century. For some reason, for nearly nine years, this mental weed, this troublesome belief, held its Rasputin-like powers over runners from every nation. The runners were not struggling physically; instead, they were battling limiting beliefs from a weed that had grown for thousands of years. The negative voice reigned supreme over the mile runners, while the positive voice was silenced through nearly three thousand years of failed attempts.

Enter medical student Roger Bannister, one of the new breed of runners who believed that the four-minute barrier could and should be broken. For Bannister, breaking the long-standing barrier was a personal challenge, having heard repeatedly that it was "impossible." It's interesting to note that while most get demoralized when hearing the negative voices of others, winners get energized turning the crowds' negative voices into a personal challenge to overcome. Bannister was a winner, and this negative stimulus only strengthened his positive voice resolve. Training alone, he deliberately avoided the coaches and managers, believing they were subconsciously holding the runners back through their limiting beliefs and attitudes. By 1953, by applying his own training regimen and using his medical field experience, he had reduced his time to 4:03.6, still short of the mythical standard, but progressing forward. With constant practice, both mental and physical, Bannister slowed his heart rate to less than 50 beats per minute (BPM), significantly below the 72 BPM of the average man. The lower heart rate allowed him, under the intense strain of running, to maintain a larger oxygen reserve, which prolonged the time he could run under anaerobic conditions. This made the four-minute mile physically possible. Nevertheless, it was more than just hard training. Bannister, naturally scientific in outlook, analyzed his performance after every practice, placing focus on continuous improvement. He wrote, "Improvement in running depends on continuous self-discipline by the athlete himself, on acute observation of his reaction to races and training, and above all on judgment, which he must learn for himself." This belief, along with his research on the latest running mechanics and his scientific methods for training, convinced him that he could break the record, ending, once and for all, the three-thousand-year quest.

Bannister might have trained alone, but he certainly was not alone in his quest for the coveted four-minute mile. Two other runners, Wes Santee and John Landy, had impressive credentials, both publicly stating the goal to be the first to break the coveted *paidea*. These three men were in a race against time for track-and-field immortality.

Santee, an American, was probably the best natural athlete of the three. The son of a Kansas ranch hand, he amazed crowds with his athletic prowess and confident spirit. He was the first to publicly state his intention of breaking the four-minute barrier. John Landy, on the other hand, was an Australian. He trained harder than anyone, desiring to win this international honor, not only for himself, but for his home country. He ran everywhere—in the woods, in the sand dunes, and on the beach—revealing an inner drive to be the best that he could be.

Each of these three runners understood that on any given day, with the right conditions, he could break through the four-minute barrier. This led to a three-dimensional race against time. On the one hand was the race itself and the quest to break through the four-minute barrier, certainly pressure enough. On the other hand was the race against the unknown since only one of the three could be the first in history to run a sub-four-minute mile the first time. None of the runners knew how much time each of them had before one of his competitors broke through the barrier. Each runner understood that each opportunity could be his last.

Neal Bascomb described the hoopla created by these three elite runners: "For weeks in advance of every race, the headlines heralded an impending break in the barrier: 'Landy

Likely to Achieve Impossible!'; 'Bannister Gets Chance of Four-Minute Mile!'; 'Santee Admits Getting Closer to Phantom Mile.' Articles dissected track conditions and the weather forecasts. Millions around the world followed every attempt. When each runner failed—and there were many failures— he was criticized for coming up short, for not having what it took. Each such episode only motivated the others to try harder." This three-man drama created a buzz throughout the athletic world, starting endless debates about who would be the first man to break the four-minute mile.

On May 6, 1954, on a chilly spring evening, the debate ended, and Bannister's date with destiny arrived. He traveled to the Iffley Road track in Oxford for their annual track meet. The "dream mile" had been scientifically plotted for years by sports physiologists and coaches, believing that it would take ideal conditions to achieve it. It was theorized that temperatures needed to be around sixty-eight degrees with no discernible wind and a track made of hard dry clay in order to set the stage for the "dream mile." In addition, along with the perfect weather and track conditions, a planned sequence of quarters needed to be run, the first quarter clocked the slowest, with each subsequent quarter becoming faster, closing with the fastest time being the final quarter. Nearly everyone believed that without perfect conditions and planning, the "dream mile" would remain just that—a dream.

The conditions, however, in Oxford on this chilly May day were far from ideal, forcing Bannister to break nearly every one of the "dream mile" theories. Rain had drenched the cinder track, making the surface slippery. Meanwhile, the wind had been blowing at practically galelike force for most of the day, reducing the crowd to a mere 1,500 spectators at the historic event. Thankfully, with the late six o'clock start time, the rain had died down, but not the biting wind that was cutting across the track. In spite of these conditions, Bannister believed that he must make this race count, knowing that Santee or Landy could break the record at any of their upcoming races. Bannister reached deep inside himself, listening to his positive voice, revealing the inside champion to the outside world through his now-legendary performance.

At six o'clock in the evening, the runners were at the starting line. Bannister, with two of his teammates from the BAAA (British Amateur Athletic Association), lined up with three Oxford runners. In a methodical plan, developed before the race, Chris Brasher, a teammate of Bannister's, was set to play the jackrabbit, the pacesetter for Bannister. Brasher's first lap set a blistering pace, with Bannister, running right behind him, timing in at 57.5 seconds. This was too fast, an impossible time to maintain for even two laps, let alone four, making many believe that the record was safe, at least for today. Brasher, however, regaining his composure and pace, completed his two laps before collapsing to the side of the track, exhausted. Bannister's half-mile time was 1:58.2, within the range he had set beforehand, leaving the goal within his reach. Near the start of the third lap, Chris Chataway, the third BAAA runner, in accordance with the plan, sprinted to the front, allowing Bannister to draft behind him. Chataway ran a stellar third lap, giving it all he had, until, depleted of energy, he fell off the pace. But Bannister, thanks to the pace set by his friend, completed the third lap in 3:00.7, a mere fraction of a second off the prized pace. The million-dollar question was, how much gas did Bannister have left after his grueling first three laps? He didn't wait long to answer this question. With three hundred yards to go, he began his final kick, tapping into a reservoir of energy known only to himself. He lengthened his stride, rolled his head back awkwardly, and gave it everything he had, literally collapsing as he broke the tape, passing out momentarily from the extended physical and mental exertion. Pensively, the crowd awaited an official announcement, which finally came over the loudspeaker: "A time which is a new meeting and track record, and which, subject to ratification, will be a new English native, a British national, a British all-comers, European, British Empire, and world record. The time was three minutes....fifty-nine and four-tenths seconds." The audience erupted, and pandemonium ensued as people realized the momentous event they had just witnessed. Bannister had run the fourth lap in a scintillating 58.7 seconds, smashing through the four-minute-mile barrier with a final time of 3:59.4! After his superhuman effort, Bannister regained consciousness quickly, even though he suffered momentary color blindness from his physical exertions. Indeed, his standard heart rate of 50 BPM had soared to over 155 BPM, not returning to normal for over three hours. He completed his 1954 dream season in style, winning the British and Empire championships in the mile run, along with the European title in the 1,500-meter event. After completing his record-breaking season, Bannister announced his retirement from athletic competitions and pursued his medical career full-time.

In 1955, he wrote a book on his track-and-field exploits, titled *The Four-Minute Mile*. He earned his medical degree from Oxford, becoming a neurologist. In 1975, he received the honor of being knighted by Queen Elizabeth II, a fitting close to an extraordinary career.

Bannister raised the bar on what was possible and faced more than his fair share of criticisms, carpings, and naysayers along the way, but he didn't hear them. He chose, instead, to listen to his positive voice. The most incredible part of this story isn't even Bannister's four-minute mile, but rather what happened to the other runners when Bannister accomplished the "impossible." The mile record, the Greek *paideia*, which had never been run in under four minutes and had stood at slightly over four minutes for nearly nine years, was suddenly broken thirty-seven times in the following two years. How did this happen? It certainly wasn't improved physical conditioning, better tracks, or lighter weight shoes, since none of these changed. What did improve were the beliefs and subsequent attitudes through Bannister's example of listening to his positive voice, which gave others permission to listen to theirs. Today, breaking through limiting beliefs is called "the Bannister Effect."

In the third year, things really went crazy, with over three hundred runners breaking the four-minute mile—all because of a changed belief window, which led to each runner now consulting with his positive voice rather than his negative voice. What was once thought impossible has now become routine, simply because a man with better beliefs and a positive attitude proved that it could be done. Guardian News, in an interview with Bannister fifty years after his historic accomplishment, reported: "Until then, there had been a widespread belief that it was physically impossible for a man to run the mile in less than four minutes. People claimed the human body would burst amid such a trial of speed and endurance." Bannister, slipping into his best Inspector Clouseau–style accent, remembered: "a Frenchman once said to my wife, 'but 'ow did 'ee know 'ees heart would not burst?' Even Landy spoke of a 'cement wall' protecting the four-minute mark. But I knew it could be done." Bannister knew it could be done, and this made all the difference because the real barrier to breaking the four-minute mile wasn't physical, but mental. Bannister's personal breakthrough pulled a three-thousand-year-old weed for humanity, removing the mental roadblocks, allowing millions to achieve success through "the Bannister Effect."

CHAPTER 4

# VISION
## Resolved: To Align My Conscious (Ant) with My Subconscious (Elephant) Mind toward My Vision

*I know that ending the civil war between the two is crucial for all achievement.*

### The Ant and the Elephant

Achievers in every field visualize successful outcomes before they make them a reality. From athletes to salespeople, musicians, business owners, and many others, top performers understand the power of visualization for goal achievement. In fact, Jack Canfield, in his book *The Success Principles*, wrote that people have control over only three things in life: "the thoughts you think, the images you visualize, and the action you take." The conscious mind thinks in words, while the subconscious mind thinks in images. The images formed in the subconscious mind lead a person toward his dominating vision, but this visualization process is little known and rarely applied by most people. In reality, if someone desires to break out of the crowd, then learning to feed the subconscious mind his vision for the future isn't just a nice add-on but an essential part of the success journey.

> **The conscious mind thinks in words, while the subconscious mind thinks in images.**

Author Vince Poscente in *The Ant and The Elephant*, described the difference between the conscious mind and the subconscious mind, teaching that the conscious (ant) mind, in one second of thinking, stimulates two thousand neurons, while the subconscious (elephant) mind, in a second of imagining, stimulates four billion neurons. That's four billion neurons to two thousand neurons; literally, two million times more neurons are stimulated in the subconscious mind than in the conscious mind in a second of mental activity. Since "neurons are the cells essential for brain activity," according to Antonio Damasio, a noted brain researcher, the subconscious (elephant) mind's four billion neurons are the brain's prime mover for high-performance achievers. Moreover, author Michael Gelb shared the differences in storage capacities of the two brains, saying, "Brain researchers estimate that your unconscious data base outweighs the conscious on an order exceeding ten million to one. This data base is the source of your hidden, natural genius. In other words, a part of you is much smarter than you are. The wise people regularly consult that smarter part." Simply stated, success cannot be achieved without tapping into both the ant and the elephant. As Erik Calonius describes in his book *Ten Steps Ahead*, "Scientists are discovering that the brain is a visionary device—that its primary function is to create pictures in our minds that can be used as blueprints for things that don't exist. They are also learning that our brains can work subconsciously to solve problems that we cannot crack through conscious reasoning, and that the brain is a relentless pattern seeker, constantly reinventing the world." "The ant and the elephant" analogy teaches us how to create successful results through the power of programming the subconscious mind with the positive thinking and visions from the conscious mind. In fact, Albert Einstein strongly believed in the subconscious mind, saying, "Imagination is everything. It is the preview of life's coming attractions." He also said, "Imagination is more important than knowledge." Both the ant and the elephant are important, but research concludes that unless a person unleashes the elephant, no world-changing results are possible.

## The Civil War

Dr. Maxwell Maltz wrote, "The brain and nervous system constitute a marvelous and complex 'goal-striving mechanism,' a sort of built-in automatic guidance system which works for you as a 'success mechanism,' or against you as a 'failure mechanism,' depending on how YOU, the operator, operate it and the goals you set for it." Sadly, most operate the elephant as a "failure mechanism," repeatedly feeding it fears and negativity, leading to dismal results. Henry David Thoreau, a famous American transcendentalist, wrote, "Most men lead lives of quiet desperation," believing few ever accomplish what they truly want, instead, quietly resigning themselves to their fate.

The "quiet desperation" is the result of a civil war between the ant and the elephant. A battle is started between the two, both fighting for control over which direction to move, causing a protracted civil war, with frustration, indecision, and inaction as the predictable results. The civil war short-circuits a person's success, not his environment, history, or talent. French thinker Émile Coué shares a law he called "the law of reversed effort," saying, "When the will and imagination are in conflict, the imagination invariably wins the day." Coué's law confirms that outside circumstances do not count nearly as much as inside alignments. A person doesn't control his outside issues, but he certainly is responsible for his inside conditions.

## The Power of Alignment

When a person assumes responsibility for what is fed to his ant and elephant, he changes his thoughts. The moment that happens, he changes his destiny forever. Every winner has realized the confidence inside him, knowing that by visualizing with the elephant mind, aligning the ant and the elephant in a common cause, that any dream is obtainable through consistent efforts toward the vividly imagined future. Similar to how actors perform a movie script, a person acts out his life according to the script provided to his elephant. In order to move in the direction of one's dreams, he must train the ant to think in a positive manner in order to feed the elephant the proper life script. How, in other words, can a negative fearful ant feed a positive faith-based image to its elephant? Peter Vidmar, an Olympic gymnast, stressed his point, saying, "Visualization is not a substitute for hard work and dedication. But if you add it to your training regimen—whether in sports, business, or your personal relationships—you will prepare your mind for success, which is the first step in achieving all your goals and dreams." After character, this is probably the single most neglected resolution, leading to lives of quiet desperation instead of thankful celebrations. If a person becomes the script he feeds to his elephant, then by changing the food it is fed, he changes his script, thus changing his destiny. My author friend Richard Brooke sums it up nicely: "Your mind

> When a person assumes responsibility for what is fed to his ant and elephant, he changes his thoughts.

doesn't care what you want—or what you are willing to work hard for. It only cares that you perform in accordance with what you expect of yourself."

## Who Is Feeding the Elephant?

The expectations that are fed to a person's elephant become his reality. The elephant will feed on something, as it must eat. If a person does not feed his elephant, then someone else gladly will. Sadly, most people's subconscious minds are deluged daily by the images fed to them from their television sets. Latest research shares that the average American is watching over five hours of TV every day. Calonius wrote on the impact of repeated exposures on the mind: "The researchers found that the subjects like the pictures they had already seen. Researchers call this the 'mere exposure effect.' That's why advertisers pound ads repeatedly down our throats. It's why chain restaurants (you get the same meal coast to coast) thrive." It's interesting to note that advertisers skip right past the ant mind, displaying their ads as food to the elephant brain. Every single advertisement feeds your elephant with an image and a vision for the offered product. A person will never view an ad that invests thirty seconds or a minute to share copious details on the functions, features, and benefits of a product. Instead, the advertisers share an image intended to create a feeling inside each TV viewer, creating a hunger to satisfy that feeling by buying a company's products. Why do advertisements feed the elephant mind and not the ant one? Simply stated, it's because giving a list of functions, features, and benefits to your ant doesn't produce results; however, the ads that feed the elephant an image of success produce the feelings that lead to purchases. Advertising agents have learned to speak past the ant mind, instead feeding the starving elephant, creating perceived needs in the consumer's elephant mind through constant repetition of appropriate images. Because of this, people end up buying things that they don't really need based on emotion, not rationally understanding why they did it. Psychologist Timothy Wilson, author of *Strangers to Ourselves*, wrote, "The adaptive unconscious plays a major executive role in our mental lives. It gathers information, interprets and evaluates it, and sets goals in motion, quickly and efficiently." Remember, people make decisions emotionally (elephant) and then will explain it rationally (ant) to themselves and others. Advertisers, in other words, replace a person's imagination with images of their own making, literally programming the minds of people who seem unwilling to program their own minds themselves.

As an example, think of the commercials aired during sporting events. Most kids love watching sports on TV, viewing football, basketball, and baseball every time they can. Through the years of watching TV sports, the children have viewed thousands of beer commercials. Remember the 1980s beer commercials? Songs like "Tonight, Tonight, Let It Be" and slogans like "Tastes great; less filling still" ring in the heads of viewers, even after thirty years has passed since the last commercial was actually experienced.

These products were sold through images and slogans that were meant to be catchy and appealing. Has anyone ever seen a beer ad where they explained the ratio of carbonated water to barley and hops? Can a person imagine an ant-version beer ad explaining how alcohol blocks the oxygen from the brain, causing impaired thinking and motor skills? That's an ad that is not likely to be produced in our lifetime. Instead, ads implant images into people's elephant minds. Since the market for beer is, in the majority of cases, single guys, the ads target this market. They run images of guys popping open a beer, and meanwhile, mysteriously, beautiful bikini-clad women appear out of nowhere. Rationally, the young men understand this isn't going to happen, but the elephant charges to pick up the beer anyway. Maybe the first time they see the ad, their elephants resist; but through constant exposure, a continuous daily feeding of the elephant, eventually, young men act out the elephant's implanted visions.

Companies understand the power of their ads; otherwise, ad executives would not pay big bucks for time slots during sporting events. Many young men resist, or at least minimize, beer drinking in high school because they are training for athletic events; but after high school, this no longer constrains them. Not in training for competitive sports, these young men, after finishing a pickup sports game, head to the bar for some male bonding and a cold one, just as their elephants were trained years before through commercials. Few have any idea why they desire to drink beer with guys, but the marketing executives know perfectly well why: this desire has been implanted into their elephant minds by repeated exposures during their youth. In other words, advertisers take advantage of a child's love of sports to capture his attention long enough to program his elephant. Young men act out the elephant programming provided to them "free of charge" by high-paid TV advertising executives with an assignment. Make no mistake, the elephant mind will be fed; the only questions are: What is it feeding on? And who is feeding it? To seize his future, a person must assume responsibility for feeding his elephant mind the proper food needed to reach his goals and dreams.

## Controlling the Inside Conditions

In order for a person to assume responsibility for his mind, he must first identify what conditions he has currently created through his thoughts and actions because they are the thought food that his ant feeds to his elephant. By identifying what a person is feeding his elephant, he can accurately predict his future. The Wallenda factor, named for Karl Wallenda, a world-renowned aerial acrobat, tragically portrays this principle. Wallenda attempted to traverse a seventy-five-foot-high wire in Puerto Rico in 1978. Helen, Karl's widow, recalled, "All Karl thought about for three straight months prior to it was falling. It was the first time he'd ever thought about that, and it seemed to me that he put all his energies into not falling rather than walking the tightrope." Karl was the best in his craft, but when he consistently fed fear to his elephant, instead of faith, the outcome was predictable. Mrs. Wallenda shared that her husband, contrary to his normal behavior, personally supervised the installation of the tightrope and guide wires. He fed wrong images into his elephant mind, dividing his attention between his conscious mind's goal to cross successfully and his subconscious mind's fears of failure, thus beginning a civil war in his mind. Instead of feeding his elephant a vision of a successful wire crossing, he fed it a fear of falling, initiating his "failure mechanism" to fulfill his tragic fear-based destiny.

Imagination, then, is neutral on success or failure; it is dependent on what a programmer chooses to feed to the elephant. The French emperor Napoleon understood this, proclaiming, "Imagination rules the world." The difference between success and failure hinges on what is consistently fed to the elephant. Remember, a person cannot set himself on fire with his dream when he is busy wetting on himself with his dread. The highest achievers are not innately better than anyone else, but they have learned the importance of feeding the elephant faith, not fears. Dr. Maltz summed it up, saying, "We act, or fail to act, not because of the *will*, as is so commonly believed, but because of imagination. A human being always acts and feels and performs in accordance with what he imagines to be true about himself and his

> **The difference between success and failure hinges upon what is consistently fed to the elephant.**

environment." What a person imagines quickly becomes his reality. If dreams are *compelling* visions of the future, then worries are *fearful* visions of the future. Just as a dream incites the elephant into action, worry directs the elephant in the wrong direction, creating a civil war of the mind.

Author Jack Canfield shared another tragic example of the civil war between the ant mind and the elephant mind in the story of Nick Sitzman, a young railroad yardman who was accidentally locked in a refrigerator boxcar after the rest of the crew had gone home:

> He banged and shouted until his fists were bloody and his voice was hoarse, but no one heard him. With his knowledge of "the numbers and the facts," he predicted the temperature to be zero degrees. Nick's thought was, "If I can't get out, I'll freeze to death in here." Wanting to let his wife and family know exactly what had happened to him, Nick found a knife and began to etch words on the wooden floor. He wrote, "It's so cold, my body is getting numb. If I could just go to sleep. These may be my last words." The next morning, the crew slid open the heavy doors of the boxcar and found Nick dead. An autopsy revealed that every physical sign of his body indicated he had frozen to death. And yet the refrigeration unit of the car was inoperative, and the temperature inside indicated 55 degrees Fahrenheit. Nick had killed himself by the power of his own thoughts.

Protect the thoughts sent to the unconscious mind, for both the fears and the dreams that the ant feeds to the elephant consistently unleash the elephant to fulfill his programming.

## Uniting the Ant and the Elephant

After understanding how the mind works to process images and thoughts, it's time to learn how to join them together by learning to properly program both the ant and the elephant. For when the ant learns to feed the elephant, a breakout from the crowd is in the making.

Many people will discipline the ant to perform work, creating habits that produce routine results, like waking up, driving to work, scheduling one's day, performing various tasks, all routinized by the daily ant habits. But imagine if people disciplined their elephants in the same way that they disciplined their ants; we would have a worldwide productivity revolution. Some may argue that they don't have time, or that they are not disciplined enough to do this, but that really isn't true. Anyone who has a job is disciplined enough to get up at a certain time, whether he prefers to or not. In life, discipline is a given; the only question is, is it going to be internal discipline or external discipline? Jobs provide external discipline to ensure the proper outcomes, while feeding the elephant requires internal discipline in order to consistently feed it a success-oriented vision for the future.

When a person disciplines the elephant, he aligns the elephant to move in the same direction as the ant, allowing the ant to hop on the back of the more powerful elephant in a drive toward success. He must feed the elephant and the ant together, uniting both parts of the brain for a common purpose, making the success trip not only possible but also enjoyable.

A person's goal should be to feed the elephant images of the oasis (the dream) off in the distance, inspiring the elephant to charge ahead with the ant hopping on its back to help direct the elephant's charge to success. Do not misunderstand the point; this isn't some magical elixir, but rather a logical plan to utilize the entire brain for goal achievement. It will still take work, effort, and drive to achieve; but by aligning the ant and the elephant, the civil war inside one's mind is ended, creating the right conditions that lead to massive results. Claude Bristol, author of *The Magic of Believing*, instructed one to feed the elephant through the ant, when he wrote: "This subtle force of repeated suggestion overcomes our reason. It acts directly on our emotions and our feelings, and finally penetrates to the very depths of our subconscious minds. It's the repeated suggestion that makes you believe." If a person wants true success, then he shouldn't waste another day riding the ant; instead, he should go back to base camp and fire up the elephant, uniting the ant and elephant with a common vision for a brighter tomorrow. He should cease the tug of war between the ant and the elephant, a war that the elephant is sure to win. Instead, he should replace it with a common goal and dream for the future. The success journey needs both the ant and elephant to achieve the desired results. Ants have neither the size nor the power to create radical change, but they do make great team players, working with the elephant to achieve alignment and direct success.

For example, Eugene Ferguson, writing in *Engineering and the Mind's Eye*, shared, "Pyramids, cathedrals, and rockets exist not because of geometry, theory of structures, or thermodynamics, but because they were first pictures—literally visions—in the (elephant) minds of those who first conceived them. Usually the significant governing decisions regarding an artisan's or an engineer's design have been made before the artisan picks up (ant) tools or the engineer turns to his (ant) drawing board." Calonius shared, "When we look at something . . . the same part of the brain lights up as when we imagine that something. This is called the 'mutual interference' between imagery and perception." Dr. Maltz concurred, writing, "Experimental and clinical psychologists have proved beyond a shadow of doubt that the human nervous system cannot tell the difference between an actual experience and an experience imagined vividly and in detail." Furthermore, philosopher Dan Dennett declared that the subconscious mind is the "president," while the conscious mind is its "press secretary." Regardless of where the line of demarcation falls between the ant and the elephant mind, it is clear that alignment between the ant and the elephant is crucial for massive achievement.

## Success Is a Picture in the Mind's Eye

Dr. Maltz wrote on the power of imagination in goal achievement: "The goals that the Creative Mechanism seeks to achieve are MENTAL IMAGES or mental pictures, which we create by the use of IMAGINATION." Success is pictured in the mind first, and then through the use of the mind's Creative Mechanism, it's formulated in the real world. Every achiever has learned to run what amounts to a success advertisement in his mind. The more the ad is visualized and achieved in the imagination, the more real it becomes. The mind, through the imagination, experiences the ads as real. What makes human beings different from animals is the mind's ability to imagine a better future. By contrast, animals cannot imagine or dream for a better future, only living through genetically coded instincts. Dr. Maltz explained, "Man, on the other hand, has something animals haven't—Creative Imagination. Thus man of all creatures is more than a creature; he is also a creator. With his imagination, he can formulate a variety of goals. Man alone can direct his Success Mechanism by the use of imagination, or imaging ability."

Peter Vidmar shared how he used *creative imagination* at the end of his practices to win a gold medal:

> I'd say, "Okay, Tim, let's imagine it's the men's gymnastics finals of the Olympic Games. The United States team is on its last event of the night, which just happens to be

the high bar. The last two guys up for the United States are Tim Daggett and Peter Vidmar. Our team is neck and neck with the People's Republic of China, the reigning world champions, and we have to perform our routines perfectly to win the Olympic team gold medal. . . ."

We'd close our eyes and, in this empty gym at the end of a long day, we'd visualize an Olympic arena with 13,000 people in the seats and another 200 million watching live on television. Then we'd practice our routines....

Tim would shout out, "Green light," and I'd look at the superior judge, who was usually our coach Mako. I'd raise my hand, and he'd raise his right back. Then I'd turn, face the bar, grab hold, and begin my routine.

Well, a funny thing happened on July 31, 1984.

It was the Olympic Games, men's gymnastics team finals in Pauley Pavilion on the UCLA campus. The 13,000 seats were filled and a television audience in excess of 200 million around the world tuned in. The United States team was on its last event of the night, the high bar. The last two guys up for the United States just happened to be Tim Daggett and Peter Vidmar. And just as we visualized, our team was neck and neck with the People's Republic of China. We had to perform our high bar routines perfectly to win the gold medal.

I looked at Coach Mako, my coach for the past 12 years. As focused as ever, he simply said, "Okay, Peter, let's go. You know what to do. You've done it a thousand times, just like every day back in the gym. Let's just do it one more time, and let's go home. You're prepared."

He was right. I had planned for this moment and visualized it hundreds of times. I was prepared to perform my routine. Rather than seeing myself actually standing in the Olympic arena with 13,000 people in the stands and 200 million watching on television, in my mind, I pictured myself back in the UCLA gym at the end of the day with two people left in the gym.

When the announcer said, "From the United States of America, Peter Vidmar," I imagined it was my buddy Tim Daggett saying it. When the green light came on, indicating it was time for the routine, I imagined that it wasn't really a green light but that it was Tim shouting, "Green light!" And when I raised my hand toward the superior judge from East Germany, in my mind I was signaling my coach, just like I had signaled him every day at the end of hundreds of workouts. In the gym, I always visualized I was at the Olympic finals; at the Olympic finals, I visualized I was back in the gym.

I turned, faced the bar, jumped up, and grabbed on. I began the same routine I had visualized and practiced day after day in the gym. I was in memory mode, going yet again where I'd already gone hundreds of times.

I quickly made it past the risky double-release move that had harpooned my chances at the world championships. I moved smoothly through the rest of my routine and landed a solid dismount, where I anxiously waited for my score from the judges.

With a deep voice the announcement came through the speaker, "The score for Peter Vidmar is 9.95."

"Yes!" I shouted. "I did it!" The crowd cheered loudly as my teammates and I celebrated our victory.

Thirty minutes later, we were standing on the Olympic medal platform in the Olympic arena with 13,000 people in the stands and over 200 million watching on television, while the gold medals were officially draped around our necks. Tim, me, and our teammates stood proudly wearing our gold medals as the national anthem played and the American flag was raised to the top of the arena. It was a moment we visualized and practiced hundreds of times in the gym. Only this time, it was for real.

Vidmar proved that in life, a person doesn't always get what he wants or what he deserves, but he always gets what he expects. For what a person consistently feeds his elephant is eventually what a person expects out of life.

## Success through Visualization

Most people fail in life, not from lack of potential, but from lack of planned, focused feeding of their elephant minds. This focus begins when a person identifies what his true dreams in life are. The journey of a thousand miles begins with one step, but not until one identifies in which direction he is heading. Without a doubt, this is the most underutilized aspect in a man's quest for a successful life, causing most people to exhaust themselves without achieving the results that they deserve. Author Charles Garfield shared a compelling personal story of how belief acts on both the conscious mind and the subconscious mind. A former amateur weight lifter, he sat down with Soviet sports scientists, who mentally prepared Soviet Bloc athletes for Olympic competition. The Soviets claimed they had tapped into what they called psychophysiology, hidden reserves of energy through mental preparation. Garfield, skeptical of the results claimed by the mental visualization techniques, believed that most of the Soviet results were due to steroid use. He listened to the Soviets, asking questions, while seeking to understand the process behind the mental training techniques. The Soviets, in an effort to alleviate any doubts, proposed that Garfield subject himself to their training exercises. The Soviet trainers urged him to attempt a three-hundred-pound bench press—something he hadn't accomplished in several years. He surprised himself as he accomplished the goal, straining every muscle to bench-press three hundred pounds. The Soviets began a series of measurements, blood tests, and calculations designed to measure the full potential inside Garfield. Finally, they were ready to demonstrate the mental aspects of psychophysiology. Here are Garfield's words:

Eventually we went to the next step. They asked me to lie down on my back. Then they guided me into a deeper state of relaxation. "Imagine your arms and legs becoming increasingly heavy and warm...." Fully awake and alert, I began to feel more at ease.

When nearly an hour had passed, they asked me to get up slowly and gently. They had added 65 pounds to the 300 I had barely pushed off my chest earlier. Any weightlifter knows that you go up in smaller increments; you just don't make a 21 percent increase all at once. That didn't bother them. Firmly, thoroughly, they talked me through a series of mental preparations. In my mind's eye I saw myself approaching the bench. I visualized myself lying down. I visualized myself, with total confidence, lifting the 365 pounds. I imagined the sounds I would hear, the clink of the metal as I tipped the bar and the weights shifted, my own breathing...

Suddenly, I became apprehensive. They actually thought I was going to try and lift 365 pounds! I "knew" I could not do it. I knew my limits. The needles on the monitors jerked back and forth, reflecting my anxiety. Patiently, they talked me through more relaxation, more visualization. They asked me to zoom mentally in and out of the images now becoming familiar imprints in my mind: ap-

proaching the bar, grasping, lifting smoothly and confidently. All the while, they checked my responses on their
monitors and gauges.

At length, everything began to come together for me,
just as it does an instant before you know you are going
to succeed in some task for which you have been preparing. One more time they talked me through the lift. In my
mind I became convinced I could do it. The world around
me seemed to fade, giving way to self-confidence, belief in
myself, and then to deliberate action. I lifted the weight.
Astounded, exhilarated by the triumph, I wanted to go on, I
felt ready to challenge the world record. But more rational
minds prevailed.

Garfield, after an eight-year layoff, had achieved his peak
bench press through the power of mentally aligning his conscious
mind and his subconscious mind: the ant and the elephant. The
Soviet scientists had united Garfield's conscious beliefs with his
unconscious images, creating a successful outcome.

Nearly every world-class athlete has learned the secret of
aligning the ant and the elephant, and it's just as effective in other
fields. In 1987, a struggling actor, barely able to pay his bills, drove
his old Toyota up Mulholland Drive into the Hollywood Hills. As he
stared down at the City of Angels' lights, he ended the internal civil
war, aligning his ant and his elephant. He wrote himself a check,
dated for Thanksgiving 1995, "for acting services rendered," in the
amount of $10 million. Few actors or actresses of any caliber were
receiving checks of this amount, making it especially far-fetched
that an unknown actor would believe in so absurd a ritual. But Jim
Carrey knew what he was doing, uniting his ant and his elephant.
When his conscious ant mind wrote the $10 million check, he was
purposefully feeding his subconscious elephant mind the vision
of his future reality. Today, Carrey, thanks to his united ant and
elephant, surpasses $20 million for his acting services. Imagine
how many people, with near-unlimited talent inside of them, never
achieve success because, unlike Carrey, they never align the ant
and the elephant.

People will discipline their conscious ant mind to make a living,
but few will discipline their subconscious elephant mind to achieve
their dreams. Aligning the ant and the elephant toward a person's
dream is essential for achieving success. His elephant is always
charging; the only question is, is it charging toward dreams or fears?

## Will Smith

Willard Christopher Smith Jr., otherwise known as Will Smith, is a testament to the power of a mind with an aligned ant and elephant. The actor, a number one box office phenomenon, has accomplished something that has never been done before—eight consecutive movies grossing over $100 million in revenue. He learned early to tap into his subconscious mind, aligning his ant and his elephant, sharing, "I don't know what my calling is, but I want to be here for a bigger reason. I strive to be like the greatest people who have ever lived."

Smith's story isn't a fairy tale of dream, victory, and a happily-ever-after kind. Rather, it is more like American Dreams of old—a kid with a huge dream, massive struggles, and sweet victories. A story similar to so many past American Horatio Alger successes.

Smith didn't start with a silver spoon in his mouth. He was born to a lower-middle-class West Philadelphia family. But he did start with something infinitely more powerful: a huge dream. His dream to do something great filled him with hope, leading to an unquenchable hunger to learn.

According to Smith, the turning point in his life happened when he was sixteen years of age, after his first girlfriend cheated on him. "In my mind, she cheated because I wasn't good enough. I remember making the decision that I will never not be good enough again." Instead of hosting his own pity party, he intuitively understood that massive success would be the best revenge, incubating in his mind a plan for worldwide fame, fortune, and excellence. How many other sixteen-year-old kids respond to setbacks in this manner?

Smith gained his wisdom early in life when he learned the value of reading to borrow ideas from the greatest men and women who ever lived. He stated:

> The idea that there are millions and billions of people who have lived before us, and they had problems and they solved them and they wrote it in a book somewhere—there is no new problem that we can have that we have to figure out by ourselves. There's no relationship issue, there is no issue with your par-

ents or your brother or your government, there is no issue we can have that somebody didn't already write a thousand years ago in a book. So, for me, that concept of reading is bittersweet because you know it's in a book somewhere but you've got to find the right one that is going to give you the proper information.

Passing on the engineering career offered him by attending MIT, Smith instead partnered with DJ Jazzy Jeff, releasing their first album while still in high school. The pair's PG-rated rap earned them the first-ever Grammy Award for a hip-hop act. Some believe Smith was lucky, but in an interview with Travis Smiley, he said, "Just decide, and the universe will get out of your way. You're in a universe that says 2 + 2 = 4; 2 + 2 is going to be what I want it to be."

After winning his Grammy, Smith, still a teenager with no financial experience, spent his income freely, leading to an Internal Revenue Service's audit resulting in a tax lien of $2.8 million against his dwindling estate! One can only imagine the pain and embarrassment felt by the young Smith with the IRS seizing his assets and garnishing his future wages. Few would have bounced back from this setback, but Smith's elephant vision refused to die, regardless of the challenges.

Facing the mockery of friends and nearing bankruptcy, Smith parlayed his popularity as a Grammy-winning rap act into an NBC sitcom titled *The Fresh Prince of Bel-Air.* The series became an overnight hit, surging his career forward, erasing his financial setbacks through his united ant and elephant. This show set the foundation for Smith's meteoric rise in the entertainment industry.

Smith's troubles were far from over, however, as he also endured a difficult divorce leading to a $900,000 lump sum settlement to his former wife with $24,000 per month for alimony and child support. He views setbacks like a broken-down car on a road: "Every once in a while, it's your turn to be broken down. And you wait for the tow truck to come. That's how I viewed that difficult time in my life." He understood that it wasn't what happened to him but how he handled it that mattered.

Both of these setbacks, a multimillion-dollar tax lien and a multimillion-dollar divorce, could have knocked down

Smith for the count; instead, they only fueled his hunger to do and become more. This is the power of an elephant-sized dream, turning rejection into more fuel for growth. Only with true belief, formed when the conscious mind's words align with subconscious mind's images, will the multitude of setbacks, in the pursuit of any worthwhile dream, be overcome. In fact, it's the size of the dream that determines the size of the comeback. What if Smith surrendered to bankruptcy? What if he surrendered to negativity, blaming the world for his problems? That is exactly what the majority of people do when faced with setbacks—even those setbacks that are minuscule in proportion to those faced and overcome by Smith. A person must never give up on a worthwhile goal or dream, refusing to ever surrender.

Smith set the goal early to become "the biggest movie star in the world," and in order to achieve this elephant-sized dream, he had to overcome elephant-sized obstacles. In fact, any person who dreams of success at the highest levels must expect the same level of obstacles. A person becomes a champion on the inside long before the rest of society acknowledges it on the outside.

With the success of *The Fresh Prince of Bel-Air*, one would have thought it would be an easy step into movies, but nothing could have been farther from the truth. Despite his growing fame, Smith couldn't buy a meeting with any of the studios or directors, having to work for over five years before his first successful meeting occurred. Indeed, Smith's business partner James Lassiter, frustrated by the apparent lack of interest, explained the skepticism of the studios this way: "Nobody cared. You're a rapper. You got lucky, and you got this television show, but that's all you can do."

When Smith was asked if he had ever thought of a plan B during this time, since plan A seemed closed, he responded quickly, almost shocked by the thought, "I don't want to get too metaphysical, but by even contemplating a plan B, you almost create the necessity for a plan B." Smith expresses so well the near-mysterious power that a unified ant and elephant have in propelling people to their dreams. He refused to contemplate a plan B, knowing that by merely contemplating it, he was subconsciously surrendering his plan.

When a person contemplates a plan B, the elephant is

confused on whether to pursue plan A or a new plan. Surrender starts the civil war between the conscious mind and the subconscious mind—a civil war that leads to failure.

Later in his career, while on the set of the Mohamed Ali movie, Smith had another breakthrough. "When I was doing *Ali*, I realized that he kept saying, 'I'm the greatest, I'm pretty,' to make himself believe it," Smith explained. "He doesn't believe it, but he was dealing with racism. He was reacting to pain and rejection. He said it so much that he started to believe it. That's what I've tried to do for myself." Aligning the conscious words with the subconscious images brings added power to all subsequent actions. Will Smith's success is not by accident, but by design—a design available to all who hunger after a dream. Smith understands the metaphysical nature of words, teaching himself to take command of his inner voice. He explained, "I think of the universe as this big master computer. The keyboard is inside each of us. I have a keyboard inside of me. I just have to figure out what to type, learn the code, to make the things happen that I want." Where others see limits, Smith trains his conscious and subconscious to imagine the limitless. Truly, vision is tomorrow's reality expressed as an idea today. Smith, displaying his vision for tomorrow, shared with Smiley, "I want to be an idea. I want to represent possibilities. I want to represent the idea that you really can make what you want."

Smith creates what he wants through the power of his words. He stated:

> I said reading and running and the running aspect is how you can connect with your weakness. When you get on the treadmill you deprive yourself of oxygen. What kind of person you are will come out very, very quickly. You're either the type of person who will say you're going to run three miles or you stop the treadmill at 2.94 and you hit it and you call 2.94 3 miles, or you get off after a mile. Or you're the type of person that runs hard through the finish line and when you get to 3.0 you realize, "God, I could really do 5," and you go ahead and do two more. And that little person talks to you and says, "Man, do you feel our knee? We should stop. I feel we should stop

ourselves right now. This is not healthy anymore."
When you learn to get command over that person on
that treadmill, you learn to get command over that
person in your life.

Smith took command of his positive voice, aligning his thoughts, talk, and, walk toward his goals and
dreams—a true example of the ant and the elephant in
alignment.

It's been nearly twenty years since Smith made his sitcom splash as the humorous, fast-talking fresh prince. Today, his films gross over $130 million per movie on average,
making him one of the elite of the elite in his profession. His
most financially successful films are *Bad Boys*; *Bad Boys
II*; *Independence Day*; *Men in Black*; *Men in Black II*; *I, Ro-
bot*; *The Pursuit of Happyness*; *I Am Legend*; *Hancock*; *Wild
Wild West*; *Enemy of the State*; *Shark Tale*; *Hitch*; and *Seven
Pounds*. He also earned critical praise for his performances in
*Six Degrees of Separation*, *Ali*, and *The Pursuit of Happyness*,
receiving Best Actor Oscar nominations for the latter two. He
discussed the connection between the proper thinking necessary for success and the hard work necessary to achieve the
success:

> Paulo Coelho in *The Alchemist*, which is my fa-
> vorite book, talks about the whole of the universe,
> and it's containment in one grain of sand. For years
> I've been saying that, and now it's really starting to
> expose itself to me. My own grain of sand has been my
> story. The next 10 years will be my peak of innovation
> in filmmaking and just as a human being. I was read-
> ing Malcolm Gladwell's *Outliers*, and he talks about
> the concept of 10,000 hours—that you don't really
> settle into any level of mastery until 10,000 hours,
> and I feel like I've just completed my 10,000 hours of
> story structure and filmmaking.

It's exciting to imagine what Smith can accomplish next,
having already, at forty-two years of age, broken many of the
all-time records. But one thing the world should understand
about Willard Christopher Smith Jr. is to never bet against

him. He has aligned his ant and elephant, charging ahead, forging onward with his superhuman work ethic and believing in his dreams while others are doubting theirs.

We can all learn from Smith, setting our sails based on our dreams and goals, not merely following the direction of the wind. Jesus, in Matthew 17:20, says, "For verily I say unto you, If ye have faith as a grain of mustard seed, ye shall say unto this mountain, Remove hence to yonder place; and it shall remove; and nothing shall be impossible unto you" (King James Version). What if all people removed the mountains holding them back from their destinies?

One final thought from Smith: "I consider myself an alchemist. An alchemist who took lead and made it gold." Imagine if people refused to live with lead in their lives and instead chose to play the part of the alchemist, converting their leaden lives into gold. What a difference would be made by having faith.

Smith's unyielding belief in his mission is what has helped him succeed. "If it was something that I really committed myself to, I don't think there's anything that could stop me becoming president of the United States."

## CHAPTER 5

# PLAN AND DO
## Resolved: To Develop and Implement a Game Plan in Each Area of My Life

*I know that planning and doing are essential parts of the success process.*

Now that a person has committed to the mastery of the first four resolutions, he is ready to actively pursue success in his chosen field. To achieve in life, he must have a plan because failure to plan is a plan for failure.

### Success Never Goes on Sale

Success never goes on sale, and most people spend their entire lives dickering over the cost but never making the purchase. The price for success is high, but then again, so is the price for failure. One enjoys the fruits of success yet suffers the recurring pain of the failure to act. His gifts, talents, and energies are given to him for his time on earth; and like time, once they're wasted, they can never be restored. A person has one life in which to do something. The reader is experiencing that life as he reads this; what he does with his remaining time is the subject of this chapter. Since a person must surrender his gifts anyway, why not invest them in the path toward a meaningful success? There are three simple, but not easy, steps to success:

1. What do you want?
2. What does it cost?

3. Pay it.

As a person reads these three statements, he probably thinks to himself that it can't be that simple. But truthfully, it is that simple, just not that easy. Why is success so difficult if it only requires three steps? It's so difficult because each step gets progressively harder. Most people can identify what they want, some will even check what type of commitment it would take to achieve it, but only a select few will apply the first two steps consistently in order to pay the full price. It's not the lack of talent or the lack of time or the lack of opportunities that denies a person success in the West; rather, it's the lack of a singular focus on what he truly wants. A person must be willing to surrender who he is in order to become who he needs to be in his quest for a significant success. This is a price that few are willing to pay and the reason game planning is one of the thirteen resolutions, for without planning and implementing a game plan and paying the price for success, one can never fulfill his purpose and vision.

The previous chapters discussed purpose, character, attitude, and the power of aligning one's ant and elephant on a dream. All of these are excellent; however, without a specific game plan to implement his dreams, they will remain fantasies. Success is a picture backed by a long-term plan and finished through hard work. Five-year plans are reasonable time frames for top achievements; however, in our microwave age, most people seem to expect top results in five days. This simply cannot be done.

> **Dreams turn into plans which turn into goals.**

One must realize that the price for success is not purchased in a lump sum; instead, it's paid in daily installments over time. Only after every installment plus interest is paid in full will one receive the prize. In fact, many times, one will pay more than the asking price; but if his commitment is nonnegotiable, he will pay whatever price legally, morally, and ethically is required. Dreams turn into plans, which turn into goals. Develop a plan for success in each area of life, making every monthly deposit to pay the price in full.

## Plan, Do, Check, and Adjust

I learned the power of the planning process at twenty-four years of age while working as an engineer at GM. Dr. Edward Deming, a man famous for helping the Japanese turn around their economy after WWII, spoke at a GM conference on the topic of statistical controls. What I learned that day improved my professional life, and even more important, it revolutionized my thinking life by changing the process I used for achievement. Deming stated that tests and experiments are performed to "make predictions" and "verify predictions based upon data from the test." He went on to explain how experiments help a person determine the accuracy of his predictions. If his thinking is correct, he should be able to predict the result of an experiment; but if the results are not predictable, then his prediction is not accurate and requires further changes before testing again.

As I listened to Deming, I realized that his process could be utilized in any area of life, not just in engineering. Indeed, his methodology, called PDCA—plan, do, check, and act—was designed for testing products and services; but the PDCA process is just as applicable a method for predicting and testing in life. I adjusted the PDCA wording slightly, making it "plan, do, check, and adjust," and started using this methodology immediately in my life. Every game plan must be developed, performed, checked, and adjusted based on the data in order to improve one's actual results versus his intended outcomes. The gap between the plan and the results leads to adjustments, closing the gap until the plan works or further learning occurs. Each experiment leads to further adjustments to fulfill the predicted objective of the plan step. A person must plan his work and work his plan, while making the needed adjustments when his plan doesn't produce his predicted result. If he repeatedly performs tests in his life, he will quickly identify whether his thinking accurately portrays reality or not. The quicker he can run PDCA tests, the sooner he can learn whether his thinking or skills are faulty, leading to further adjustments. From this, I began to think of life as an ongoing test, as an opportunity to predict results based on planned behaviors, testing the predictions in real time, determining whether my predictions were accurate or needed more adjustments. Running PDCAs allows a person to sort fact from fiction in any area of his life.

For example, I remember when I was five years old having a vivid dream that I was swimming underwater while breathing freely. When I woke up, I announced to my mother that I could swim and breathe underwater. My mom, a near saint, patiently explained to me that it was a dream, that human beings cannot breathe underwater because we have lungs, not gills. I chose to ignore this counsel, announcing instead to my brothers and sister that during our swimming lessons, I would prove that I could breathe underwater. In the afternoon, at the poolside, after ensuring my mom and siblings were watching, I proceeded to dive underwater, swimming leisurely from one end of the pool to the other. Eventually needing air, I contracted my young diaphragm, quickly inhaling chlorinated water, disproving my predicted model amidst flailing arms, gasping breaths, and a reddening face. My predicted result had failed under rigorous testing conditions. By confronting the data, I no longer believed I could breathe underwater and adjusted my behavior accordingly. This is a simple example of a PDCA. My plan (to swim underwater) was implemented (I did inhale underwater), but after checking the results (gasping for breath as water filled my lungs), I realized I had failed. I made an adjustment (I learned that human lungs need air, not water), breathing before going underwater from that day forward.

Every person's PDCAs are different, but everyone can improve in any area if he is willing to follow the disciplined PDCA process. PDCAs ensure one's predictions are accurate and not just assumptions, for assumptions are the facts of fools and fools quickly join the list of business failures. However, those who are willing to PDCA continuously, verifying their thinking by studying the results of their consistent PDCAs, will move ahead. Many people in specific areas of life have unconsciously used this process, and the plan moving forward is to consciously design one's life around continuous improvement toward one's purpose and vision through the PDCA process.

## PDCA—the Steps

Let's analyze the first two steps of the PDCA process, starting with plan.

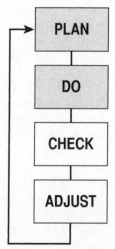

What is the plan, and how is it used to generate improvement? The plan is a way to test one's hypotheses, beliefs, or models of life. For example, if a person believes he is a poor public speaker and has a few ideas to improve, then he must PDCA those ideas to verify how the crowd would respond to his experiment. Thinking about improving won't change anything until he develops a plan. The first step in planning is to honestly review areas where he could potentially improve. Perhaps he can begin by discussing with his mentors, or by studying the best public speakers, or maybe by reading good books on the subject. A proper plan requires a person to look at himself honestly where he is, not just what he would like to be.

Asking the right questions is the second step to proper planning. What's the difference between good speakers and poor speakers? What is the plan that, if implemented, would help him make the improvements needed to become a good speaker? Excellence demands consistent planning and testing, and a person must desire the goal more than he desires comfort. Develop plans to improve in all areas of life and begin implementing them daily through PDCA.

> **Excellence demands consistent planning and testing, and a person must desire the goal more than he desires comfort.**

This leads us to the second step in the PDCA process: do. The best plans in the world are worthless unless people do them. If the road to Hell is paved with good intentions, then Hell has thickly paved roads. It's been said that the plans to fix the political mess in Washington, DC exist, but plans are worthless without someone willing to execute them. One of the books in the Bible is titled the book of Acts. Notice that it isn't called the book of Thoughts or the book of Best Intentions but the book of Acts. Greatness begins when a person takes the plan step and has the courage to act on it. "Just do it," as the Nike slogan says. If, in public speaking, a person has identified areas in which to improve, then it's time for him to start speaking. A person simply cannot improve his craft until it is performed correctly over and over, even if he has to make mistake after mistake for an extended period until he becomes good. There simply is no substitute for this. Any person who is unwilling to look bad will never become good. By necessity, the PDCA process pushes a person to failure, forcing him to revise his plans. This isn't actually a failure; it is just an opportunity to learn where one can improve. Sadly, most people refuse to execute the PDCA process because they fear feeling like a failure more than they fear being a failure. Indeed, the only true failure in the PDCA process is someone who fails to plan and do the test since any results that occur lead to "teachable moments" and further learning and adjustments. Every PDCA leads to learning what went wrong, which then becomes the knowledge necessary in order to run a better test in the future. A person will never get to the check and adjust steps, which will be covered in the next chapter, without the discipline to plan and do.

## PDCA and Ten Thousand Hours

With the PDCA process, the more one does, the more he learns. Samuel Goldwyn wrote, "The harder I work, the luckier I get." People like Goldwyn aren't really lucky as much as they are learners. Successful people just appear lucky because most people cannot comprehend the ten thousand hours of painful effort already paid by the time anyone notices that they are successful. People who consistently win follow the steps in the PDCA process. Luck is a loser's excuse not to make a winner's commitment. No one lucks into long-term success. Malcolm Gladwell referred to K. Anders Ericsson's study, describing how work ethic trumps talent:

> The striking thing about Ericsson's study is that he and his colleagues couldn't find any "naturals," musicians who floated effortlessly to the top while practicing a fraction of time their peers did. Nor could they find any "grinds," people who worked harder than everyone else, yet just didn't have what it takes to break the top ranks. Their research suggests that once a musician has enough ability to get into a top music school, the thing that distinguishes one performer from another is how hard he or she works. That's it. And what's more, the people at the very top don't work just harder or even much harder than everyone else. They work much, much harder.

The number that reappears consistently when researchers study top achievers is ten thousand hours for mastery in any field. It takes a minimum of ten thousand hours of study, practice time, actions, improvements, and adjustments to develop skills, making success look and feel natural. This dedicated work ethic explains why the haves separate themselves from the have-nots in life. But if everyone works for forty years or more, doesn't everyone eventually reach mastery? Simply logging hours isn't enough, a person must endure the pain of "teachable moments" over and over in the PDCA process, becoming a continuous improvement machine. It's only PDCA hours that count in the ten thousand hours. Lamentably, for most people, twenty-five years of experience is actually one year's experience twenty-five times. When a person has logged ten thousand hours of PDCA time, improving in key areas on a consistent basis, then, and only then, will he develop mastery.

Since mastery requires ten thousand PDCA hours in a specific profession, focus becomes crucial because there simply aren't enough ten-thousand-hour segments to master every field. One can become great in nearly any field, but he cannot become great in all fields. By understanding this, a person should ask the next logical question: in which areas is he willing to invest ten thousand PDCA hours to develop mastery?

For example, the Beatles didn't start out as master musicians; they needed to invest ten thousand PDCA hours to become so. And the key was they focused in the field of music until they reached mastery. Many assume that the Beatles were incredibly talented musicians and that talent alone catapulted them to success. Philip Norman, author of *Shout!* set the record straight. He described the group's eighteen months of live nightly performances in Hamburg, Germany. He wrote, "They were no good onstage when they went there and they were very good when they came back. They learned not only stamina. They had to learn an enormous amount of numbers—cover versions of everything you can think of, not just rock and roll, a bit of jazz too. They weren't disciplined onstage at all before that. But when they came back, they sounded like no one else. It was the making of them." Just how many hours did the Beatles play during that year and a half? They performed 270 times in that period, many times for eight hours or more! It's not shocking that the musical skills and showmanship of the Beatles improved dramatically with thousands of hours of live performances in Hamburg.

When Beatlemania exploded on the USA music scene in 1964, the Beatles had performed at live events over 1,200 times, more than most bands will perform in their lifetimes. Simply put, the Beatles were willing to work harder than other bands, improving their skills through the PDCA process. Gladwell reflected, "The Hamburg crucible is one of the things that set the Beatles apart." Every leader or performer needs his Hamburg crucible, practicing while others are playing, dreaming while others are complaining, enduring while others are quitting. Indeed, no great achievement is accomplished without great sacrifice, and the ten thousand hours is the price to be paid for mastery in any field.

## Deliberate Practice

Abraham Lincoln, amidst many trials and tribulations, invested his ten thousand hours in personal development and people, commenting, "I will work, I will study, and when my moment comes, I will be ready." Lincoln set out to deliberately build himself by working, studying, learning, and improving—all key aspects of any person's PDCA process. Geoff Colvin, in his book *Talent Is Overrated*, explained that all high achievers go through a process called deliberate practice, another name for PDCA, writing, "Deliberate practice is characterized by several elements, each worth examining. It is activity designed specifically to improve performance, often with a teacher's help; it can be repeated a lot; feedback on results is continuously available; it's highly demanding mentally, whether the activity is purely intellectual, such as chess or business-related activities, or heavily physical, such as sports; and it isn't much fun." Deliberate practice separates the amateurs from the professionals in any field. The amateurs practice skills that they are comfortable with, while the professionals work at the uncomfortable limits of their skills, pushing to failure, in an effort to move their mastery of skills past their current competence and comfort levels. Only through pushing past a person's comfort zone will he improve his level of skills. Few are willing to endure the consistent "teachable moments" experienced from a properly running PDCA. Deliberate practice demands a level of focus and endurance to withstand the constant assault on a person's current skill limits, making a high pain tolerance an absolute must. Colvin discussed the importance of pushing past the comfort zone in deliberate practice, sharing:

> **Only through pushing past a person's comfort zone will a person improve his level of skills.**

> Great performers never allow themselves to reach the automatic, arrested-development stage in their chosen field. That is the effect of continual deliberate practice—avoiding automaticity. The essence of practice, which is constantly trying to do the things one cannot do comfortably, makes automatic behavior impossible.... Avoiding automaticity

through continual practice is another way of saying
that great performers are always getting better.

Clearly then, no one lucks into success at this level. LUCK, properly defined, is "laboring under correct knowledge." Consistently hard and painful work is the only recipe known for developing mastery.

## Success—the Pain of Greatness

Success isn't for the weak of heart because when the going gets tough, only the tough will get going. Winners will choose to get better; whiners will choose to get bitter. The PDCA process is designed to reveal shortcomings in a person's thinking, but this can be a painful experience. Professor Robert Grudin explained the role of pain in creativity and innovation:

> To be truly open to any experience, the mind must be open to all. The willing endurance of pain is a key factor not only in human dignity, but also in human creativity. It would seem to follow that individuals who spend their lives in the persistent avoidance of pain are not likely to amount to much...The process of achieving their professional level is usually full of pain. Such mastery demands endless practice of technical operations, endless assaults on seemingly ineluctable concepts, humiliation by teachers, anxious and exhausting competition with peers. To gain such mastery, one must face the sting of pertinent criticism, the shock of a thousand minor failures, and the nagging fear of one's own un-improvable inadequacy....A tiny minority gets through to the top, to memorable excellence or profound understanding. The rest of us stop along the way, perhaps for a temporary rest, perhaps for a period of reassessment. But once we stop, we are unlikely to start up again. Security is suddenly far sweeter than enterprise.

Grudin pointed out the deliberate practice difference between nonachievers and achievers. Nonachievers settle for less than excellence, valuing security even if it comes with ignorance. In contrast, achievers strive for nothing less than excellence, valuing learning even if it comes with pain. The highest achievers, because they concede in areas where others are better than they are, work harder to close the gap. In fact, one of the biggest drivers that allows a person to endure the pain of deliberate practice is the criticism of others who look down on him in an attempt to make him feel inferior. Winners turn rejection into energy, as psychologist Henry Link described, in his book *The Rediscovery of Man*:

> A sense of inferiority, we find, is not a disease. I have told hundreds of complaining parents: You should be thankful that your child has a sense of inferiority. The children to worry about are those who always think they are smart, who know better than their elders, who see no reason for painful practice or humble effort. The child, however, who feels inferior, can usually be trained to develop abilities which in time will make him truly superior. All genuine superiority grows out of a sense of inferiority.

In an interview, Will Smith stressed his work ethic, saying, "I'm not afraid to die on a treadmill. I will not be outworked. You may be more talented than me. You might be smarter than me. And you may be better looking than me. But if we get on a treadmill together, you are going to get off first or I'm going to die. It's really that simple. I'm not going to be outworked." The person who admits his inferiority and then does something about it develops superiority. Life, then, isn't easy; but if people have to work hard anyway, then they should work not just for existence but for excellence in their purpose.

## Work as a Game

The work demanded to win at the highest levels is tough, but it can be developed by anyone. Furthermore, although there isn't a shortcut past the ten thousand hours for mastery in any field, there is a shortcut through the monotony of it. When work becomes a game, the tasks of work turn into the plays of the game. A person doesn't even realize that he is working because the tasks are enjoyed as part of advancing in the game. Therefore, the secret to mastery in any field hinges on learning to enjoy the deliberate practice by turning the grueling effort into the joy of competing and winning a game. Consider a man on a hot autumn day having to choose between playing tennis and raking the lawn. He can play for hours, sweating profusely, while enjoying the thrill of the game. On the other hand, he can look at raking with dread, procrastinating as long as possible, only completing through sheer strength of will. Why the difference? Both require effort and discipline and are exhausting, but one is perceived as a fun game, and the other is viewed as miserable work. When a person views his work as a game, he no longer does tasks; instead, he plays the game to win. All top performers have learned to do this in their fields of mastery, whether in business, sports, or music. Work isn't simply work anymore; rather, it's part of the process to win the game that they love. Weekend warriors are similarly motivated because they give 100 percent effort to their weekend sports for no pay. Why? They do it for the love of the game. Highly successful people have tapped into this reservoir of energy, creating a game out of their professions, thus falling in love with the process and the quest for excellence in order to win. Imagine the productivity if everyone worked their professions as hard as they worked their hobbies. Better still, imagine if everyone's professions were their passions, leading to purpose-filled work.

Ozzie Smith, a baseball Hall of Famer, is an excellent example of a person who turned his passion into his profession by playing baseball. Ozzie loved baseball, but growing up in poverty didn't allow him to have the best equipment. He wanted to develop his skills in fielding anyway, so he used his imagination. He created a game where he bounced a tennis ball off his cement porch. He challenged himself daily, moving closer and closer to the porch, testing his ability to field the tennis ball cleanly. The goal was to field as many balls rebounding off the porch as he could, and this developed his hand-eye coordination. By making it a game, Ozzie played for hours on end, attempting to field the ball again and again and again. No coach would ever ask the same level of discipline out of a Little League team, but since it was a game, it hardly felt like discipline at all. Smith's love of the game allowed him to stay focused while he endured through the hours of deliberate practice, developing mastery as a baseball infielder. His game made his hours of deliberate practice fun, leading to his being a perennial Gold Glove performer and the best shortstop in baseball. He made the tough plays look easy because they were easy for him after so many hours of deliberate practice, amazing the fans with his highly developed hand-eye coordination. He credited his childhood game for developing the skills he applied to his profession. Few will subject themselves to the pain of deliberate practice unless, like Ozzie, they create a game out of the deliberate practice needed for mastery. Ozzie made his practice a game, thus creating the skills he needed while enjoying the PDCA time—a lesson to learn for anyone in a quest for mastery.

## Quitters, Campers, and Climbers

Another painful lesson to be learned in order to achieve mastery is that when a person succeeds, he should expect many to admire his accomplishment as well as many to hate him. There is even a name for this today: haters. What is it about these hero haters (anti-heroes), who seem to hate everything about character-centered people? In today's age, not only are there only a few who are willing to pay the price for success, but many discredit those who dare to strive for personal excellence. Author George Roche, in his book *A World without Heroes*, explained:

> The anti-hero dismisses all purpose as illusion. It sees us as helpless pawns, unable to act or even think on our own, fully shaped and determined by outside forces. It reaches this position with tortuous chains of inference, with misused "scientific assumptions" and fanciful formulas that dare to tell us what we can and cannot know, what is and is not real. But all this is contrivance, serving not the search for knowledge and truth, but the rebel's own dark purposes. And it is all belied in an instant by that one purposeful, death-defying act of a hero. That act, a reality known to us all, tells us more about the human condition than all of the empty and life-hating mutterings of modernist philosophers. It serves a Good we all may turn to for fulfillment in our lives.

To succeed in today's world, a person must not only endure the price of success, paying the same price that Washington, Franklin, and Edwards paid, but also decide to do so regardless of the antiheroic behaviors of others. Sadly, critics throw tomatoes at achievers because achievers remind them of what they might have been. When a person develops mastery today, he must expect the pain of the process, along with the pain of criticisms from the anti-heroes. Author Marc Simmons, addressing the Western writers of America, said, "You see they must discredit the Western hero because if just one person can be shown to have achieved wholeness, then it becomes evident that the possibility is open to all."

> **When a person develops mastery today, he must expect the pain of the process, along with the pain of criticisms from the anti-heroes.**

If success is open to all, but only a few make it, then the rest have to either admit that they didn't do what it takes or attack the person who did do what it takes to make themselves feel better. Dr. Paul Stoltz described three types of people. All of them begin in the valley, staring at the mountain of life: quitters, campers, and climbers. Even though all human beings are born with the urge to climb, and there are billions of people in the world, the mountain-top remains practically empty. What happens to all of life's mountain climbers? Most end up compromising what they truly want for what is immediately available because they are unwilling to endure the painful climb, so they become "given-ups" instead of grownups.

Life's quitters see the mountain's jagged cliffs, threatening storms, and endless paths as dangerous, deciding to pass on the climb entirely, avoiding the PDCA process rather than risking failure. By denying their God-given urge to climb, they make major compromises in their lives. Quitters are typically people who entertain themselves to death, escaping into drugs, sex, or other noncontributing time-consuming activities. They keep themselves busy doing mindless activities in order to avoid the mountain; they are doing everything not to climb. They suffer the worst pain of all—the pain of regret—for a life spent in service to self, not to others. They lead compromised lives, selling out convictions for conveniences. However, when confronted with the truth of their pitiable lives, they obfuscate the facts, attempting to justify the unjustifiable, and live a completely wasted life. The worst quitters, those having no more conscience, solicit others to join their lamentable condition.

Campers, on the other hand, start climbing the mountain by using the PDCA process. They are excited about the opportunities on the mountainside, beginning life's climb enthusiastically. However, at some point, through a combination of successes already achieved and the pain associated with further climbing, they cease the PDCA process, compromising their ideals and selling out their courage for the comfort of camp. They may achieve a nice mountain view, but their best days are behind them, surrendering their future for doing "pretty good." Although campers know the price of the climb, they are unwilling to pay it any longer. They may convince themselves that they are only resting for a season, but few will ever break camp. Some of the most talented people are content in camp, having achieved a good lifestyle, fooling themselves that this is more important than their purpose. Don't misread this; everyone needs a vacation once in a while to refresh, but not a vacation for the rest of one's life. Take a break when needed, but never compromise your calling for your comforts. Vacations end, but a person's purpose only ends when his life ends.

Climbers are the last group. These are people who refuse to compromise their calling and convictions, deciding to press on with their PDCA processes, no matter how painful the climb is, as far as they can go. They know they were called to climb the mountain and are willing to do the work in order to accomplish it. Climbers are a rare breed—they never sacrifice their convictions for conveniences since they understand that life isn't about obtaining the best spot in camp or gathering the most items in the tent. Life isn't about possessions, but about purpose; it's about the climb. Climbers have learned that one of the keys to a happy life is fulfilling one's purpose, becoming who he is intended to be, not necessarily by reaching the top, but through the constant effort to improve. A true climber battles his mountain, and in the process, he conquers himself. His climb leaves a path for others to follow in pursuit of their purpose, teaching other climbers the lessons he has learned through life's mountain climb. Each person must make his own decision while staring at life's mountain. Will he quit, camp, or climb? If he chooses to climb, the PDCA process will be an invaluable aid in his journey to improve, helping him learn life's lessons so that he can pass them on to others. This is what true success in life is all about.

## Lou Holtz:  Planning and Doing

How does a young man from a broken home—his parents separated while he was in college and had no wealth or contacts to give him a step up or in—become one of the all-time greats in his field? What is even more impressive is achieving it despite a lisp, an undersized physique, and low self-esteem. Lou Holtz's rise to success in football coaching is one of the most inspiring stories in America.

Lou Holtz was born in 1937 in the small town of Follansbee, West Virginia, to a poor family. Lou describes his financial environment when he was growing up: "We needed a raise to be considered poor. Every day we awoke to hardship, and every night we fell asleep thankful for one more day of sustenance." Lou, unlike many people, did not seek a life of ease, hoping to avoid challenges; instead, young Lou learned from his challenges, growing with a resolution to persevere and succeed through hard work, no matter what. The men of the Holtz family worked in either the coal mines or the steel industry as manual laborers. No one in the Holtz clan had gone to college—not his dad, who quit school in the third grade, nor his mom, even though she graduated valedictorian of her high-school class.

When Lou's high-school coach visited his parents and suggested that Lou attend college and become a coach, the Holtz family didn't know how to respond since they lacked the funds and Lou lacked the grades. At first, Lou thought the idea of going to college was ludicrous, but he later warmed to it, saying, "I was not a good student, but I received a good education, not only academically but also in the intangibles everyone must have to succeed." Thanks to his mom for taking a night job and Lou for signing up for ROTC, he was able to enroll at Kent State.

A turning point in Lou's life came shortly before he left for college, transforming an academically unmotivated youth into a determined young freshman. It happened in a local grocery store. As he was picking up several items, he heard two ladies on the next aisle in a conversation. Lou told the story:

Mrs. Hoback said, "I can't believe Anne Marie

Holtz is wasting her money sending that boy Lou to college." Mrs. Toft then said, "I know what you mean. She took a night job and everything. It's such a waste."

They didn't know I'd overheard them, since I was one aisle over, but those comments cut me deeply and burned inside me throughout my freshman year. I knew that my mother was sacrificing for me, but to have her friends, the people in my town, think that I was not worth the effort, that I was bound to fail, turned my wounded feelings into something quite different. My "want" to do well became a fiery determination. I would do whatever it took to pass, especially as a freshman, a year when the adjustment to college life can take its toll.

This incident formed the fire inside Lou to set and hit his goals. Notice how Lou turned this negative criticism into a positive energy. This is a crucial point when a person is setting goals since many will laugh at a person and his goals, at least when the goals are big ones. But the more the critics laugh, the more determined a person needs to be, finishing what he started through the strength of his convictions.

Lou did finish school and moved into a coaching career. He worked as an assistant defensive football coach at several schools until, in 1967, while at South Carolina, he was fired, along with all the other assistant coaches, when the head coach left. Lou had just bought a house in South Carolina, so the available funds were as low as his available opportunities. Beth, his wife, in a gesture of confidence and love, bought him the classic book *The Magic of Thinking Big*. He devoured the book, and like every good student should, he followed the instructions in it, writing out his goals. He captured 108 goals, some of them crazy at the time since fired assistant coaches didn't live in the same stratosphere as the items on his list demanded him to be in, but that was exactly the point. A fired assistant coach cannot achieve big things, but any person with a dream, a goal, and a commitment can, simply because he will develop into the person necessary to achieve the goals.

Few people plan with specific intent and then put enormous action behind the plan as well as Lou. He shared how goal planning and action transformed his life: "I've been amazed at how many people have wanted to talk about my list over the years. I can't believe more people don't have a similar list of goals." For without goals, it's difficult to create the passion and energy needed to accomplish an assignment. Lou constantly exhorted his children and athletes: "Be a participant; don't be a spectator. Do things. Just decide what you want to do and then ask the question, 'What's important now?' Now what do I have to do to accomplish such and such? And that will tell you the action you have to take. It's not a wish list, it's a set of things I wanted to accomplish and it really hasn't changed that much."

After identifying what's important, then a person must give it all he has in order to accomplish the task, similar to Ben Hogan's practice philosophy: "Playing a tournament is almost an anticlimax. Tournaments are won and lost in preparation. Playing them is just going through the motions." In his book *Wins, Losses, and Lessons*, Lou shared the value of hard work in making people better:

> You work hard and suffer because it makes you a better man. If the rewards you seek are found in the praise and adulation of others, you are destined for disappointment, because the moment you drop one pass, or lose one game, the cheering stops and the praise goes away. Internal rewards, the ones you gain from pain, sweat, and tears, stick with you forever . . . People perform to the level expected of them . . . If I had expected the scout squad to go through the motions and pump up the egos of our starters, that's exactly what they would have done. But because I demanded nothing short of greatness, the players elevated their performance far beyond anyone's expectations. This is the way I was coached and the only way I know how to coach.

Without Lou's ability to set goals and apply maximum effort to achieve them by following a PDCA process, he would have never achieved the level of success and fame he later accomplished. But the PDCA process doesn't promise an easy life or one without challenges. Indeed, Lou's life is a model of the ups and downs that will occur, regardless of how hungry or driven one is. Nonetheless, in order to accomplish goals, one must accept responsibility for the PDCA results, both the good and the bad. He doesn't fail in life until he blames someone else for his results, surrendering the PDCA process to the blame game. Lou refused to make excuses, building his life around personal responsibility and teaching that life is a series of choices, writing, "The choices we make determine how successful we are. When you acknowledge that you and only you are responsible and accountable for the choices you make, and when you refuse to blame others for the choices you have made, you have in your hands the blueprint for success. When you allow others to choose your path so that you can then blame someone else when things don't go your way, you are fooling no one and cheating no one but yourself." Lou believes that people are where they are in life because of the choices that they make. Additionally, if a person wants better results, then he should realize that planning and doing are crucial steps in beginning a change. For no one can determine his results in life except himself through his plans and actions. Better plans and hard work pave the way for improved outcomes. High achievement requires rigorous implementation of the PDCA process and disciplined thinking to set plans and goals. Lou Holtz added personal responsibility, work ethic, and a positive attitude to achieve uncommon results. Lou Holtz has set college football records, perhaps never to be broken, as he has helped four schools finish in the top 10 rankings, a feat never before accomplished.

Not surprisingly, like all achievers, he received his share of criticisms. In fact, all great achievements demand a thick skin since most people view life as one huge game of King of the Mountain. Do you remember playing that game where one person or a group of people battle to get to the top of a mountain, only to be knocked off by another group still climbing? Since criticism is viewed as the easiest way to knock someone off the mountaintop, requiring no effort and no results, all champions are criticized by nonachievers. It's a fact of life. The smallest minds with the smallest ideas always criticize the biggest minds with the biggest ideas. Imagine if Holtz shared his 108 dreams or plans with his critics. They would have laughed at a fired assistant coach's hubris for daring to plan such audacious plans, but Lou did dream and plan them, and he has accomplished nearly all of them.

Lou shared his thoughts on critics: "The only people who aren't going to be criticized are those who do absolutely nothing. And the critics, the people who just observe, are never on the inside, never really had to make decisions that affect people's lives." Holtz learned, as all successful people do, that tearing down others' successes is the easiest thing for people to do and that succeeding is much more difficult for them to do. He said, "I welcome all the suggestions in the world from people who have been involved in doing something . . . but somebody who has never done anything except observe and criticize, I don't weigh that at all." The key is to live life based on one's resolutions and refuse to listen to the barking dogs who accomplish nothing of substance. Holtz summed it up well: "The higher up you go and the more things you try to accomplish, the more people try to find fault. There are so many things in life that are not fair. You work all your life to do something and people try to tear you down. You can't control it or do anything about it. When you look at the options of dealing with criticism, there's really only one option—to pray to God that you have the courage and the strength that you won't become bitter and move on with your life."

Such wise advice from a modern sage of success like Lou Holtz is an inspiration to anyone who is ready to make the success leap. Your life will change direction only when, like the captain of a ship, you seize the helm. Perhaps it's time to take goal setting seriously. Dust off that paper where you wrote your goals several years back. Or better yet, start with a fresh piece of paper and dare to dream again. But don't just try to hit goals; decide to do whatever it takes legally, morally, and ethically to achieve them. Lou expounded:

> Every athlete who has ever played for me has heard me preach against the pitfalls of entering anything halfway. In my mind, a half-hearted commitment is worse than no commitment at all . . . If you're on a team, you owe your coaches and teammates your total commitment. If you don't—if you're unhappy because the coach doesn't start you, or because you

aren't getting as many touches as you think you should—you are hurting yourself and the entire organization. You and the team would be better off if you played somewhere else . . . Commitment is the most critical component in any relationship. A marriage based on the premise "Well, let's give this a shot, and if it doesn't work out, or if we 'grow apart,' we can always get divorced," is doomed before the vows are complete.

Goal setting works when one commits to following the PDCA process. Lou Holtz's life is a living example of the power of goals and work ethic to achieve one's dreams. When a person makes a 100 percent commitment, backing it up with 100 percent effort to achieve the goal, and perseveres over the long haul, greatness is developed within, just as it was developed inside a fired assistant coach named Lou Holtz.

CHAPTER 6

# SCOREBOARD
# Resolved: To Keep Score
# in the Game of Life

*I know that the scoreboard forces me to check and confront
the results, making the needed adjustments in order to win.*

You either hate losing bad enough to change, or you hate changing bad enough to lose. As people further look into the PDCA process, many of them plan, some do, but very few finish the process with the check and adjust steps. If one doesn't perform the check step, he will hinder his ability to learn from the PDCA process. For most people, the check step is the most difficult to apply correctly, having to honestly review their real results, not their perceived ones. Ronald Reagan said, "Trust but verify." When it comes to personal growth, the overwhelming majority would rather trust without verifying. Improving the check step, for most people, would make the most significant difference in their personal growth.

The Check step is the scoreboard of life. Without a scoreboard, a person simply cannot identify the areas where he needs to improve. For example, the scoreboard and statistics in a basketball game help communicate who is

> **The Check step
> is the scoreboard
> for life.**

winning. A good coach studies the data during the halftime break to determine why his team is winning or losing, making the necessary adjustments based on what the scoreboard reveals in order to achieve victory. In the same way, the check step provides the scoreboard for people following the PDCA process, helping them identify their current performance and potential areas for improvement. To refuse to study the check step is to reject a learning experience.

Even so, it's surprisingly common for someone who has disciplined himself to plan and do to not evaluate his results extensively in the check step.

Why do so many resist the check step? Simply put, a person's defense mechanisms kick in, which are designed to protect his fragile ego from the painful revelation of his current performance. It can be embarrassing when a person discovers the gap between the skills he wants and the skills he has. Most people, in other words, would rather delude themselves and be happy than confront themselves and exert the effort to improve. But running from the data doesn't change anything; rather, it only changes or blocks a person's ability to improve it. An ostrich, for example, may stick his head in the sand, avoiding his fear of lions by refusing to look at the lion. Sadly, that has no bearing on the lion's dinner plans. A person must check his results, identifying the gaps between his stated objectives and his current results.

When the gaps are identified, it's time to make the adjustments needed in order to advance. Plan it, do it, check it, and adjust it; this is the PDCA process for any area of life. After each test, check the results, evaluating what can be done to make the plans better. Every plan and do, no matter how good or bad it is, ultimately helps because it reveals, through the check step, how to improve.

If a person has invested the time to plan, do, and check, then he only has to make adjustments based on the scoreboard to advance. It's important to find a defeat in every victory (to improve) and a victory in every defeat (to maintain morale). In other words, the defeats keep one humble, while the victories keep one hopeful. Balance is the key here, keeping both pride and hopelessness at bay. There has never been, nor will there ever be, a perfect performance. Therefore, the key is to point out the failure mode, the main area where one is currently deficient that, if enhanced, would make the biggest impact. When such areas are identified, one must follow through and make the adjustments. There is always room to get better, no matter how great one's present achievements are, so he shouldn't be upset when he finds areas that need work. A student must check the data, examining it from all angles and perspectives and then adjust anything that is necessary in his thinking, actions, and beliefs in order to grow. It takes courage to make adjustments personally and professionally since most people value comfort over change. But leaders are different; they value results more.

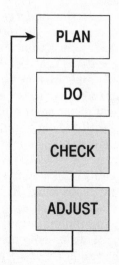

After the adjust step, completing the full PDCA loop, it's time to start again from step 1, making new plans. The best in any field repeats the PDCA cycle continuously, gaining mastery of the PDCA process. The goal is to improve both personally and professionally, closing the gap between where one is and where one desires to be. Success is practically ensured when a person realizes that he is responsible for his own perpetual personal development process. This means anyone can win in life as long as he is willing to surrender himself to the PDCA process, opening himself up to his failures as part of the learning process to improve. The PDCA process reveals a person to himself, forcing him to either change or quit. For when truth is revealed, he can either deny it, protecting his ego and sacrificing excellence, or embrace it, protecting excellence and sacrificing his ego. Success, then, is only for the few—not the talented few but the courageous few who are willing to know the truth about themselves, disciplining their lives through the PDCA process to improve and grow consistently in the game of life.

> **Success is practically ensured when a person realizes that he is responsible for his own perpetual personal development process.**

## The Emperor's New Clothes

An excellent example of a person who chose ego over excellence, thus falling into self-delusion, is found in a short story writ-

ten by Hans Christian Anderson in 1837 titled "The Emperor's
New Clothes." The story, in abbreviated form, is about an emperor
who cared more about his clothes than about anything else. He
was so obsessed with his attire that he changed his suits every
hour, flaunting his wealth and prestige to his subjects. One day,
two shysters, pretending to be weavers, presented themselves to
the emperor. They bragged about their ability to weave the finest
clothes with the most beautiful colors and elaborate designs. The
clothes, according to the charlatans, were invisible to any simple-
tons or anyone unworthy of his office. The emperor, impressed by
their claims, paid large sums of money to the weavers for the new
clothes. The two weavers, requesting the most expensive fabrics
and threads, set up two looms, pretending to weave on the looms
night and day while placing the materials inside their sacks. The
emperor, impatient with the wait, sent one of his loyal ministers to
examine the clothes. The minister, discovering nothing, not even
a single strand on the loom, feared that he must be a simpleton.
He listened to the impostors describe the beautiful colors and patterns as he watched them working diligently on the empty looms.
Not wishing to appear unworthy of his office, the minister reported
back to the emperor of his genius in hiring such competent and
talented weavers. The emperor, after further delays, sent another
official, hoping to encourage the completion of the suit. The official
saw nothing but, fearing the emperor's wrath, reported in a manner similar to the minister's.

Finally, the day arrived for the emperor to preview the weavers'
work. The emperor, seeing nothing, but fearful of being considered
unfit for his kingdom, played along with the deceit, proclaiming his
love for the patterns and colors in his new outfit. The two con men
proceeded to ask the emperor to remove his clothes, raising their
arms as if holding something to put on him. The court officials, not
daring to speak the truth, pretended to agree with the emperor,
lauding his genius and the weavers' design. The people, in antici-
pation of the king's most expensive and wondrous clothes to date,
gathered for the parade to view the new clothes. The emperor pa-
raded through his capital city, listening as the people lavished complements on him and his new clothes. Nearly everyone was spell-
bound by the beauty of his clothes, but over the din of praise and
hoopla was heard the cry of a child, shouting, "The emperor has no
clothes on!" The father of the young boy quickly reprimanded him,
but everyone around the boy had heard the truth. The emperor,
although secretly agreeing with the child, continued the parade
as the crowd fawned in endless adulation and displayed his new

clothes only to those of intelligence and worthy of their high offices.

## Confronting Reality

"The Emperor's New Clothes" explains why so many people fail in the game of life. Most of life's participants, like the crowd surrounding the emperor, will not confront reality. Even if a person performs the PDCA process, if, at the check step, he suffers from self-deception, a distortion between reality and his perceptions, he will not be able to confront the data and adjust his plans to win. Indeed, the majority of people prefer comfortable illusions rather than disturbing realities. Even though they have near-limitless potential, most people seem to go through the motions, doing just enough to survive but not enough to excel in the game of life. On the one hand, in order to make winning a habit, a person must apply the PDCA process consistently, hating to lose so badly that he will endure nearly any pain to change the scoreboard (check step) results. On the other hand, in order to make losing a habit, a person must delude himself consistently, hating to change so badly that he will create whatever distortion of reality is necessary in order to deny what is undeniable to others—his mounting failures. In both situations, a person escapes the pain of losing: one by learning to confront, change, and win; the other by learning to escape, excuse, and lose. As discussed earlier, people must choose between these two options: ego or excellence on a daily basis. Regretfully, most choose the easier route, escaping the pain of losing through self-delusion (like the emperor). But one can change at any time, choosing to confront the check step head-on, eliminating the pain of losing by adjusting and winning.

Confronting issues requires more up-front work than escaping does, which is probably why most people choose the latter, the perceived easier route. But leaders are not like most people; leaders refuse to run from issues. They allow setbacks to build an increasing internal level of frustration, until finally, sick and tired of being sick and tired, they explode past previous limiting beliefs when the pain of defeat becomes stronger than the pain of changing. If, at any point in the process, one allows himself to escape from the pressure, change won't happen, but plenty of losing will. Anyone can be a leader, but he must refuse the tempting avenues of escape that lead to mediocrity. Reject outright the temporary mental comfort that escape offers from

> **When the going gets tough, the tough get going.**

135

the scoreboard of life. Don't settle for mental peace and mediocrity. Rather, embrace the mental tumult needed to confront brutal reality. Don't settle for anything less than your personal best; declare war on mediocrity in a quest for excellence in everything that you do. Ultimately, there are only two choices in the game of life: surviving or thriving. When the going gets tough, the tough get going. People will either get going to win or get quitting to whine. Admittedly, changing is tough, requiring internal strength and fortitude; but the point is that not changing is even tougher, requiring increasing doses of self-delusion, literally lying to oneself, in order to deflect the responsibility for mounting setbacks in the game of life.

How is it possible to confront the brutal facts, both personally and professionally, without losing confidence in an eventual victory? Jim Collins wrote, "In every case, the management team responded with a powerful psychological duality. On the one hand, they stoically accepted the brutal facts of reality. On the other hand, they maintained an unwavering faith in the endgame and a commitment to prevail as a great company despite the brutal facts. We came to call this duality the Stockdale Paradox." Great companies and individuals confront facts routinely, not hiding their heads in the sand; regardless of the current score, they maintain an unwavering belief that they will overcome and win, no matter how painful the change process is. Stockdale, even though he was never given an ounce of hope that he would be released when he was a prisoner of war in Vietnam, refused to lose faith, saying, "I never doubted not only that I would get out, but also that I would prevail in the end and turn the experience into the defining event of my life, which, in retrospect, I would not trade." Optimists, unlike Stockdale, fail to assess situations properly, suffering from self-delusion. They build false hopes (like the emperor's clothes), leaving them exposed when confronted with brutal facts. Stockdale, embodying the quote "A man who is down need fear no fall," was down but never out because of his unyielding faith, no matter how long his suffering took. He confronted the brutal facts of his situation, knowing that he was in for the long haul, suffering no false illusions because he refused self-delusion. Leaders fail, just as non-leaders do, but they are different in one crucial thing: leaders accept responsibility for their failures and study the data, thus learning and growing.

## Developing the Scoreboard

Collins, when comparing good-to-great companies, noticed, "The great companies continually refined the path to greatness with the brutal facts of reality." The comparison companies in his study, on the other hand, did not. In order to confront reality, one must collect relevant data. Bill Gates, in the book *Business @ the Speed of Thought*, wrote, "The most meaningful way to differentiate your company from your competition, the best way to put distance between you and the crowd, is to do an outstanding job with information. How you gather, manage, and use information will determine whether you win or lose." Actually, gathering it isn't enough because unless a company confronts what the data is truly saying, it is still deceived. In fact, Collins wrote, "Indeed, we found no evidence that the good-to-great companies had more or better information than the comparison companies. None. Both sets of companies had virtually identical access to good information. The key, then, lies not in better information, but in turning information into information that cannot be ignored." With that said, Gates's scoreboard is still essential in business, or as he calls it, "the digital nervous system," because a company cannot confront data when it has none. Just as this is true at the corporate level, it's also true at the individual level.

Negative information shouldn't be downplayed; instead, it should be confronted head-on, looking for areas that can be improved. Negative information should be sought out, knowing that the health of an individual or a company depends on learning and confronting brutal reality quickly, avoiding the pitfalls of self and corporate deception. Without a scoreboard, how does one know whether he is winning, losing, or even advancing? Only with an updated scoreboard can a person tell if the strategies he is employing are moving him toward or away from his personal and professional objectives. People must learn to track the score in each area of life because it is an essential step in mastering the game. In fact, productive individuals and companies can be determined by how fast negative facts are confronted. Leaders address negative information quickly, maintaining the perspective that no matter what, they will overcome. Non-leaders, on the other hand, fall quickly into self-delusion, which leads to even bigger issues by not dealing with reality.

> **People must learn to track the score in each area of life because it is an essential step in mastering the game.**

The scoreboard for life and business isn't a new concept. As a matter of fact, Albert Sloan, one of the founders of modern management, learned the value of keeping score to improve General Motors' performance in the 1920s. Sloan created working relationships with the GM dealers nationwide, knowing that his business was complete not when he sold to his dealers but when the dealers sold to satisfied customers. He intuitively understood that his business needed a scoreboard, and that without one, it was operating blindly. Sloan traveled the country in a private railroad car, visiting GM dealerships, collecting data, and building the scoreboard in order to make decisions based on customer preferences. If the CEO of the largest corporation in the world traveled extensively to gather the right data, what should people, in our computer age, do to ensure collection of the right data? In God we trust; all others must have data. What data is essential in order to determine the difference between winning and losing in each area of a person's life?

In the financial realm, perhaps the data collected is the percent of income spent after taxes. In this case, a person's defined win is saving a minimum of 10 percent after all expenses. The data collected produces the scoreboard, not allowing him to be deceived by thinking everything is good when the scoreboard reveals the true picture. Successful people seem to hunger for data, even if it paints a poor picture, believing that only by determining the real picture can they confront it, making changes to win. While most people are deluding themselves, winners are gathering data, studying it voraciously, and making changes. Michael Dell, in the book *Direct from Dell*, wrote, "It was clear that in 1993 we didn't have the information we needed to run our business. We didn't fully understand the relationship between costs, revenues, and profits within the different parts of our business. There were internal disagreements about which businesses were worthwhile and which were not. We were making decisions based on emotions and opinions. In leadership, it's important to be intuitive, but not at the expense of facts. Without the right data to back it up, emotion-based decision-making during difficult times will inevitably lead a company into greater danger. That's precisely what was happening to us." Dell was being deceived by rumors, false opinions, and turf building. Only after developing a working scoreboard could Dell sort out fact from fiction and deal with reality.

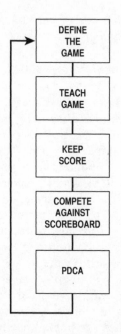

Sloan, Gates, and Dell, like all the best business entrepreneurs, would not think about building a business without a scoreboard. (For more reading on the development and implementation of the scoreboard, see the chapter on the Leadership Resolution.) Most people would agree that keeping score in business is a must, but surprisingly, these same people aren't keeping score of the results in their personal lives. Life's scoreboard plays the same role as a sports scoreboard, helping a person make adjustments during the game of life. In fact, the better information a person has, the better predictions he can make. Dell's example of inventory management exemplifies the method of turning the scoreboard into information that improves actions: "The concept behind the direct model has nothing to do with stockpiling and everything to do with information. The quality of your information is inversely proportional to the amount of assets required, in this case excess inventory. With less information about customer needs, you need massive amounts of inventory. So, if you have great information—that is, you know exactly what people want and how much—you need that much less in inventory." Dell kept score, confronting his business's brutal reality, leading to a multibillion-dollar competitive advantage in his twenties.

Non-leaders, on the other hand, pass the buck and point fingers, thus blaming others and excusing themselves. Here are three of the most popular methods of self-delusion, leading to hiding from the brutal reality displayed on the scoreboard.

## Blame Game and Passing the Buck

The first and most popular way that so-called leaders use to escape a confrontation with brutal reality is to play the blame game. No one likes to lose, but when potential leaders blame others for losses in an effort to protect their fragile egos, they may ease their pain momentarily, but only by abdicating personal responsibility for results. If a person doesn't own his losses, he won't own any victories. Any time one assigns his lack of results to poor mentorship, lazy teammates, unsupportive spouses, the economy, etc., he surrenders control of his life, waiting for others to get better in order for his life to improve. Real leaders cannot stand the thought of passively waiting for others to improve before their lives do. Leaders refuse to pass the buck, knowing that if they do, they will release the tension created by the pain of losing; this tension is what generates the motivation to change. In fact, the amount of time that someone spends pointing fingers at anything outside of himself is the same amount of time that he is not leading. Don't fall for this seductive self-delusional blame game. Instead, search for ways to be responsible, working on better skills rather than on better excuses. One can make a million dollars or a million excuses, but one cannot make both. Moreover, if a person won't accept responsibility for his current results, then he won't learn how to change his results. Don't play the blame game, regardless of the alleged temporary relief it provides, because in the long run, it only produces self-delusion and a habit of losing.

Lou Holtz, former coach of Notre Dame wrote in *Wins, Losses, and Lessons*, "The person who has never made a mistake in his own mind, who obfuscates and attempts to deflect blame, is someone you should approach cautiously. I've fouled up plenty in my life. In most circumstances, I've done my best to own up to my mistakes and take whatever steps I could to correct them." Is it any surprise that Lou won a national championship and led six different universities to bowl games? Lou learned early in life that passing the buck was a recipe for disaster. Passing the buck is the most costly of luxuries, which no true leader can afford. Lou, instead of protecting his ego and blaming others, accepted responsibility, con-

> **Real leaders cannot stand the thought of passively waiting for others to improve before their lives do.**

fronted brutal reality, and changed. His courageous actions led to world-class results. He, like all winners, hated losing but accepted responsibility for it, creating the drive to change in order to win.

## Winning Isn't Worth It

The second way that would-be leaders use to escape a confrontation with brutal reality is by denying that victory would be worth the sacrifice. One may hear statements like, "Well, I'm just not willing to work that hard for success," or "I'm doing pretty well." Many people seem to forget that they work hard whether they are successful or not. The physical work difference between winning and losing is negligible; it's the mental work that makes the difference. Only when a person is willing to give his all to a worthy cause, willing to sacrifice for his team and his dream, mastering the patterns of success in his chosen field, will he feel the exhilaration that only a winner experiences in his quest for a noble victory.

Society today has experienced a growing material abundance and, simultaneously, a growing happiness scarcity. In the pursuit of happiness, people make two common errors. First, they believe that by ceasing to strive for excellence, they can enjoy peace and happiness in mediocrity. Second, on the other side of the pendulum, they believe that material wealth can make them happy. The truth is that happiness cannot be pursued directly at all; rather, it is a result of striving to improve every day on life's journey. True success isn't the destination but the journey, and happiness is the by-product in the pursuit of a goal or a dream bigger than oneself. Both sides of the pendulum steal true joy, the first with boring complacency, the other with restless discontent.

Another principle existing in both is that each chooses self over others, the first by desiring peace, the second by desiring affluence, making neither of them focused on serving other people. One of life's biggest lessons is that it's not success that creates happiness; rather, it's what one becomes on the journey by pursuing a worthwhile goal or dream. God, in the larger scope of things, is infinitely more concerned with the state of your heart than with your net worth. The sacrifices made for others on the journey to success create self-worth, producing happiness (joy) long before the dream is obtained. By taking sacrifice out of success, one also halts the building of self-worth, making the attainment of the dream empty of its true value.

## Vicarious Victories

The third way that people take to delude themselves is by hiding in the stands of life, vicariously winning through others' score boards while ignoring their own. Nearly everyone loves sports, and one of the main reasons for this is that the scoreboard is updated real time, providing instant feedback on each team's performance. When a person arrives at a sporting event late, the first thing he asks upon sitting down is, "What's the score?" Can one imagine going to a professional game without keeping score? It would be laughable in sports, but it is so common in people. People love sporting events because the game is clearly defined. Winning and losing can be measured instantly by the scoreboard.

**Winning and losing can be measured instantly by the scoreboard.**

When a team loses, the members must make adjustments in their strategies with the goal of improving their performance in the next game. The PDCA—plan, do, check, and adjust—process is applied constantly in sports, but not so often in a person's life.

It's a common phenomenon in sporting events for a spectator to berate one of the players on the field, yelling at the player for not executing the plays flawlessly. Remember, the player on the field has reached a level of achievement that few ever will by playing for a professional sports team. On the other hand, what level of performance does it take to be a fan, besides buying a ticket? Isn't it ironic that, many times, a man criticizing a player's performance isn't criticizing his own, even though his personal statistics are far inferior to the player's? Although living paycheck to paycheck, barely keeping his head above water, he is disgusted by the player's lack of excellence. Doesn't this seem peculiar? Most fans maintain a strange dichotomy. The fan seems to have higher expectations for the excellence of his sports team than he does for himself. Don't misread the point—athletes ought to do their personal best night after night, but why shouldn't the fans do the same in their chosen fields? The fans religiously keep track of the scoreboard at sporting events, but few seem to maintain high standards when the spotlight is placed on their professional fields of play.

Imagine what would happen if all sports fans who expect the coaches to lead their teams chose to lead their families with a similar level of expectation for excellence. The paradox of success is solved only when it's realized that most people have substituted their personal scoreboards with the scoreboards of their favorite sports teams, musical bands, or hobbies, believing that they themselves cannot win. Since human beings are hardwired to keep score, they cannot surrender the urge to compete and score in the game of life. Instead, they transfer life's competition from themselves to others, seeking to vicariously live for excellence through others' achievements. What else could explain why a person would spend his time, money, and energy as a fan of someone else's success journey, while claiming not to have time, money, or energy for his own success journey? It appears that people, after years of struggling with little success, surrender the hope that they could ever win. Fans feel the thrill of victory and the agony of defeat, albeit vicariously, with no personal growth or results included or required. They are beautiful people with amazing potential and great passion but are missing out on their calling due to a faulty belief system. Only by confronting the true scoreboard in their lives, feeling the pain of losing without attempting to escape, can people get back to the game and out of the spectator's section of life. Life is keeping score anyway, whether the person is tracking his score or not.

Confronting brutal reality is the only path out of self-delusion and to personal success. The key is to accurately define one's life game in order to satisfy all his customers (wife, children, coworkers, neighbors, etc.) consistently. There simply isn't a substitute for defining the game and keeping score. Until a person honestly confronts the facts, refusing to deceive himself like the emperor with his clothes, he will not win the game.

In the end, leaders must either sacrifice their egos on the altar of truth or sacrifice the truth on the altar of their egos. Life is a game, and the game is being played now. Isn't it time to start keeping score?

## The PDCA Success Summary

Success is simply the PDCA journey of learning. No one ever arrives because there are always more PDCAs to do. Of course, people suffer defeats in the PDCA process, but setbacks only reveal false models in need of more testing. People disciplined enough to apply the PDCA process to each area of their lives will improve rapidly, leaving friends and family puzzled on how they changed so profoundly. Sam Walton exclaimed, "I've made it my own personal mission to ensure that constant change is a vital part of the Wal-Mart culture itself. I've forced change—sometimes for change's sake alone—at every turn in our company's development. In fact, I think one of the greatest strengths of Wal-Mart's ingrained culture is its ability to drop everything and turn on a dime."

Be patient with the PDCA process when implementing it in your life, remembering that most people overestimate the amount of change one can achieve in one year, while underestimating the changes that can occur in ten years. Rome wasn't built in a day, oak trees do not mature overnight, and success will take time. By consistently forming new skills and habits through the PDCA process, a person will grow toward his vision.

## Sam Walton: Tracking the Scoreboard

The year was 1966. Little did the world know that an unknown merchant from Arkansas had enrolled in an IBM school for retailers, and he was about to change the face of shopping in America.

In Poughkeepsie, New York, Abe Marks, the first president of the National Mass Retailing Institute (NMRI) trade association, was one of the speakers for a class. Marks recalled his first meeting with the man:

> So he opens up this attaché case, and, I swear, he had every article I had ever written and every speech I had ever given in there. I'm thinking, "This guy is a very thorough man." Then he hands me an accountant's working column sheet, showing all his operating categories all written out by hand. Then he says: "Tell me what's wrong. What am I doing wrong?" I look at these numbers—this is in 1966—and I don't believe what I am seeing. He's got a handful of stores and he's doing about $10 million a year with some incredible margin. An unbelievable performance!

This thorough man that Marks was referring to was none other than Sam Walton. He had enrolled in the IBM school, desiring to learn about computers, specifically how to use them to control his merchandise inventory. His meeting with Abe Marks was the start of a lifelong friendship.

Walton intuitively understood that if he wished to keep growing, he must leverage computers as the scoreboard to track the results at each store, which allowed local leadership with centralized oversight. In the book *Sam Walton: Made in America*, Marks shared Walton's philosophy: "He knew that he was already in what the trade calls an 'absentee ownership' situation. That just means you're putting your stores out where you, as management, aren't. If he wanted to grow, he had to learn to control it. So to service these stores you've got to have timely information: How much merchandise is in the store? What is it? What's selling and what's not? What is to be ordered, marked down, replaced?...The more you turn your inventory, the less capital is required." Marks brought clarity to Walton's thinking on one of the secrets to explosive growth—keeping score. Keeping score is the only way for a leader to confront the reality of the data and make adjustments based on the scoreboard. Walton refused to run his business on hunches or gut feelings; instead, he allowed the data to speak and corrected his course when necessary.

Walton understood that keeping score was vital to Walmart's success because as Marks shared, "He couldn't expand beyond that horizon unless he had the ability to capture this information on paper so that he could control his operations, no matter where they might be. He became, really the best utilizer of information to control absentee ownerships that there's ever been, which gave him the ability to open as many stores as he [opened], and run them as well as he [ran] them, and to be as profitable as he [made] them." Walton utilized computers to help him track the scoreboard, one that both the local stores and Walton's leadership team could study. This held local managers responsible for store results, while allowing the leadership to offer suggestions for improvements from other more successful stores. Indeed, Walton would not have grown into the business success that Walmart is today if it weren't for the computer age; however, even before the digital age, he was learning already. Marks recalled, "He was really ten years away (in 1966) from the computer world coming. But he was preparing himself. And this is an important point: without the computer, Sam Walton could not have done what he's done. He could not have built a retailing empire the size of what he's built, the way he built it. He's done a lot of other things right, too, but he could not have done it without the computer. It would have been impossible."

Once Walton had a scoreboard in place, he was able to bring the lessons he learned to the masses in several ways. One way of doing this was by implementing a Saturday-morning meeting with the goal of sharing ideas, confronting brutal reality, and making course adjustments where necessary. This meeting allowed the leaders, both local and top management, to discuss the same data, everyone having the same scoreboard to review, celebrating their victories and learning from their failures. Walton valued the scoreboard, saying:

That's why I come in every Saturday morning usually around two or three (a.m.), and go through all the weekly numbers. I steal a march on everybody else for the Saturday morning meeting. I can go through those sheets and look at a store, and even though I haven't been there in a while, I can remind myself of something about it, the manager maybe, and then I can remember later that they are doing this much business this week and that their wage cost is such and such. I do this with each store every Saturday morning. It usually takes about three hours, but when I'm done I have as good a feel for what's going on in the company as anybody here—maybe better on some days.

No one understood more than Walton that you have no right to expect what you are not willing to inspect. Walton expected a lot from his leaders, trusting them to achieve excellence, but he also reviewed the scoreboard, verifying that the trust was merited. A. L. Johnson, a former vice chairman of Walmart, said, "As famous as Sam is for being a great motivator—and he deserves even more credit than he's gotten for that—he is equally good at checking on the people he has motivated. You might call his style: management by looking over your shoulder." Because Walton was expanding so fast, he constantly needed more leaders to run his local stores. This forced a level of delegation higher than most businesses will ever have to sustain, but thanks to his scoreboard, Walton could quickly identify people who were in over their heads. Ferold Arend, former president of operations of Walmart, said:

Sam would take people with hardly any retail experience, give them six months with us, and if he thought they showed any real potential to merchandise a store and manage people, he'd give them a chance. He'd make them an assistant manager. . . . In my opinion, most of them weren't anywhere near ready to run stores, but Sam proved me wrong there. He finally convinced me. If you take someone who lacks experience and the know-how but has the real desire and the willingness to work his tail off to get the job done, he'll make up for what he lacks. And that proved to be true nine times out of ten. It was one way we were able to grow so fast.

Walton's delegation of responsibilities, coupled with his zeal for inspecting the scoreboard, was one of his key secrets to leadership development, producing leaders who confronted reality based on data, not on daydreams.

Walton developed a culture at Walmart where high achievers could win. In order to do this, he intuitively created a business game following a four-step pattern. The game followed this equation: *low prices + good quality + friendly service = high value and satisfied customers*. Each Saturday morning, participants of the game would gather to review the scoreboard, identifying areas where they had achieved goals, in which case, they celebrated, as well as areas where stores or corporate leadership fell short of the mark, in which case, adjustments were made. The goal of the leaders at the store level was to produce results that would be recognized at the Saturday-morning meeting. Walton's goal, by studying the data, was to identify the variance between good performance and poor performance, leading to recognition for the good performance and "teachable moments" for the rest. Walton, always competitive, could not stand the thought of losing, driving change whenever the scoreboard pointed a weakness in their strategy.

The highly competitive game was a measure of store profitability, and when wins were added together, they made the total profitability of Walmart. Many people say that money is not a proper measurement of success, but in a competitive marketplace, with many choices for customers to choose from for their retail dollars, profitability measures the consistent ability of an organization to satisfy its customers. If they are not satisfied, they will vote with their feet by shopping at other stores. Walton's simple equation—*low prices + good quality + friendly service = high value and satisfied customers*—was the only constant. How to achieve this equation requires leaders to constantly innovate, leading to one of the most creative and execution-oriented cultures in the world. Walmart was difficult to beat because if a competitor started to make inroads in the game, the data would reveal this at Walmart's next Saturday-morning meeting, leading to adjustments in the PDCA—plan, do, check, and adjust process. Walmart, in a nutshell, refused to lose, willing to consistently change in order to stay ahead of the competition. No other organization had such unit discipline to allow the data to speak directly to the entire management team. In fact, most management teams avoid negative data, as one avoids a plague, but Walton was simply more interested in results than his management team's ego. David Glass, former CEO of Walmart, shared, "Two things about Sam Walton distinguish him from almost anyone else that I know. First, he gets up every day bound and determined to improve something. Second, he is less afraid of being wrong than anyone I've ever known. And once he sees he's wrong, he just shakes it off and heads in another direction." Walton, an over-the-top optimist by nature, never allowed the data to reduce his confidence in ultimate victory; instead, he allowed it to help him question his current methods, leading to continuous improvement, since his ego was attached not to his current methods but to the results produced by using improved methods. For example, if customer satisfaction is the ultimate principle for existence, then all methods can be questioned in order to obtain that end. But if the boss's ego, salary, and power are the ultimate principles for existence, then customer satisfaction, as well as the company's well-being, is easily sacrificed on the altar of pride and self-preservation, a shrine where Walton refused to worship.

Once the data is tracked, the key is to make the business a game. Walton did this in a variety of ways, and one of the best was by using the Volume Producing Item (VPI), a merchandising program designed to encourage different regions and stores to compete based on the amount of merchandise moved. Walton wrote, "We have a lot of fun with all this item promotion, but here's what it's really all about. The philosophy it teaches, which rubs off on all the associates and the store managers and the department heads, is that your stores are full of items that can explode into big volume and big profits if you are just smart enough to identify them and take the trouble to promote them." Competition created cooperation within the stores and the regions as they pushed each other to reach for levels previously thought impossible. The scoreboard made this possible by providing real-time sales data from each store.

Anything that worked was quickly cross pollinated to different regions, recognizing the originators of the innovative promotion to the rest of their sister stores. Many games were played by tracking the numbers, focused on reducing costs or increasing sales.

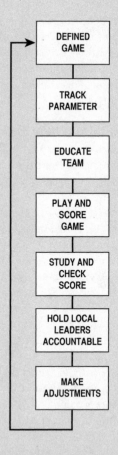

Without a doubt, the most well-known game in the history of Walmart was in 1984, when Walton agreed to wear a grass skirt and do the hula on Wall Street if the company could achieve 8 percent pretax profits. This energized the entire

Walmart team, wanting to see if their conservative founder would really dance the hula on Wall Street in front of the financial cronies. Walmart hit its target, and Walton followed through on his word on the front steps of Merrill Lynch. He slipped on a grass skirt and Hawaiian shirt and danced the hula

**Any friendship that cannot laugh at itself isn't real.**

with real hula dancers and ukulele players. Walton said, "It was one of the few times one of our company stunts really embarrassed me. But at Walmart, when you make a bet like I did—that we couldn't possibly produce a pretax profit of more than 8 percent—you always pay up....Most folks probably thought we just had a wacky chairman who was pulling a pretty primitive publicity stunt. What they didn't realize is that this sort of stuff goes on all the time at Walmart. It's part of our culture, and it runs through everything we do....we always have tried to make life interesting and as unpredictable as we can, and to make Walmart a fun proposition." Games are fun, and this was Walton's forte. He wrote, "If you are committed to the Walmart partnership and its core values, the culture encourages you to think up all sorts of ideas that break the mold and fight monotony."

The bigger Walmart grew, the more important it was for individual stores to score the game since the total sales and volume of the company boggled the mind. But in order to do so, each store must receive information in a timely manner, studying and adjusting at the local level, not waiting for the corporate leadership to issue edicts. Walton wrote, "Sharing information and responsibility is a key to any partnership. It makes people feel responsible and involved....In our individual stores, we show them their store's profits, their store's purchases, their store's sales, and their store's markdowns. We show them all that on a regular basis, and I'm not talking about just the managers and the assistant managers." Walton understood that in order to build an absentee ownership enterprise, local leaders must have access to the scoreboard in order to be held responsible for the results. Leaders who accomplished the objectives moved up; those who didn't learned lessons. In Walmart's culture, due to the constant focus on results rather than mere talk, managers either improved or were removed since hiding out was not an option in the scoreboard-based culture because everyone knew who was winning or losing.

By keeping score and traveling to the stores, Walton created more "teachable moments" than any other retailer did, allowing his stores to learn faster through the PDCA process. Without an accurate scoreboard, people can spin the story to their own liking, avoiding the harmful data, thankful that their bosses are not inspecting the delegated assignments. But when one tracks the scoreboard, holding those who are in leadership positions responsible, the company's culture is changed, making confrontations with brutal facts a standard operating procedure in the company's DNA. Sam Walton, consciously or unconsciously, followed a four-step process, creating a culture of winning throughout his company. Any business leader can do the same by developing his own criteria in this four-step process. Here are the steps: define the game, play the game, analyze the game, and execute the playbook to win the game.

CHAPTER 7

# FRIENDSHIP
## Resolved: To Develop the Art and Science of Friendship

*I know that everyone needs a true friend to lighten the load when life gets heavy.*

True friends give the most when they receive the least. The Ancient Greeks had four distinct words that communicated the concept of love: *agape*, *eros*, *storge*, and *philia*. *Agape* embodies sacrificial love; *eros* describes sensual love; *storge* pertains to familial love; and *philia*, the subject of this chapter, symbolizes brotherly love (like Philadelphia, "the City of Brotherly Love"), the love between true friends.

Aristotle described *philia* as loyalty to friends, family, and community, requiring virtue, equality, and familiarity. It is best represented by the love shared between two longtime close friends. *Philia*-type relationships, however, are not thriving today. In fact, the quality and quantity of friendship, according to the 2006 study of the *American Sociological Review*, is declining. In a survey among 1,467 people, data was collected and compared to a survey from nineteen years earlier. The findings revealed that the average number of people with whom Americans can discuss matters of importance had dropped by nearly one-third, from 2.94 people in 1985 to 2.08 in 2004. One of the researchers, Lynn Smith-Lovin, a professor of sociology at Duke University, commented, "The evidence shows that Americans have fewer confidants and those ties are also more family-based than they used to be. This change indicates something that's not good for our society. Ties with a close network of people create a safety net. These ties also lead to civic engagement and local political action." The study also revealed that the number of people who have no one with whom to discuss important matters more than doubled to nearly 25 percent of survey respondents. Sociologists believe that discussion networks, a person's friends and family, are an important social resource, providing encouragement, counseling, and support.

Some may argue that Facebook and Twitter connect people to discussion networks, but the high-tech world will never replace the warmth of high-touch relationships. In fact, author Robert Putnam, in his book *Bowling Alone*, asked, "What is the single most common finding from half a century of research on the correlates of life satisfaction?" His extensive research can be summarized in one sentence: "That happiness is best predicted by the breadth and depth of one's social connections." C. S. Lewis described the change in the value of friendship: "To the Ancients, Friendship seemed the happiest and most fully human of all loves; the crown of life and the school of virtue. The modern world, in comparison, ignores it.... It is something quite marginal; not a main course in life's banquet; a diversion; something that fills up the chinks of one's time." Sadly, if true happiness is based on a person's friends and social connections, then the future of the Western world is dismal at best. But perhaps, with enough resolve, the principles of true friendship can be restored, turning the tide of Western decline.

## The Eight Principles of True Friendship

After enjoying decades of true friendships, living and breathing leadership principles in a thriving community, and doing extensive research in the field, I have identified eight essential principles for building and maintaining long-term *philia*-friendships:

1. True friends form around a shared insight, interest, or taste, enjoying the common bond uniting them.
2. True friends accept one another, loving each other despite their human imperfections.
3. True friends approve of one another, protecting each other's weaknesses while enhancing each other's strengths.
4. True friends appreciate one another, encouraging, serving, and believing in one another's gifts and talents.
5. True friends listen with empathy, learning the hopes, dreams, fears, and struggles of each other.
6. True friends celebrate one another's success, proud of each other's accomplishments without a hint of envy.

7. True friends are trustworthy, maintaining all confidences shared with unimpeachable honor and self-respect, knowing that gossip separates the best of friends.
8. True friends are loyal, respecting and defending one another's character, reputation, and motives, as far as truth allows, while addressing any issues or concerns between them promptly and privately, ensuring misunderstandings never fester.

## 1. True Friends Form around Shared Insights

True friends begin as companions, but soon go further, developing a love and respect for one another. Author Fred Smith shared a poignant description about love: "Love is willing the ultimate good for the other person." Only deep friendship will build loving bonds of this magnitude. C. S. Lewis depicted the process of discovery from companions into friends:

> Friendship arises out of mere companionship when two or more of the companions discover that they have in common some insight or interest or even taste which the others do not share and which, till that moment, each believed to be his own unique treasure (or burden). The typical expression of opening Friendship would be something like, "What? You, too? I thought I was the only one"…In this kind of love, as Emerson said, 'Do you love me?' means 'Do you see the same truth?'—Or at least, 'Do you care about the same truth?'" The man who agrees with us that some question, little regarded by others, is of great importance, can be our Friend.

There is an indescribable joy in the discovery of, and in being discovered by, another human being, providing a brief respite from the loneliness of life. Emerson shared the feeling: "The glory of friendship is not the outstretched hand, not the kindly smile, nor the joy of companionship; it is the spiritual inspiration that comes to one when you discover that someone believes in you and is willing to trust you with a friendship." Aristotle distinguished between a genuine friendship and two counterfeit types—one founded on utility, the other on pleasure. A friendship based solely on utility, like a mailman, survives only as long as both parties receive benefit, while a friendship based only on pleasure, like golfing buddies, ends when one party no longer finds the activity pleasurable.

Genuine friendship, on the other hand, is based on something more enduring. According to Aristotle, "It is those who desire the good of their friends for the friends' sake that are most truly friends, because each loves the other for what he is, and not for any incidental quality." Genuine friendship, then, will last as long as both parties remain committed to virtue, since a virtuous person desires good for his friends as much as for himself. Virtue, however, doesn't mean lack of fun. The best of friends laugh often and heartily. Just as one can tell a man's character by his ability to laugh at himself, so in a friendship, one can tell the quality of one's friends by their ability to laugh at each other—not a derisive or condescending laughter, but simply one that acknowledges the imperfections inherent in the human condition. Any friendship that cannot laugh at itself isn't real. True friends enjoy one another's company. When a person finds someone who can help him become better while enjoying fellowship, he is on his way to having a true friend. Everybody ought to strive to be this type of friend to others and seek friendships of this caliber, magnifying one's blessings by both giving and receiving true *philia*-friendships.

> **Any friendship that cannot laugh at itself isn't real.**

## 2. True Friends Accept One Another

The value of a true friend is immeasurable. Everyone makes mistakes, but "love covers a multitude of sins" (I Peter 4:8, New Living Translation). In other words, a friend loves his friends enough to see past their faults and foibles and recognize the talents and treasures buried within. Friends have built bonds of trust that cannot be unwound easily, especially when the relationship is coated with forgiveness and grace. Friends offer one another grace when they make mistakes, recognizing that in the future, they may need grace themselves. They also see the hidden hurts, fears, and vulnerabilities but love their friends' warts and all anyway. Author Les Giblin shared a Triple A Formula—*accept*, *approve*, and *appreciate*—that, if practiced from the heart, builds strong relationships.

Acceptance that one human being shows another creates peace, which allows one to relax and share openly. When someone is constantly judging what another person says or does, he doesn't allow the other person to relax, making friendship nearly impossible. Acceptance doesn't mean that one approves of everything that his friend does; rather, it means that he accepts his friend as a human being. A friend's acceptance stills troubled waters, allowing his friend some space to grow. It's only when a person is accepted as he is that he is free to become what he desires to be. Acceptance is for the soul what food is for the body, providing nourishment and energy for improvement.

When people are accepted as they are, they desire more of the feeling that comes with acceptance, leading them to seek approval, which creates a process for change and growth that is nurtured by the Triple A Formula. Many people get this wrong, thinking that they cannot accept someone until he does things right. No one does everything right, making all of us unacceptable and lonely. Everyone needs personal growth, and it's only through acceptance that the soul is nourished to pursue approval and appreciation. A person shouldn't judge the faults of others too critically since he has to work on a full-time project, which is himself. As the proverb says, "Blessed are the flexible, for they shall not be bent out of shape." The following story displays the power of acceptance:

A water bearer in China had two large pots, each hung on each end of a pole, which he carried across his neck. One of the pots had a crack in it, while the other pot was perfect and always delivered a full portion of water. At the end of the long walk from the stream to the house, the cracked pot was only half-full. For a full two years, this went on daily, with the bearer delivering only one and a half pots of water to his house.

Of course, the perfect pot was proud of its accomplishments, perfect for what it was made to do. The poor cracked pot, on the other hand, was ashamed of its imperfection. It was miserable that it was able to accomplish only half of what it was made to do.

After two years of feeling a bitter failure, the poor cracked pot spoke to the water bearer one day by the stream. "I am ashamed of myself, and I want to apologize to you. I have been able to deliver only half my load because this crack on my side causes water to leak as you walk all the way back to your house. Because of my flaw, you have to do all of this work, and you don't get the full value of your efforts," the pot said.

The bearer said to the pot, "Did you notice that there are flowers only on your side of the path, but not on the other pot's side? That's because I have always known your flaw. So I planted flower seeds on your side of the path, and every day, while we walk back, you water them. For two years, I have been able to pick these beautiful flowers to decorate the table. Without you being just the way you are, there would not be this beauty to grace the house."

Every person has cracks and flaws, and it doesn't take a genius to find them since everyone is a proverbial cracked pot. Gaining acceptance of one's imperfections from a friend and from oneself is the starting point for change. When a person is accepted, despite his flaws, a foundation is provided upon which to build and hope for a better future. Since he has no need to deny his present reality, thanks to the acceptance, he can confront the facts as they are in order to begin changing, knowing that he is loved and accepted. Moreover, when people accept a person, they allow him to accept himself, leading to an honest look at reality, not with a negative self-criticism but with a hopeful expectation of a better tomorrow. All of this occurs because someone simply accepted another human being as he is, freeing him to become what he ought to be.

### 3. True Friends Approve of One Another

If acceptance is viewed as withholding criticisms, then approval can be viewed as releasing commendations. A true friend approves of his friends' gifts and talents. But how does one approve of others if he doesn't feel approved by them? A person, having heard many conversations among new friends where everyone attempts to impress the others, reaches the conclusion that the best policy is first to allow himself to be impressed, and then impress if necessary. By providing relationship oxygen to others, the person can breathe easier, feeling approved, making it much easier for him to now listen and approve. Seeking first to understand, then to be understood, is the principle to apply here. Seeking first to understand costs a person nothing (unless self-pride is more important than others' self-worth), but it makes huge deposits in a relationship. Approval moves beyond acceptance of people and extends to acclaim for specific abilities and actions. In order to approve of others, therefore, a person must look for the qualities and attributes that he respects. Few people invest the time to approve of others because most are too busy focusing on themselves. Typically, it's only when a person feels approved that he can offer approval to others. Imagine the friendship revolution that would be experienced if everyone approved of his friends' strengths by sharing what he respects and admires about them. Regretfully, many times, these good words are spoken only at a deceased friend's funeral, but why wait for the funeral to tell a friend what is admirable about him?

Do not withhold approval until the funeral is held; instead, liberally apply approval any time it's appropriate. Just as oil works in an engine, approval makes relationships run smoother, with less friction. Don't just approve a friend's obvious attributes; rather, point out lesser-known strengths that others may not have noticed. For example, a professional driver is known for having good racing skills, but if someone pointed out that he has excellent parenting methods, the driver would never forget the kind words. Be a professional observer of excellence, but don't just observe; share the approval with the one observed and with others. The oil of approval reduces heat and friction in relationships, strengthening the resolve of one's friends to fulfill their purposes. In fact, a *New York Times* article on friendship revealed, "Last year, researchers studied thirty-four students at the University of Virginia, taking them to the base of a steep hill and fitting them with a weighted backpack. They were then asked to estimate the steepness of the hill. Some participants stood next to friends during the exercise, while others were alone. The students who stood with friends gave lower estimates of the steepness of the hill. And the longer the friends had known each other, the less steep the hill appeared."

"People with stronger friendship networks feel like there is someone they can turn to," said Karen A. Roberto, director of the Center for Gerontology at Virginia Tech. "Friendship is an undervalued resource. The consistent message of these studies is that friends make your life better." Notice that in this study, the friends didn't help carry the load; they only conversed with the participant, building his confidence by telling him that the hill was manageable. Greek philosopher Epicurus noted, "It is not so much our friends' help that helps us, as the confident knowledge that they will help us." Approval is the shining of one's light into another's darkness; although the words cost one little, their value to others is priceless. How many people would benefit from feeling approved when climbing life's mountains?

> **Approval is the shining of one's light into another's darkness; although the words cost one little, their value to others is priceless.**

## 4. True Friends Appreciate One Another

If acceptance is the appetizer, then approval is the main dish, and appreciation is the dessert in the buffet for the soul. When a person appreciates somebody, he communicates to him that he is unique and that he no longer is just another face in the crowd. When something depreciates, it loses value; but when something appreciates, it gains value. Therefore, appreciation helps others gain value. For example, when a person sets an appointment, he should make sure that he is on time since that communicates to the other person that his time is valued. To really appreciate people, one should share all the good he can find in people with others. It's good to appreciate someone personally, but one should also feel free to share that appreciation with everyone. This is the proper form of talking behind someone's back—all the good that you know about them. Author Fred Smith wrote, "Another characteristic of friendship above acquaintanceship is the genuine desire of friends to help each other. They really want others to do well and are happy to contribute to that welfare. Friends look for ways to help each other. They think of each other when opportunities arise."

One of the greatest benefits a person can offer a friend is to help him turn up his positive voice, as discussed in Chapter Three. Every day, inside every person is a battle, a battle of whom to listen to. One of the greatest things that a true friend can do for a friend is help him turn up his positive voice while simultaneously turning down the negative voice. Friends help friends think better about themselves and their opportunities by pointing out the positive and minimizing the negative. This way, a true friend helps his friend win his battle of the mind by loaning him his positive belief. This is what makes association so important because this concept works in reverse as well. Bad friends turn up the negative voice, predictably leading to trouble. A person should choose his friends wisely because one becomes whom he associates with. True friends magnify each other's positive voice because friends accept, approve, and appreciate each other, providing the volume to drown out the negative voice and creating the belief needed to grow and change. An individual should forget about complaining, condemning, and criticizing his friends; they do enough of that to themselves. One catches more bees with honey than with vinegar. He should put away the vinegar jar and replace it with appreciation honey. A true friend will never forget a friend who helped him believe in himself. This poem sums up the essence of how true friends help one another:

*A friend is someone who knows you as you are,*
*understands where you have been, accepts who you*
*have become, and still gently invites you to grow.*
*- Unknown*

## 5. True Friends Listen with Empathy

One of the best ways to show acceptance, approval, and appreciation is through listening. A person has two ears and one mouth, and they should be used in that ratio. People learn more from listening than from talking. Cultivate listening as one of your most developed skills. People can tell when someone is truly listening or just going through the motions, waiting for a person who is sharing his feelings to pause long enough so he can begin speaking again. Active listening requires discipline, allowing others to share. One of the biggest complements a person can give someone is to genuinely listen to him. For example, Abraham Lincoln, in the midst of the emancipation question during the Civil War, sent a telegram to Leonard Swett, a longtime friend, saying, "I need to see you." Swett, having earned Lincoln's trust and having served him in many capacities, accepted the president's request, packing his bags and heading to Washington. Author Douglas Wilson shared, "Lincoln asked Swett to listen as he read from letters and position papers and then laid out, in his own words, various arguments both for and against issuing a policy of emancipation. Swett was an old friend and close confidant, and he was surely expecting Lincoln to say, 'Now, what do you think?' But he didn't. Instead, when he finished he said, 'Tell all the folks 'hello' when you get back to Bloomington, and I really thank you for coming.' He asked Swett to come to Washington simply to listen." Swett was a true friend, with whom Lincoln had the trust to unburden his heart, and in the process of speaking with Swett, Lincoln solidified his thinking. Perhaps a friend will ask for advice, but not always, since many times, he just needs a trusted person to listen to him. In her novel *A Life For a Life*, poet and author Dinah Maria Mulock Craik described the joy when a friend truly listens as follows: "Oh, the comfort—the inexpressible comfort of feeling safe with a person, having neither to weigh thoughts nor measure words—but pouring them all right out—just as they are—chaff and grain together; certain that a faithful hand will take and sift them—keep what is worth keeping—and then with the breath of kindness blow the rest away." What a beautiful picture of true friendship and the joy of being truly understood!

## 6. True Friends Celebrate One Another's Success

True friends celebrate victories together. This is essential for true friendships as friends should be one another's greatest cheerleader.

Friends refuse to let petty jealousies or envy rot a friendship, as each friend desires the other's good as much as he desires his own. Moreover, friends aren't competitors; rather, they are huge fans and encouragers of one another. Why wouldn't a true friend celebrate another friend's success in any worthy endeavor? A friend's victory lifts the tide for everyone surrounding him, and even if it doesn't, true friends are still always proud of their friends' accomplishments. Friends dream together, laugh together, struggle together, lose together, win together, and celebrate together. One should be the most enthusiastic cheerleader for a friend's success, even when he is struggling personally. A person must let his friends know how much he admires their strengths, sharing how thankful he is for being a part of their lives. Celebrating with a friend in this fashion lets one know that his work is not in vain and that his search for excellence is making a difference in the lives of others.

> **One should be the most enthusiastic cheerleader for a friend's success, even when he is struggling personally.**

There are two ways of reacting to a friend's success: *admire and emulate* or *envy and denigrate*. A true friend admires and emulates when possible and celebrates a friend's accomplishments to the same degree he would his own. This forms stronger bonds of fidelity as he displays to his friends that the smallest hint of jealousy and envy is not tolerated in his heart. Friends lift one another when they are together, as well as when they are apart. Talking behind each other's backs is perfectly acceptable, as long as only the good qualities are talked about. One should applaud the accomplishments of his friends behind their backs because doing so builds the friends' reputations to match their level of character, while raising the tide of the entire community.

John Maxwell shared Andy Stanley's story about overcoming jealousy and envy. Stanley explains, "Louie and I have been friends since the 6th grade . . . We met at youth camp under a bunk bed while seniors battled it out over our heads. Louie is just a phenomenal communicator. When I announce at our church that Louie Giglio is going to be speaking next week, they all start clapping and we have high attendance Sunday. And then for four or five days the rest of the week everyone's going, 'Oh, Louie, Louie, Louie.'" If it weren't for the love and loyalty shared between these two stellar performers, jealousy and envy would creep into their relationship, damaging their friendship; but both friends refuse to let this happen. In fact, Maxwell wrote, "When Louie delivers a great message,

Andy goes out of his way to praise him and celebrate with him. And Louie does the same with him. Andy said, 'It's not enough to think it. I have to say it because that's how I cleanse my heart. Celebration is how you defeat jealousy.'"

## 7. True Friends Are Trustworthy

Without trust, a person won't open his heart, making his relationships shallow. But how does someone build trust with others? The simple answer is by following the golden rule: "Do unto others as you would have them do unto you." A friend hears, empathizes with, and protects the innermost thoughts of his friends. When a person shares his fears, struggles, ambitions, or dreams, a true friend can be counted on to listen without judging, empathize without pitying, and guide without lecturing. Trust is built when one can hear the burdens of another person's heart, listening empathetically and offering earnest advice when requested. True friends don't exit the scene when life gets tough; instead, they exhibit loyalty and sacrificial love, supporting a friend in his time of trouble. False friends, on the other hand, are merely acquaintances who perceive a personal gain through association. Fair-weather friends depart when the storms of life arrive; a true friend, however, endures the storms, hurting when his friend hurts.

Pepper Rodgers, a former UCLA football coach, in the middle of a tough season, jestingly said in an interview, "My dog was my only friend, and I told my wife that man needs at least two friends. She bought me another dog." John Maxwell commented, "False friends are like shadows, keeping close to us while we walk in the sunshine but leaving us when we cross into the shade, but real friends stick with us when trouble comes. As the old saying goes: "In prosperity, our friends know us; in adversity, we know our friends." Any man is considered blessed if he has a couple of true friends who can be counted on in both prosperity and adversity.

## 8. True Friends Are Loyal

A trusted friend is loyal to his friends when he is in front of them and, more importantly, when they are not present. As Martin Luther King Jr. said, "In the end, we will remember not the words of our enemies, but the silence of our friends." Loyalty doesn't mean taking a friend's side on any issue, right or wrong; rather, it means one is a friend, right or wrong. People must defend a friend's character, honor, and reputation as far as the truth allows, while helping to resolve any issue privately and promptly. Lincoln said, "A friend is one who has the same enemies as you have," which is true as long as the truth is on the side of the friend. The key principle to follow is "loyalty to the absent," protecting the character of those not present to stand up for themselves. For example, if you wouldn't say something about a person who is in the room you are in, then why would you say it when he isn't in the same room? Sadly, when this principle is abused, a person quickly gains the reputation of being a talebearer who can no longer be respected or trusted as a true friend.

What if two friends fall into a conflict and place their mutual friends in the middle? In this situation, a mutual true friend would bring the two conflicting friends together in a spirit of reconciliation. Both parties must follow the conflict resolution principles (to be covered in the Conflict Resolution Chapter). If either side refuses to follow the principles, the refusing party violates the trust of all who are involved. What good is it to have principles if they are not followed when needed? Self-deception can blind a friend. As Maxwell wrote, "If you are not honest with yourself, you will not be capable of honesty with others. Self-deception is the enemy of relationships. It also undermines personal growth. If a person does not admit his shortcomings, he cannot improve." At this point, a person must address his friend privately and promptly, hoping to point out his friend's blind spot, praying that his friend return to the principles that are based on virtue and that are expected from all true friends. Friends are loyal to one another, only abandoning a friendship when a friend refuses to return to the principles of virtue and honor after numerous attempts by friends to help. Simply put, loyalty to a friend only ends where untruth begins. Even in this sad situation, former friends should maintain confidence where possible, holding on to the hope that in the future, restoration will happen when principles of virtue are restored in the lost individual. Loyalty, fidelity, and honor are the foundations of lifelong friendships, though they are seldom seen in today's society. Next to truth as the most valued principle of friendship is loyalty, which forms the glue that holds friendships together during the storms of life.

## Summary

True friendship is a lost art in today's "me" generation, and this increases the value of a friend. The best way to find friends of such caliber is to be one, which is why friendship is one of the thirteen resolutions. If someone dies having had several true friends, then he is a blessed man. A person must make a commitment to give to each of his relationships more than he receives. Although simple in theory, this is much tougher in practice, especially with true friends. A friendship brings so much joy and fun into one's life that it should be cultivated as a fine art. Conversely, damaged relationships bring so much pain into one's life that conflicts should be resolved promptly. Resolve the issues rather than dissolve the friendship, if at all possible. A person's real wealth isn't his net worth but his relationships with God, his family, and his friends. No amount of money can mend a damaged relationship or purchase the joy and happiness experienced in a true friendship. Regardless of the fickleness and fecklessness witnessed in the world, resolve today to give others the fidelity and faithfulness of a true friend.

## C. S. Lewis and J. R. R. Tolkien: Friendship

Two Oxford professors, both founding members of a writing club called Inklings, became two of the greatest writers and best-selling authors of all time. These two formed a friendship that embodies the power of encouragement and love to change people.

The relationship between C. S. Lewis and J. R. R. Tolkien bonded them together and formed into something special in September of 1931. Tolkien, Lewis, and Hugo Dyson walked down Addison's Walk on the grounds of Magdalen College. On this walk, Lewis surrendered his materialistic worldview in favor of a Christian worldview and a personal relationship with Jesus Christ. Tolkien and Dyson, both Christians, repeatedly pointed out the untenable position that Lewis had placed himself in with his materialistic worldview, which separated his power of reasoning from his power of imagining. Author Ethan Gilsdorf shared his thoughts on the three friends' discussion:

> "Myths are lies," Lewis had said that night.
> "Myths are not lies," Tolkien countered, among the swaying trees of Magdalen Grove. "Materialistic progress leads only to the abyss," Tolkien said, "but the myths we tell reflect a fragment of the true light."
> He argued the Christ story functions as a myth, just like the Scandinavian myths they had loved, with one difference: The Christian myth was true.

As the night wore on, Lewis began to see the hopeless divide in his materialistic mind-set, leading to his eventual conversion. In his book *Miracles*, Lewis described the content of the conversations between Tolkien, Dyson, and himself:

> The heart of Christianity is a myth which is also a fact. The old myth of a Dying God, without ceasing to be myth, comes down from the heaven of legend and imagination to the earth of history. It happens— at a particular date, in a particular place, followed by definable historical consequences. We pass from a Balder or an Osiris, dying nobody knows when or

where, to a historical Person crucified (it is all in order) under Pontius Pilate. By becoming fact it does not cease to be myth: that is miracle. To be truly Christian we must both assent to the historical fact and also receive the myth (fact though it has become) with the same imaginative embrace which we accord to all myths.

Lewis envisioned God as the storyteller who enters his own story, completing the work of redemption according to his plan, making all other stories and myths pale in comparison, since his story is myth made real in history by the direct intervention of God through the birth of Christ. Lewis personally discovered the reason fantasy and myth were so popular, mainly because they provide a foretaste, a foreshadowing of the greatest story in redemptive history: the true story told in the Bible of the birth, the life, the death, and the resurrection of Jesus Christ.

With Lewis's conversion, both authors now understood the critical role that fantasy and myth could play in leading people to the true myth of Christ. Duriez explained it well when he wrote:

> The two friends had a tangible confidence that the separation of story and fact had been reconciled, which led them to continue in a tradition of symbolic fiction, telling stories of dragons and kings in disguise, talking animals and heroic quests, set in imagined worlds. For them, heaven at a particular, definable moment in space and time came down to earth, and our humanity subsequently was taken up by the ancient fall of humanity, have met and fused forever because of the heroism of Christ. Their confidence in the reconciliation of myth and fact directly led Tolkien and Lewis to create Middle-earth, Narnia, Glome, and Perelandra, which aim to present a true picture of reality that combines heaven and earth, spirit and nature.

Lewis's conversion directly led to the Narnia series since it was his Christian worldview, along with his understanding of the role of fantasy and myth, that inspired him to write the books. Tolkien played such an important role in Lewis's journey because he was able to confront his friend's untenable worldview while still communicating his love for him as a person. Without Tolkien's friendship, the Lewis of Narnia fame would not have existed. Tolkien played the key role of a true friend, which is to help sharpen the thinking of his fellow life passengers, all the while encouraging and loving them through and through. Although Lewis was brilliant, he had swallowed a poison that needed an antidote, and Tolkien provided the antidote for Lewis's pessimistic worldview, allowing Lewis, for the first time in his life, to merge his reason and imagination, leading directly to his modern fiction classics.

The authors' relationship was not a one-way street, however. Lewis impacted Tolkien in different, but equally important, ways. If there could have been no Lewis classics without Tolkien, the same could be said in reverse: There could have been no Tolkien classics without Lewis. For without Lewis's constant encouragement of the hyper self-critical Tolkien, the Lord of the Rings series would have not existed or, at best, would have existed as a story shared only in the Tolkien family. Tolkien wrote of Lewis's impact on him two years after the latter's death: "The unpayable debt that I owe him was not 'influence' as it is ordinarily understood, but sheer encouragement. He was for long my only audience. Only from him did I ever get the idea that my 'stuff' could be more than a private hobby. But for his interest and unceasing for more I should never have brought the *Lord of the Rings* to a conclusion." Tolkien found an enthusiastic listener and encourager in the younger Lewis, and this encouragement was regularized with the founding of the Inkling's Thursday-night readings. Lewis and Tolkien sharpened each other, clarifying the thinking of one another, encouraging one another to finish the projects that would ultimately impact the world.

*Christian History* managing editor Chris Armstrong interviewed Colin Duriez, the author of *Tolkien and C. S. Lewis: The Gift of Friendship*. Armstrong was seeking the keys to the powerful influence that each had on the other, so he asked Duriez, "You have said that if it hadn't been for the friendship between Tolkien and Lewis, the world would likely never have seen *The Narnia Chronicles, The Lord of the Rings,* and much else. What was it about 'fairy stories' that led these two men to want to rehabilitate them for a modern audience—adults as well as children?" Duriez answered:

> They had both personal and professional reasons for this interest. Personally, they had both read and enjoyed such stories as they were growing up, in collections by the brothers Grimm, Andrew Lang, and others. Lewis had also heard Celtic myths—his nurse had told him some of the folk tales of Ireland. Professionally, they studied and taught the literatures of medieval romance and, in Tolkien's case, the background of Norse myth. And they realized that it was only quite recently that such stories had become marginalized as "children's stories." Through much of history these were tales told and enjoyed by grown-ups. Even strong warriors enjoyed them, rejoicing in their triumphant moments, weeping at tragic turns of events. These stories told them important things about life—about who they were and what the world was like, and about the realm of the divine. It dawned on both men that there was a need to create a readership again for these books—especially an adult readership.

There might have been a need to create again a readership for "fairy stories" or "children's stories," but for two academic professors with no financial backing or worldwide connections to believe they could impact culture as greatly as they did is a fairy tale in itself. Although both men were greatly concerned about the rampant materialism of the modern age, believing it divided the mind of humanity by separating man's reason from his imagination, most professors, when confronted with this dilemma, only expressed their concerns, folded their hands, and did nothing. But Tolkien and Lewis were not like most professors.

Duriez recreated a dramatic scene or discussion between Tolkien and Lewis, two barely published authors who had the desire to reintroduce imagination through fantasy and myth. The two daydreamers discussed the dearth of good fiction, fiction that exemplified the spirit of recovery and escape through using the power of myth. After reviewing various authors and their works, Tolkien and Lewis developed a plan, a plan so audacious that it was barely conceivable given the amount of time and effort it entailed. Nonetheless, these professors, not afraid of hard work, agreed to write fiction with a purpose, which was to lead people to truth through the power of myth. They aspired to reconnect reason and imagination for the divided modern world. Duriez wrote:

> "You know, Tollers," Lewis says decisively, pipe in hand. "I'm afraid we'll have to write them ourselves. We need stories like your Hobbit book, but on the more heroic scale of your older tales of Gondolin and Goblin wars. One of us should write a tale of time travel and the other should do space travel."
>
> Tolkien reminds his friend of a rather similar challenge well over a century ago—Lord Byron, at Lake Geneva in 1816, had challenged Percy Shelley and Mary Shelley to write a ghost story....and Mary, a mere girl at the time, went on to write Frankenstein. "They needed" Tolkien continues, his eyes brightening, "stories today that expose modern magic—the tyranny of the machine."
>
> "Let's toss for it, Tollers. Heads, you write about time travel; tails, you try space travel. I'll do the other." Tolkien nods his agreement, grinning. Lewis fishes in the pocket of his crumpled and baggy flannels and a coin spins in the air. "Heads it is."

The unknown authors of 1936 had accomplished exactly what they had set out to do by creating fiction that captures the profound realities of life nearly impossible to capture in any other way. Lewis wrote many other books aside from his Narnia set, while Tolkien remained focused on his classic Lord of the Rings collection. Both authors eventually achieved fame through their fantasy fiction books. The audacity of these two friends when they began their quest was only surpassed by their inexperience. History, it seems, exhibits many instances in which great achievements are birthed by optimistic amateurs rather than pessimistic experts.

In a recent survey of the top five best-selling books of all time, Tolkien's Lord of the Rings series was number four, and right behind it, was Lewis's Chronicles of Narnia set, an impressive accomplishment for two best friends in the Oxford literature department. The Lord of the Rings book series has sold over 200 million books, while its movie adaptation trilogy has surpassed box office revenues, gaining over $3 billion. Lewis's Narnia series has sold over 150 million books, and its movie adaptations sales has reached just under $2 billion, with several more movies in the series still to be produced. When these staggering totals are added together, the grand total from the works of these two creative geniuses is over 350 million books sold and nearly $5 billion in movie sales. Those are pretty impressive numbers for two Oxford professors, who, on a whim, formed the Inklings. Although the organization was informal, the members, typically ten or less, perfected their crafts by reading to one another their latest works. And both Lewis and Tolkien relished the time they invested in each other.

It would be hard to fathom whether there was ever a friendship more productive than Lewis and Tolkien's. Two of the top five best-selling books of all time were birthed from a friendship that began in 1926 and was nurtured through association at the Inklings club and fueled by constant encouragement and belief in one another. Lewis and Tolkien changed each other internally, providing the world with the external fruits of their fantasy fiction books. All of these combined together to display the amazing power inherent in a synergistic friendship.

CHAPTER 8

# FINANCE
## Resolved: To Develop
## Financial Intelligence

*I know that, over time, my wealth is compounded when income is higher than expenses.*

Financial literacy and management is as valuable as, if not more valuable than, the ability to earn income. As a person moves from private achievements to public achievements, he will find that his ability to make money increases. However, if he cannot manage his finances, then it won't matter how much money he makes since it will quickly dissipate. For example, many people who make $25,000 per year believe if they made $50,000, their financial issues would be solved. People who make $50,000, on the other hand, believe their problems would be solved if they made $100,000. The truth of the matter is that a person can be wealthy or broke at any income level because wealth is less about what he makes and more about what he keeps. Learning to spend less than one makes for an extended period of time is the only way to generate wealth. But doing this requires principles—such as delayed gratification, which is learning to say no even when a person has the money to say yes—that most people do not enjoy.

> As a person moves from private achievements to public achievements, he will find that his ability to make money increases.

Another principle that is crucial for anyone desiring to improve himself is financial management. It doesn't matter how disciplined one must be to attain personal development; if one must work ten to twelve hours a day, then he should. Debt enslaves people to what is urgent, forcing long-term planning and develop-

173

ment to fall down the list of priorities. A quick look at the Founding Fathers reveals that most of them had the financial means to be able to spend years working on developing themselves, a community, a culture, and eventually, a nation. They weren't in dead-end careers with no time or money to concentrate on what was significant. But without financial independence, most Americans will burn their most productive years making a living instead of making a legacy.

It's vital to master financial literacy and financial management because no one can work hard enough to outrun the debilitating effects of compound interest working against him over decades. But anyone can become wealthy when he allows compound interest to work for him over time.

A quick review of the average American's (Canadian's and others') financial position is enough to sober the most inebriated of spenders. For example, 50 percent of Americans have less than one month's savings, making bankruptcy less than thirty days away for most. That is just the tip of the iceberg. Here are ten more disconcerting financial facts compiled from *Own the Dollar* and *Money101*:

1. Students graduate with an average of $23,186 in student loan debt and $4,100 credit card debt.
2. People spend 12–18 percent more when using credit cards than when using cash. Fast food giant McDonald's found that the average transaction rose from $4.50 to $7.00 when customers were allowed to use plastic instead of cash in its restaurants.
3. A recent study by Harris Interactive found that 57 percent of households do not have a budget.
4. Money magazine poll stated: "43 percent of readers who lent to family or friends weren't paid back in full; 27 percent hadn't received a dime."
5. The number of Americans living paycheck to paycheck is 61 percent, up from 49 percent in 2008 and 43 percent in 2007.
6. Personal saving as a percentage of disposable personal income was 3 percent in August 2009, compared with 4 percent in July.
7. There were 159 million credit card holders (separate individuals who owned at least one card) in the United States in 2000, 173 million in 2006, and an estimated 181 million in 2010.

8. At the end of 2008, Americans' credit card debt reached $972.73 billion, up 1.12 percent from 2007. That number includes both general purpose credit cards and private label credit cards that aren't owned by a bank. Average credit card debt per household was $8,329 at the end of 2008. Seventy-five percent of credit card holders have maxed out at least one credit card between 2008 and 2009.

9. In a study analyzing the impact of financial literacy, Annamaria Lusardi (professor of economics at Dartmouth College) and Olivia Mitchell (professor of insurance and risk-management at the University of Pennsylvania) quizzed people on simple calculations such as compound interest and percentages and then compared the participants' knowledge with their net-worth. The findings: More right answers matched up with greater wealth. Those who grasped compound interest, for example, had a median net-worth of $309,000 vs. $116,000 for those who missed the question.

10. Personal savings as a percentage of personal income declined from 7.5 percent in the early 1980s to 2.3 percent in the first three quarters of 2003. According to the Bureau of Economic Analysis, personal savings dropped precipitously from there to a negative 1.5 percent during the second quarter of 2006.

If anything is clear from this data, it's that most Americans have not been taught the importance of financial literacy. The good news is, with a little instruction and discipline, people can overcome their past financial mistakes and enjoy the freedom provided by financial mastery. The objective of teaching these principles is not to help a person die with the largest net worth but to help him live free from financial worries so that he can invest his time where it can make the biggest difference to others. Financial mastery, then, is an essential principle for mastering living intentionally for excellence.

There are ten principles that I have developed over the years that can help people gain financial literacy, which, when rigorously applied, will lead to financial freedom. By applying these ten principles, people can overcome nearly any financial train wreck, allowing them to regain financial control and liberty in life. If a person is married, then these principles must be reviewed with his spouse. For couples, getting on the same financial page is a must if they intend to master financial management. Remember, mastering the other resolutions without mastering finances is a foolish endeavor; it is similar to pouring buckets of water into a large barrel faster than anyone else, but ignoring the fact that the barrel has a large hole in the bottom. A person needs to fill his financial barrel, but he also must repair the holes.

> **The goal is to determine the amount of net income that a person has to make his life decisions.**

The first principle in regaining control of finances is to accurately identify how much net income one makes. Most people are like the old joke, quoting gross incomes to their friends but telling net incomes to their spouses. Only the net income can be used to pay bills, save for the future, tithe, etc. The gross income is, for all practical purposes, not relevant. The goal is to determine the amount of net income that a person has to make his life decisions. For example, a person may have a job income, a 1099 small-business income, or even babysitting income—whatever it is, he must write it down to determine the total inflow of money. Without this critical first step, a person is running blind financially, not knowing how much he makes, leading to unwise choices financially as he makes guesses or estimates rather than looking at his financial facts.

The first order of business for anyone looking to rise from the financial ash is to keep score financially, knowing exactly how much his revenues and expenses are. He should not include "if-come," or money from potential raises or bonuses that are not guaranteed, because a person must live on his income, not his "if-come." No matter how bad it may look the first time one documents his net income, it must be done since hiding from the data will never change anything. The author has witnessed many radical changes from people simply having the courage to keep score, making tough decisions that had been neglected for years. The government may be able to get away without keeping score for years, but most people do not have that luxury of time to hide from reality. Get a piece of paper, get in front of the computer, and start writing down all sources of income. Confronting brutal reality is impossible until one knows the data.

This leads to the second principle of documenting all expenses. Anything that flows out of one's possession into another entity's hands should be written down: all bills, all taxes—everything that flows out of one's money pile into someone else's money pile. One must also determine the amount of miscellaneous expenses necessary to maintain cars, houses, etc. The goal is to get as close as possible to the average monthly expenses. Remember, revenue minus expenses equals profits. Step One focuses on determining all revenue sources. Step Two focuses on determining all expenses. When the revenue and expenses are accurately documented, then by subtracting expenses from the revenue, a person can calculate his monthly profits. Sadly, many people, when performing this exercise, will learn that they have no profits and that, instead, they are falling behind every month because they are spending more than they are bringing in. Similar to a ship taking in water, this house is about to capsize and is in need of a courageous leadership in order to avoid a catastrophe.

If spending money frivolously is an issue, a person should start a cash allowance, setting aside a certain amount of cash for himself and his spouse in order to keep spending within set limits. This improves the ability to budget and reduces wasteful spending. Remember, 57 percent of people don't have a budget. When a person finishes these first two steps, he puts himself in a position to budget, which is a first-time experience for many people. Many don't like the word *budget*, because it conjures up images of limits and constraints. But in truth, everyone is on a budget; the only question is, is it self-imposed or externally imposed? In either situation, one will have to do the budgeting himself; otherwise, the banks, credit cards, etc. will do the budgeting for him. There is no escape from budgeting since money is not unlimited—regardless of what the Federal Reserve says.

The third principle is to set a financial goal, focusing on reducing expenses and increasing income to spend no more than 75 percent of what one takes in. It may take some time to achieve this goal, but one should start where he is. When a person gets his spending under 100 percent, it is a cause for celebration because, unlike our government, he is spending less than he makes. Imagine how quickly money could be saved, securing a person's financial future, by not blowing it all the moment it is received. People who spend every penny they make, if not more, are like bobbers on the water. The first financial bite that they have pulls the entire household underwater. Spending less than one makes becomes a form of insurance against the storms of life that are sure to come. Every four months lived with a spending of 75 percent of net income allows a month of freedom to be accrued because 25 percent savings multiplied by four months is a total of one month's income. In order to achieve this, a person must adopt a tough thinking on his current financial position. Does he really need all the toys that he has?

Does he need to lease the latest vehicles? Does he have to live in an expensive house? The first time he seizes control of his finances, many around him will think that he has gone mad. The Joneses will watch him reduce his house size, reduce the quality of his car, reduce his vacations, and reduce his toys, and they will think he has suffered a severe setback. But in reality, he is finally confronting the facts and severing the chains of financial bondage. Quit trying to keep up with the Joneses because they are broke. One of the key decisions in creating financial independence is to stop attempting to look wealthy and start applying the principles to actually become wealthy. By continuing to apply these principles, one can eventually increase his income while decreasing expenses by paying cash for purchases, thereby avoiding having to pay interest and fully owning one's possessions at the time of purchase. It is only then that one can live on less than 50 percent of his income. Few things allow someone to sleep better than a healthy financial position.

The fourth principle, one that would radically change the financial position of most people if applied routinely, is to never finance anything that depreciates. People believe that they can afford that motor coach because they can afford the payments, but the facts tell that if they have to finance it, they can't afford it. Paying interest on something that depreciates is a classic double whammy. One gets the right to pay for borrowing money that he didn't have, while watching the asset purchased lose its value. This can lead to situations where the asset loses 50 percent of its value in a couple of years, while the person gets to pay two times its retail value in added interest payments. For example, if one finances a $30,000 motorcycle for five years, he will have, by the time he pays it off, paid nearly $60,000 for it. At the same time, his $30,000 motorcycle at retail price has plummeted to under $20,000 in resale value. This creates a horrendous financial position where one has paid approximately $60,000 for a $20,000 asset! It isn't any wonder why most people are upside-down financially. A person should never finance entertainment or toys under any circumstances. Why would he entertain himself with a vacation on credit when it only increases his financial stress once he returns from his holiday. There are plenty of free beaches or lakes to enjoy with the family while plugging the hole in his financial barrel.

I was once asked how I learned about finances. The answer is simple: I learned mathematics. I was also dead broke when I was taking my engineering classes, so I had to either learn financial management or starve. Finances are mathematics applied in life.

As the great Albert Einstein said, "Compound interest is the eighth wonder of the world."

Even if a person must purchase a house or a car on credit, it is wise to lower the amount borrowed and reduce the length of time for which it is borrowed. For example, on a house mortgage, instead of listening to the banks, who will tell a person that he qualifies for a mortgage thrice his income, he should buy a house worth only twice his income. This allows him to either reduce the length of time for the loan or pay back the loan early as he accumulates extra money. He should also be sure that he is buying into a neighborhood where the houses are not depreciating as fast as one can pay off the mortgage. In today's environment, many houses are depreciating instead of appreciating in value. Remember, the banks want to loan a person as much money as he is capable of repaying, caring less about his financial freedom and more about their profits. But the sooner a person can pay off the mortgage on his property, the quicker he owns something rather than renting it from the banks.

Another deadly interest trap is the lease car option. Whoever conceived of the lease car option was a financial genius. In this lease, the buyer doesn't own anything at all; in fact, all he is paying for is the depreciation of the car and the profits for the car company—an ingenious method to siphon off a person's potential wealth. Hurray for the banks and car dealerships on their mathematical wizardry, but shame on the people who love new cars more than their financial freedom. Leasing a car, in most instances, is an acknowledgement that one would rather look successful than be successful. Driving a fancy car on lease payments is one of the best ways to ensure financial enslavement. Thousands of people have learned the joy of owning used cars outright, even if it is several years older than one might have preferred, because it lets hundreds or, in some cases, thousands of extra dollars go into savings. This isn't even adding in all of the extra "gotchas" that dealers charge when a person goes over the mileage limits. Sometimes people cannot even return their leased cars because they cannot afford the penalties from exceeding their mileage limits.

The fifth principle is to set a price limit on spontaneous purchases; anything above this limit must be slept on before buying. Spontaneous purchases destroy most people's budgets. Only by following this principle can one avoid the emotion of the moment and allow time for the rational mind to think through the purchase. Billions of dollars per year are lost by undiscerning buyers who make emotional decisions, only to pay for them for years. In my married life, this single principle helped Laurie and me the most. Many times, when a person sleeps on a decision, by the next morning, the spell has been broken, and he will realize that his earlier desire to purchase an item was simply a want, not a need. When one desires financial freedom more than he desires things, then he should get his freedom by allowing many things to remain unpurchased. The price limit is a personal family choice, but $100 isn't unreasonable for a starting point to help anchor this new behavior. The goal is to help one determine whether an item is really needed or if it is just a nice item that will eventually end up sitting in the garage. Look at all the rummage sales where items are sold for a tenth of the original price. Why reduce one's wealth by 90 percent to buy an item that isn't absolutely necessary, especially when one isn't financially free?

The sixth principle is if a person discovers that he spends more money when he uses a credit card, it is time to pay them off and use cash whenever possible. Credit cards have been found to increase a person's spending, helping accumulate debt that he cannot afford. Only when he can pay off the credit card balances in full each month while still building his savings can he consider using a credit card as a matter of personal convenience. However, if one is racking up debt, then credit cards become a personal convenience in which one cannot afford to indulge. The key to regaining control of a person's finances is to pay as one goes, no longer living today on next year's income, but instead, living today on last year's income. Typically, credit cards have the highest interest rates, quickly wiping out the net worth of people who lack discipline when plastic is all that separates them from their desires. In this case, one is not comprehending the massive losses associated with his inability to say no. Imagine the day when all debt is eliminated, making it the first night that one goes to bed waking up wealthier. It will take guts to leave the financial ruts, but that first night, a person will realize it was worth it.

The seventh principle is to wipe out all consumer debt before starting to save. This principle is similar to calling all hands on deck when a ship is taking in water since it will take everyone on board to help bail out the water in the sinking ship. In a financial sense, every dollar of income is needed to help bail out the debt before starting a savings plan. So many people are saving money at 2 percent interest while having a debt that they are servicing at 20 percent interest. It doesn't take a rocket scientist to realize, in this example, that the savings account is costing 18 percent interest. Wipe out all debt as quickly as possible by either selling the toys, turning in the leased cars, or paying off credit cards. Unless the savings account makes significantly more interest than the debt is costing, it's best to just wipe out the debt first. This is not even mentioning the fact that, thanks to our insatiable government, the interest earned is taxable, while most interest paid is not tax deductible. This is another reason that a simple understanding of math and a willingness to think rationally will drive one to get out of debt quickly. Remember, debt is cancer. When someone has cancer, the goal is to remove it; likewise, when someone has debt, the goal is to get rid of it quickly.

When debts are eliminated, one should start saving money, setting aside a minimum of 10 percent per month for the rainy days. Tithes to a local church aren't included as part of a savings plan because they are tithed to the Lord. Savings, in other words, is learning to save personal money, not hoarding God's tithe money.

The eighth principle is to know the difference between an investment and an expense. An investment has a return, while an expense just consumes money. For instance, if a person were to invest in the development of new skills, it would be a good investment because no one can ever take that from him since the skills become part of who he is. Learning requires an investment of money, and if it enhances a person's performance, then it returns improved results. As Ben Franklin said, "An investment in knowledge always pays the best interest." People should cut all unnecessary expenses; on the other hand, when they cut out their personal investments, they throw the baby out with the dirty bathwater. As the joke says, "Due to recent cost-cutting measures, the light at the end of the tunnel will be shut off until further notice." Great companies understand this; even when cutting back on expenses, the best companies continue to do research, investing in the future. An individual must do the same as he is the only person who can improve his circumstances. Without investing in personal development, a person is as good as he will ever get. However, when he invests in improved leadership and skill sets, his only limit is the size of his dream. He should never use lack of money as a reason to not invest in himself since what the conscious brain is telling the subconscious brain at that moment is that the investment isn't worth it. Sadly, many people do just that, thinking they are saving money, when they are actually just shutting off any hope for personal change. Remember, no economic downturn can

> **Without investing in personal development, a person is as good as he will ever get.**

ever take away better leadership abilities, better communication skills, improved attitudes, or any other positive attributes or skills.

The ninth principle is to focus on quality of life and peace of mind when one becomes wealthy. Too many people, when they are wealthy, spend all their time attempting to increase their wealth, leaving their families and peace of mind to take a backseat, if given any seat at all. For example, John Rockefeller became one of the wealthiest men in the world by building his own company, but he lost his money and added stress to nearly every investment that he ever made. He knew how to make money in the business where he was the prime mover, but he lost his shirt in other investments. A simple rule of thumb to remember is that it's easier to convince others that a person is good in business than it is to be good in business. One shouldn't lose the quality of his life, not to mention money, by falling victim to others' grandiose schemes with no results. Talks and plans are cheap, and it's proper execution that makes businesses successful. A person should never invest in someone's business more money than he can afford to lose in its entirety; otherwise, he will lose the quality of his life along with the money. Andrew Carnegie said it best: "Put all your eggs in one basket, and protect the basket." Many people talk about diversification; Carnegie, on the other hand, talked about focus. One can be good at nearly any business, but he cannot be good at all businesses. The key is to follow one's purpose into a field that cultivates his passions, potentials, and profits. In this way, a person makes money pursuing what he loves, a true recipe for a good quality of life.

The tenth principle is that once one becomes wealthy, he should remember to be a blessing to others. A person should give to causes, charities, and organizations that he believes in, providing others the opportunity to strive for accomplishments. Every wealthy person leaves every dime when he dies. Learning to pay one's financial blessings forward is a key principle in success. Hoarding is not the goal; developing a giving spirit is. Remember, it's not a person's net worth that is the ultimate criteria but his net change. Wealth is just a tool to help people invest in themselves and in others, leading to change and growth. Instead of creating generational dependence, one should support charities that inspire change in people, leading to personal responsibility and productive lives. No one can make someone win against

> **A person should give to causes, charities, and organizations that he believes in, providing others the opportunity to strive for accomplishments.**

his will, but everyone can contribute something to help hungry students gain the information and skills needed to get back up after being knocked down. Many people suffer hardships in life, and one of the best things a human being can do for another is to breathe confidence into the other person to help him overcome his obstacles. It has been said that man can live for forty days without food, four days without water, four minutes without air, but not four seconds without hope. Leaders are responsible for providing hope to others, first, by setting examples and, second, by blessing others with their blessings. The satisfaction felt when a person earns his keep by serving others is enduring. The following humorous story is about a young man who learned this lesson by working, earning, and saving. His father had built a large multimillion-dollar business from the ground up. As this father approached retirement, he brought his son into his office and told him that he wanted him to take over his company. The son was excited to take over his father's multimillion-dollar empire and asked, "When are you going to give it to me?"

The father replied, "I am not going to give you anything. You must earn it."

The son replied, "How am I supposed to do that?"

The father answered, "First, you must earn $10,000 to purchase a small portion of ownership in the company. When this is accomplished, you will get your next instruction."

As the son left the house to begin his quest, his mother grabbed him and thrust $10,000 into his hand and told him to give the money to his father. Thrilled by his good fortune, he ran to find his father. His dad was sitting by the fireplace, reading a book. The son approached his father and said, "Dad, Dad, here's $10,000 for the business."

Without even looking up, the father grabbed the $10,000 and tossed it into the fire and watched it burn. The son stood, frozen in amazement. As the money burned, the father said, "Come back when you have earned the money!"

As the son left the room, his mother once again thrust $10,000 into his hand. This time, she instructed him that he needed to be more convincing in selling his father on the idea that he had actually worked for the money. So the boy scuffed himself up a little, jogged around the block a few times, and then went to find his father again. His father was again sitting in front of the fireplace, reading a book. The boy approached his father and said, "It sure is tough earning money. Here's the $10,000. I really do want to own the business." Once again, the father took the $10,000 and, without even looking up, tossed the money into the fireplace. As the money burned, the son asked, "How did you know I didn't earn the money?"

The father replied, "It is easy to lose or spend money that is not your own."

At this point, the son realized he wasn't going to get the business unless he actually earned the $10,000. He wanted the business, so when his mother offered him money again, he declined her offer. He went out and picked some odd jobs. His jobs required him to get up early and stay up late, but he worked and worked until he finally earned $10,000. Proudly, he walked to his father and presented him the money. Like before, his father was sitting by the fire, reading a book. Again, the father took the money and threw it into the fire. As the money hit the flames, the son dove to the floor and, risking burns and pain, stuck his hands into the fire and pulled out the $10,000. The father looked his son in the eyes and said, "I see you really did earn the money this time."

When a person earns his money, he is more likely to treat it with respect. Conversely, a fool and his money are soon parted. The good news is that anyone can develop wisdom in financial matters by learning to apply the right principles at the right time. Financial success means a person owns everything free and clear, and no matter what happens to the economy, the bobber of financial life that he is riding on will not be pulled under, unless a severe economic catastrophe occurs. Eventually, he gets to the point where he is living today on money that was made years before. This is financial freedom and peace of mind. When this happens, he can now invest time on his loved ones, charities, and legacies. In the end, people will not remember others for their net worth; rather, they will remember them for the investments of time made in their lives. Building financial security allows a person to free himself from the mundane money-making tasks so that he can focus on his significant assignments in life. Don't worship things, for doing so is a poor substitute for worshipping God. But do develop financial management and discipline, and by doing so, you will have time to invest in people and the causes that truly make a difference.

## Ben Franklin:  Financial Management–
## Money and Time

Over three hundred years ago in the city of Boston, a burgeoning port town in the British American colonies, a baby named Ben Franklin was born. His impact on history boggles the imagination, with him even being recognized as "the first great American." Franklin achieved superhuman exploits in business, science, politics, and diplomacy and built a nation with his fellow Founding Fathers. Much has been written and rewritten on the achievements of this great man, but surprisingly little has been written on the economic engine that allowed this polymathic genius the leisure to dive deeply into his many areas of interest. In fact, Franklin's life progressed through three stages: apprenticeship, journeyman status, and mastership. Each was a vital step for Franklin because each built on his existing skills until mastery was reached.

Arguably, Franklin's greatest personal discovery occurred as a journeyman when he created his franchising model for the printing business. Indeed, it was this creation that provided him with the financial means to retire from business early. Without this financial freedom, he would not have had the leisure that led to most of his other discoveries. If Franklin had not created a financial engine to free his life from toil, today, he would be remembered as little more than a top-rate colonial printer.

Franklin's rise in business began at sixteen years of age when, tired of the abuse of his elder brother, he ran away from his hometown of Boston. He went to Philadelphia, where he apprenticed at a print shop. In less than three years, he built his reputation as a diligent worker with a witty pen—a man on the move up. He quickly became one of the prominent printers in the young city. He wrote, "A man may, if he knows not how to save as he gets, keep his nose all his life to the grindstone, and die not worth a groat at last." He was prudent with money, realizing that without capital, he would never own his own business. Indeed, most journeyman printers worked for others, not having the investment money to buy their own printing equipment and start their own businesses. Franklin contacted his dad, hoping to borrow money, but his dad refused, believing he was too young to handle

185

added responsibilities. Undeterred, Franklin became even more determined to start his own business, realizing savings was the key. He wrote, "Think of saving as well as of getting: the Indies have not made Spain rich because her outgoes are greater than her incomes." Eventually, with his own savings and loans from a few close friends, he launched his business, his first step in his march to immortality. He had discovered the philosopher's stone, turning a leaden life into a golden one. He wrote, "Get what you can, and what you get hold; 'Tis the stone that will turn all your lead into gold." His apprentice days were over; then began his years as a journeyman printer and business owner.

Franklin modeled one of his most popular sayings—"Early to bed and early to rise makes a man healthy, wealthy, and wise"—as he arrived to work early, diligently pursuing his profession. His reputation expanded with his growing business, so he was offered the position of South Carolina's official printer for its public records when he was only twenty-six years old. However, he declined the opportunity because he didn't desire to leave Philadelphia. Instead of rejecting the offer outright, however, Franklin, in a true win-win spirit, proposed an alternative plan. He suggested to the South Carolina officials that they hire one of his journeymen, Thomas Whitmarsh. Franklin would sponsor the project, helping the journeyman with the equipment, fonts, and funds, as well as any mentoring needs, while Whitmarsh would run the day-to-day operations in Charleston. In hindsight, all parties profited from this unique arrangement as South Carolina received a top-notch journeyman, trained under the tutelage of Franklin; Whitmarsh received capital and mentorship, both factors in short supply in the colonies, allowing him the opportunity to own his business; and lastly, Franklin received one-third of the profits for six years, after which, Whitmarsh had the option to buy his ownership out or continue with the status quo. Since Franklin had capital with little time, while the typical journeyman had time with little capital, this arrangement benefitted both sides. Both parties provided each other what they lacked, exemplifying a true win-win arrangement. Franklin's frugality permitted him to leverage capital and buy back time because he knew that time was life, as he had written, "Dost thou love life, then do not squander time, for that's the stuff life is made of." He wasn't a time waster; rather, he was a time saver, leveraging others' efforts in win-win partnerships. His franchising program expanded across many cities in Colonial America. He looked for hungry, sober, hardworking journeymen to be his long-distance proxies. These journeymen ran Franklin's many sister newspapers, each of them following the leadership of his *Pennsylvania Gazette* masthead. In time, Franklin's expansive printing empire reached all the way from Hartford in the north to as far south as Antigua, with Lancaster, New York, and New Haven, Connecticut, to mention just a couple, in between. Those are not bad results for a young man whose father would not invest in him. In fact, by 1755, eight of the fifteen newspapers printed in Colonial America were part of Franklin's powerful conglomerate. Although not all his partnerships were profitable, most of them prospered under his leadership. He forged partnerships that produced residual income streams for over fifty years, leaving him free to pursue his purpose, no longer enslaved by monetary want.

Thanks to his franchises, Franklin, at forty-two years of age, freed himself from the day-to-day oversight of his printing empire, focusing instead on his other areas of interest, which included science, politics, and local community affairs. He explained his philosophy to his mother, writing, "I would rather have it said, 'He lived usefully,' than 'He died rich.'" Nevertheless, he was a wealthy man because he never had to think about money again for the rest of his life. However, he didn't use his liberty for laziness; instead, he used it to create his legacy. He knew that there was more to life than just accumulating money. In fact, he did the polar opposite, using his money to accumulate time rather than using his time to accumulate money. He understood that money was the tool to free up his time for life. Simply put, he spent money to make time, while others spent time to make money. He wrote, "Money never made a man happy yet, nor will it. The more a man has, the more he wants. Instead of filling a vacuum, it makes one."

Reviewing Franklin's accomplishments is inspiring, especially when one considers the number of fields that he developed original insights in. Here is a partial list:

1.  He set up the world's first franchise-type model, freeing himself from the day-to-day work routine.
2.  He invented the famed Franklin stove, improving the heat efficiency of wood fires.
3.  He created America's first volunteer fire department, recruiting others into the bucket brigade.
4.  He founded an academy of learning in Philadelphia, which later became the University of Pennsylvania.
5.  He founded America's first public library.
6.  He discovered electricity, studying its nature through countless experiments, leading to the publication of his findings and international fame.
7.  He invented the bifocal lens.
8.  He was the first man to chart and study the temperatures of the Gulf Stream.
9.  He published the best-selling *Poor Richard's Almanac* yearly.
10. He wrote one of the best-selling autobiographies of all time, a classic of English literature.
11. He revolutionized the mail service delivery of the colonies as the postmaster general by implementing home delivery and one-day service.
12. He played an active part in the creation of nearly every major American document, including the Declaration of Independence, the Constitution, the war alliance with France, and the peace treaty with England. In fact, he was the only Founding Father to sign all four documents.

These achievements alone were enough to occupy a dozen men of energy. It's nearly incomprehensible that one person accomplished all of these, especially when one considers he started with no funds and no connections and lived in the backwaters of the British Empire. Nonetheless, Franklin did achieve these feats, and more, through disciplined time management, a relentless pursuit of knowledge, and the financial freedom obtained by franchising his printing business. He learned early in life the multiplying effect of good leadership, driving himself in a rigorous program of self-development, even, for a period of time, becoming a vegetarian in order to save more money to invest in books. He knew to feed his brain over his belly. In fact, he wrote, "If a man empties his purse into his head, no man can take it away from him. An investment in knowledge always pays the best interest." But he didn't stop there; he studied the greatest influencers of history, seeking to develop the right mix of charm, posture, and tact to go along with his unquestionable character, in a quest to become a leader of leaders. In fact, he developed one of the first personal development programs, freely sharing his success principles in his autobiography and in his yearly *Poor Richard's Almanac*, a pamphlet loaded with witty sayings, pearls of financial wisdom, and solid leadership thoughts. He was a hungry student, studying the principles of character, task, and relationships to improve his leadership; he wrote, "Not a tenth part of wisdom was my own." His leadership training proved significant since all of his achievements, including his business franchising, depended on his leadership mastery of self and others.

Ralph Frasca, the author of the groundbreaking book *Ben Franklin's Printing Network*, suggested that Franklin's motivation for setting up his printing empire had more to do with moral improvements than with monetary gains:

> Franklin utilized the *Pennsylvania Gazette* in the same educational manner, recalling, "I considered my newspapers also as another means of communicating instruction and in that view frequently reprinted in it extracts from the *Spectator* and other moral writers, and sometimes published little pieces of my own," which he had first auditioned for the Junto, a group of intelligent young Philadelphia men dedicated to self-improvement. Throughout his life, Franklin viewed these published moral lessons as a service to humanity, and therefore to God. Citing the Book of Matthew Chapter 25, Franklin commented in a 1738 letter to his parents that he wished to serve God through his virtuous deeds. "Scripture assures me, that at the last Day, we shall not be examined by what we thought, but what we did; and our recommendation will not be that we said Lord, Lord, but that we did GOOD to our fellow creatures.

Nine years later, Franklin advised readers of his almanac: "What is serving God? 'Tis doing good to man." He believed that by inculcating virtue, he was improving man and culture, fulfilling his life's mission, a mission that he set while still a teenager after reading Plutarch, Mather, and other morally uplifting authors. Frasca described Franklin's purpose: "Thus Franklin viewed it as one of his life's duties to teach people the 'art' of virtuous conduct and show them how to practice it daily. To accomplish this task, he used the existing organs of mass communication. In addition to his *Autobiography* and pamphlets, Franklin employed his annual *Poor Richard's Almanac* and newspapers—both his own, the weekly *Pennsylvania Gazette*, and those published by others—to convey his ideology of virtue to the masses."

Regardless of whether moral or monetary reasons were the prime motivation for Franklin's printing consortium, the fact remains that by helping others own their businesses, he received a portion of their profits. Although conservative with expenses, frugal in food, drink, and clothing, he was liberal with investments, understanding the power of leverage to duplicate his time and enterprises.

Near the end of his life, in his will, Franklin provided one more lesson on finances to the world, teaching the wonder of compounding interest. He left a £1,000 (around $6,000 in today's money) trust to both Boston and Philadelphia with the condition that the money couldn't be touched for two hundred years. The original £2,000 ($12,000) invested in the two trusts grew in two hundred years to over $7 million, an impressive return on investment for the cities, thanks to the financial mastery of Franklin.

Franklin reminds Americans that incremental gains over time become great surpluses. As he had shared many years earlier, "Human felicity [happiness or fortune] is produced not as much by great pieces of good fortune that seldom happen as by little advantages that occur every day." Financial mastery is a process of learning that small investments, compounded over time, become large amounts that can free people from the enervating effects of mindless work and open up leisure time in which to pursue their destinies. He wrote, "Your net worth to the world is usually determined by what remains after your bad habits are subtracted from your good ones." This is a fitting description of his life, which is not a perfect one, but when you subtract the good habits from the bad, his net worth in the service of his fellow men ranks near the top.

Most people spend a lifetime in apprenticeship mode, some reach journeyman status, and only a few—the hungry and driven few—reach the mastership level, freeing themselves from financial concern and investing their lives in the service of others. Through the growth of his business conglomerate, Franklin's business genius provided him the time to be of service to the world. He was an American original, a creative genius, and through his efforts, he unleashed himself upon the world stage. This is the priceless lesson we can learn from Franklin's life.

## CHAPTER 9

# LEADERSHIP
## Resolved: To Develop the Art and Science of Leadership

*I know that everything rises and falls based on the leadership culture created in my community.*

As the resolutions have progressed from private achievements to public achievements, one is now ready to move to leadership achievements.

What is it about leadership? It seems as though the more it is studied, the harder it is to understand. It is a topic that refuses to be quantified, escaping our airtight definitions, no matter how many hours we spend on the subject. Even though we are not sure how to define it, everyone knows when leadership is present and, sadly, when it is not. Leadership does not exist at a constant quantity in organizations; rather, the level of leadership ebbs and flows, depending on the character and competence of the leaders planning and directing the efforts.

The highest level of leadership is achieved by only a few individuals in any field, and it only happens when a great leader inspires other performers to become leaders themselves. It's tough enough to perform, let alone to perform while leading others to step up their game; but championship teams are created when leaders surround themselves with other leaders, raising the bar of excellence throughout their organization.

Michael Jordan is a great example of top leadership. Returning from his eighteen-month minor league baseball sojourn, Jordan became a great leader. For the first time in his career, he understood the weaknesses of others by experiencing firsthand his own weaknesses in baseball. In basketball, he had worked so hard for so long that he practically had no limits. Upon his return, his newfound empathy for his teammates catapulted him from a good leader to a great leader because leadership at the highest level demands a lifetime of service to others. This service involves empathy for others' strengths and weaknesses and sharing all recognition with the goal of building leaders throughout the organization. Dynasties, like Michael Jordan's Chicago Bulls, are created when teammates learn to complement each other, not criticize.

## Sports Leaders and Business Leaders

Leaders in sports win by consistently developing and executing game plans to fulfill the purpose of an organization. The coach has clearly defined rules on how to play and win the game. The winning coach is the one who executes the game plan better, scoring more points than his competitors. He cannot change the rules of the game, but he can develop and implement a plan that is better than his competitors' and thereby win more games. If his team doesn't put enough points on the scoreboard, he will suffer a loss, leading to PDCA adjustments in an effort to execute more effectively and score more points.

Business leadership is similar to sports leadership, although the two have one significant difference. In a free-enterprise environment, a business leader doesn't just execute a game plan; he must first create a game out of his business. This includes setting the ground rules on how the game is played and won, thus satisfying customers. In business, the game isn't predefined; instead, it's developed by an organization's leaders by studying its customers' needs and competitors' strategies. Moreover, competitors can, at any time, change the rules of the game, making the former game plans obsolete. A business leader, therefore, must make sure his game definition and ground rules keep up with the latest rules, ensuring that customers will be satisfied if he implements his game plan correctly. This is a crucial difference between sports coaches and business leaders—one that must not be overlooked.

Without a clearly defined game, one that satisfies current customers when it's played, a team will flounder, having no objective on which to focus. For without a game, there isn't a scoreboard. Without a scoreboard, there isn't an objective way to determine who is winning and losing. And without a win or a loss, no one can ascertain who is accomplishing a company's purpose. When an organization doesn't utilize a scoreboard, political maneuvering for personal advancement becomes the default mode. The gameless organization focuses less on the scoreboard to advance both the customers and the organization; instead, the organization's members focus more on serving bosses to advance themselves. Only the game and the scoreboard keep leaders honest with their own and their team's performances, ensuring that the game plan doesn't degenerate into self-centered political tactics designed to advance personal careers at the expense of the customers' satisfaction and the organization's well-being.

## Business, Scoreboards, and Game Plans

Even when a leader keeps his eye on the scoreboard, he must not delude himself with the changing business conditions caused by his competitors' moves. Since the rules can be changed at any time by any leader who conceptualizes a new way of satisfying the customers through creative use of technologies, processes, or systems, another level of complexity is added to the load for business leaders. In fact, many times, it's an outsider (someone who isn't an industry expert) who redefines the game, leaving the former game and its strategies on the scrap heap of business history. Because an outsider isn't a prisoner of the current operating paradigms, he doesn't feel beholden to the old rules.

If, by keeping score, one discovers that the old strategies no longer satisfy the customers, then most likely, someone has changed the rules of the game. Henry Ford changed the rules of the transportation game when he created his Model T automobile. No matter how good a manufacturer was at building horse carriages, he was left in the dust, forced to either play by the new rules or leave the industry.

A modern example of an upstart changing the rules is Amazon. com, which is in rivalry with Barnes & Noble. Jeff Bezos, founder of Amazon, changed the rules of the game, offering books online for the ease of making purchases from home. Furthermore, with the advent of digital books, shopping for books is going through another major transformation. Amazon is now selling more digital books than paper books every month. Imagine the competitive pressures the new game is placing on the traditional bookstores with huge dollar amounts in inventory and store space, which must attempt to compete with digitally-based Internet companies with little inventory or overhead. The book business will never be the same again, thanks to an outsider (Bezos) who refused to play by the old rules. The myopic businesses who hold on to the glory of yesterday's game suffer an embarrassment similar to that of the fabled emperor. The emperors of business, ignoring the savvy entrepreneurs who stripped them of their glory, parade around naked in front of their customers, who are exiting to join the prince of business who has developed a more effective game to satisfy the emperor's former customers. Business leaders, then, must constantly examine the horizon, ensuring that the current game, when executed properly, still satisfies the customers. Every savvy business leader must break his business before his competitors do. Remember, the only constant in the game of business is satisfied customers; the only way to achieve this is through constant and never-ending improvement both in the rules and in the game plan.

### Business as a Game

When the game is defined properly, communities are attracted to the competition inherent in the game. Michael Gerber wrote, "People—your people—do not simply want to work for exciting people. They want to work for people who have created a clearly defined structure for acting in the world—a structure through which they can test themselves and be tested. Such a structure is called a game. And there is nothing more exciting than a well-conceived game." Just as every game has well-defined "rules of engagement" as well as rules for how to score points and win the game, so must a business define its game properly.

Remember Collins's hedgehog concept? Another way of thinking about the game is to define the game plan through a company's hedgehog. By clearly defining and then updating the three circles as conditions change to determine the intersection point of passion (What are we passionate about?), potential (What can we be the best at?), and profits (What drives our economic engine?), the game plan is built around the hedgehog concept in order to win. Imagine two football teams that, although both are successful, have different game plans based on how they answer the hedgehog questions. One team relies on a bruising ground game, while the other uses a lightning-quick passing game. Both win games following the same football rules, but each team uses specific strategies based on its own core strengths.

A business leader develops, defines, and sells the game to everyone in his community. Gerber elaborated, "The degree to which your people 'do what you want' is the degree to which they buy into your game. And the degree to which they buy into your game doesn't depend upon them but upon how well you communicate the game to them—at the outset of your relationship, not after it's begun." To define the game, a leader must decide which criteria are essential to satisfy the customers. Then, he turns the criteria into a game, helping everyone buy into winning the game to satisfy the customers. After this, it's time to reward the leaders and the team who execute the plays effectively. When the game is defined in this manner, it helps each team keep score by applying the PDCA process for continuous improvement.

Playing a worthwhile business game brings meaning and purpose into one's life, forming communities that play the game to win. Gerber explained, "Part of what's missing is a game worth playing . . . What most people need, then, is a place of community that has purpose, order, and meaning. A place in which being human is a prerequisite, but acting human is essential." The game creates a sense of community, a team, as people focus together on achieving worthwhile results, producing meaning in their lives and satisfaction for the customers. Since true competition creates cooperation, the more a team competes with other enterprises, the more it unites together as a community, achieving victory in the game. Military units, championship sports teams, and elite business teams all unify around common objectives, building relationships that last a lifetime. Competition creates cooperation because winning the game becomes more important than protecting an individual's perks. The only word of caution here is to stay alert to the changing rules of the business game. A company can become very efficient at game plans that have ceased to work. Businesses that endure must sacrifice their sacred cows because as Spencer Johnson said, "When the cheese has been moved, it's best to go find where it moved."

There are six steps for developing the business game and scoreboard in every field.

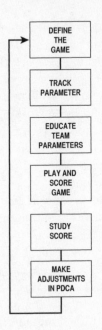

## Aligning Culture to Create Current

Now that the game is defined, the leader must create a culture to win the game. Organizational theorist Edgar Schein has defined culture as "a pattern of shared basic assumptions that the group learned as it solved its problems that has worked well enough to be considered valid and is passed on to new members as the correct way to perceive, think, and feel in relation to those problems." The thirteen resolutions are basic assumptions about life that, when learned, help solve problems personally and professionally. They can be taught in communities, which create a culture around the thirteen resolutions. Emerson's statement, "Every great institution is the lengthened shadow of a single man. His character determines the character of the organization," conveys the same message. An entrepreneur's beliefs become the cultural principles of the institution. Great cultures, then, demand great character-based leaders. By making his business a game and adding the thirteen resolutions, a person creates a character-centered, leadership-oriented culture that loves to compete and win the game. The culture determines how a group responds and solves problems in order to score points to win the game and satisfy its customers. For if a culture cannot satisfy the customer, then it will not be in business for long since other organizations will develop cultures that satisfy the former patrons of the failed company. Culture is like water current in a swimming pool. When leaders jump into the pool, triggering the community to move in the same direction, they create a current that influences everyone in it. New members jumping into the pool will be pulled along by the current flowing in the positive direction, thanks to a moving leadership team. Think of each of the resolutions as a jet pump placed in the pool, positioned to help reverse the cultural current of decline.

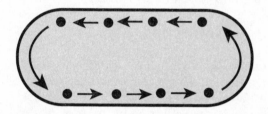

## Vision Commitment versus Economic Dependence

One of the essentials in developing an effective culture is ensuring that all behaviors are aligned to run in the same direction in the pool. If principles conflict with each other, a leader will not have unity in his pool. Purpose, vision, and core principles help align a culture so that it will run in a certain direction in the pool, carrying new people along in the current until they learn to run with the current. In fact, the goal is to teach as many people as possible in the community to run in the same direction in the pool. Leaders must master culture since a vision-led culture drives a community's behavior better than a bureaucratic control-led culture ever will. Gary Hamel described the difference:

> When it comes to mobilizing human capability, communities outperform bureaucracies . . . In a bureaucracy, the basis for exchange is contractual—you get paid for doing what is assigned to you. In a community, exchange is voluntary—you give your labor for the chance to make a difference, or exercise your talents. In a bureaucracy you are a factor of production. In a community you are a partner in a cause. In a bureaucracy, "loyalty" is a product of economic dependency. In a community, dedication and commitment are based on one's affiliation with the group's

aims and goals.

Leaders deny the urge to control others, realizing that other leaders don't need to be controlled but rather unleashed with common goals and visions. Leaders buy into the great leader; then they buy into the leader's vision for the future, aligning themselves personally and professionally to achieve greatness together. Championship teams are created when communities buy into a common vision formed around purposes and principles to accomplish that vision, surrendering their personal egos and replacing them with a team ego to accomplish the team's vision.

## Expecting and Inspecting

For leaders to create a leadership culture, they must create a culture of expecting and inspecting results. Great leadership, then, is less about how effective a person is at accomplishing tasks—although leaders are very effective in their tasks—and more about who a leader is and the culture he creates. Leaders create culture; culture creates results. The results are good or bad, depending on whether the culture aligns with the game plan to produce the desired results. A culture of execution demands excellence from each individual, compelling others to raise their game, not by force, but by the positive peer pressure of a unifying vision backed by the trust in the leaders.

In order to reach excellence, however, many tasks must be delegated to other leaders and team members who demand excellence from themselves. Delegation is essential for large-scale results; however, the mistake of many new leaders is that they delegate both the assignment and the inspection of the scoreboard. This is a recipe for failure. Proper delegation is delegating a task but maintaining responsibility for inspecting the scoreboard. If one delegates the scoreboard, he shouldn't be surprised when an underling gives his interpretation of the facts rather than the reality of the facts, since only a few will confront reality. And who, if given a choice, would confront his own inadequate performance and admit the poor reality to his supervisors? If one would review the history of organizations, he would find that improper delegation has caused as much damage over the years as proper delegation has caused good. Remember, the toughest part of delegation is teaching a subordinate how to accurately study his scoreboard so as not to spin the data into a fantasy story that, over time, will turn into a nightmare. Only by consistently inspecting the results will the leader develop a confidence that the new leader will confront his own brutal reality. Developing a leadership culture is the peak of leadership, creating a vision from the mountaintop, a culture of expecting excellence and subsequently inspecting results, ensuring the birth of a new dynasty.

## Culture of Execution—Runners, Bobbers, Obstructionist

If every organization has a culture, why do so many fail to execute effectively to serve their customers? A company that is playing the right game but still losing is suffering from a poor culture of execution, meaning, the pool current is flowing in the wrong direction. It takes a united leadership team willing to jump into the pool together and run against the current of decline for an extended period of time to reverse the negative current. Under good conditions, creating a cultural current requires unity, trust, and buy-in to the leadership team; attempting to turn around a culture that is in decline is even more demanding.

Turnaround leadership is so highly valued because it's so rare. It demands guts, tenacity, and persistence to stay in the pool, even when the current is pulling in the wrong direction. Turnaround leaders must quickly determine which people are just "bobbing" in the pool, not helping to run against the current, or worse, which people are obstructionists, literally running with the negative current. Without disciplined people, who unify into a team willing to run against the current, no turnaround is possible. Collins writes, "Discipline by itself will not produce great results . . . No, the point is to first get self-disciplined people who engage in very rigorous thinking, who then take disciplined action within the framework of a consistent system designed around the HedgeHog Concept." The hedgehog concept, in this case, is the direction in which one desires to flow the current in the pool. A leader must find others who will help him move the water in the right direction, creating the leadership culture for growth.

## Attracting and Developing Leaders

If a person expects to win in business, he must find and influence talented, disciplined people who will buy into the cultural current being created. They must be willing to learn the thirteen resolutions, applying them to life, and study the scoreboard in each area, while hating to lose badly enough to change when necessary. No coach, not even the best ones, can win without talent, but the bad ones seem to lose even with talent. A leader must surround himself with the right people, or he is doomed to mediocrity. The fewer "runners" a leader has in the pool, the more "bobbers" and "obstructionists" will fill the pool, leading to little chance of reversing a negative current.

> A leader must surround himself with the right people, or he is doomed to mediocrity.

Even the best trainers in the world will lose the Kentucky Derby if they train donkeys. Covey explained why in a new Afterword of *The 7 Habits of Highly Effective People*, where he emphasized the importance of having the right people: "I am convinced that although training and development is important, recruiting and selection are much more important." Thoroughbreds, unlike donkeys, make leadership easy because, after learning the thirteen resolutions, all they need is a description of the game, an explanation of how to score points and win, and lastly, directions to the pool. Everything else a thoroughbred will either figure out, or he will seek out a leader who knows. One can always tell the quality of a leader by that of the leaders surrounding him.

## Leadership Cultures and Freedom

Leadership cultures need freedom for leaders to blossom and grow. Ironically, Collins writes, "Most companies build their bureaucratic rules to manage the small percentage of wrong people on the bus, which in turn drives away the right people on the bus, which then increases the percentage of wrong people on the bus, which increases the need for more bureaucracy to compensate for incompetence and lack of discipline, which then further drives the right people away, and so forth." This is the chicken-and-egg scenario. Is it ineffective leaders that lead to bureaucratic rules, or is it the bureaucratic rules that drive out the good leaders, leaving only the less capable to remain? Either way, the companies who provide people the freedom to pursue scoring points in the defined game will attract more leaders, while quickly developing or weeding out non-leaders. In today's competitive environment, companies that force people to follow oppressive rules and regulations will quickly lose any leaders to companies that give them the freedom to play the game and win. Leaders sail the tumultuous seas of change, seeking to win, while non-leaders coast on the calm seas of mediocrity, seeking to stay afloat.

Sam Walton loved giving people freedom, but that freedom came with responsibility. Indeed, he had two objectives in developing the culture of his teams through the scoreboard: praise and teaching. He wrote, "All of us like praise. So what we try to practice in our company is to look for things to praise. Look for things that are going right. We want to let our folks know when they are doing something outstanding, and let them know they are important to us." On the one hand, Walton praised people who used their freedom to move the company ahead. On the other hand, what happens if someone isn't producing results? How does a person praise someone who isn't achieving the desired outcomes? Walton explained, "You can't praise something that's not done well. You can't be insincere. You have to follow up on things that aren't done well. There is no substitute for being honest with someone and letting them know they didn't do a good job. All of us profit from being corrected if we're corrected in a positive way." The goal, then, isn't to ruin a person when he misses the mark but to instruct him on the proper thinking and actions, helping him become more effective as a leader.

## Trilateral Leadership Ledger and Sturgeon's Law

In our *New York Times* best seller *Launching a Leadership Revolution*, Chris Brady and I teach people how to become more effective leaders through the Trilateral Leadership Ledger (TLL). Every leader must grow in his character, task, and relationships to become a great leader. The TLL measures each of these three areas on a scale of 0 to 10; then one multiplies all three of these scores to obtain the total score. For example, if someone rated himself 2 on character, 1 on task, and 2 on relationships, then the total score is 4 ($2 \times 1 \times 2 = 4$). The lowest score, one that many—including the author—score when they start their leadership journey, is 0. The highest score, one that no reader will ever obtain, is 1,000 ($10 \times 10 \times 10 = 1,000$). Perfection, although strived for daily, will never be achieved since no one reading this book is perfect, but the TLL has helped tens of thousands of people evaluate their current leadership scores, helping them identify areas in need of improvement.

Theodore Sturgeon, a science fiction writer, knew perfection would never be reached. In fact, he refuted many of the critics of the science fiction genre at the 1953 World Science Fiction Convention when he said:

I repeat Sturgeon's Revelation, which was wrung out of me after twenty years of wearying defense of science fiction against attacks of people who used the worst examples of the field for ammunition, and whose conclusion was that ninety percent of Science Fiction is crud. Using the same standards that categorize 90 percent of science fiction as trash, crud, or crap, it can be argued that 90 percent of film, literature, consumer goods, etc. are crap. In other words, the claim (or fact) that 90 percent of science fiction is crap is ultimately uninformative, because science fiction conforms to the same trends of quality as all other art forms.

Sturgeon's law validates a truth proven again and again in our mass-participation Internet age. For example, if a person were to review all YouTube videos, he would find that the majority (90 percent) are crud, but the remaining 10 percent are informative or entertaining. *Wikipedia*, the free online encyclopedia, displays the same trends, with less than 10 percent of the content authors providing around 90 percent of the useful content. Another example is the *American Idol* television show, where numerous contestants audition for the opportunity to showcase their talents. Can one imagine having to listen to every person who auditions for the show? Tens of thousands audition, but only the best are viewed by TV audiences. It isn't shocking that 90 percent of the contestants are eliminated since *American Idol*, as a human endeavor, is subject to Sturgeon's law. The remaining 10 percent with talent and a level of mastery are evaluated further, eventually filtering down to a select group, who appear on TV. *American Idol* isn't criticized because 90 percent of those who audition lack excellence since it couldn't be otherwise.

Before a person gets depressed, realizing that only a few people will become top leaders, he should recognize that Sturgeon's law is positive for aspiring leaders because it states that anyone can be a leader if he is willing to work at it. In other words, the reason that only a few become leaders isn't talent but tenacity. Unlike other leadership experts, I strongly believe leaders can grow beyond their believed limitations through the mastery of the thirteen resolutions in their lives. By studying and analyzing Sturgeon's law further, one realizes that it represents beautifully the art of leadership—the idea that anyone can lead but few will, simply because leadership is tough, requiring focus and relentless discipline. This doesn't mean that the rest of the people are crud; rather, this only means that their leadership abilities still need work.

The TLL reveals how one can grow as a leader by stating that leaders must be effective and advance into the elite 10 percent in the three key attributes—character, task, and relationships. Sturgeon's law, when applied to the TLL, reveals that only 10 percent of the people will excel in one of these attributes, but a top leader must excel at all three. Only 10 percent × 10 percent × 10 percent will do that, which explains why, on average, true leadership occurs only once in a thousand people. Only 1 out of 1,000 people will ever discipline his character, task, and relationships to break through Sturgeon's law and enter a select group of leaders who influence others. This number, 1 out of a 1,000, is the estimate used by leadership gurus around the world, even those who have never heard of Sturgeon's law or the Trilateral Leadership Ledger. Gladwell reported that a performer can build and maintain a community of around 100–150 people, but a leader, someone who is mastering leadership, who leads performers of these 100–150 people, will develop about one in a thousand people. In any community, a thousand people don't just gather; instead, gathering them requires an elite leader who attracts, serves, and leads them. If one is building a community of thousands of people, then elite leaders are required, leaders who break through Sturgeon's law on all three TLL attributes.

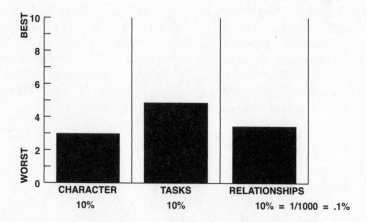

Study each of the three attributes of leadership in the TLL. The common tendency is for a person to overrate himself when tabulating his TLL score. A simple reality check for scoring is to compare one's results with the number of his following. If a person has around 100 people in his community, then his TLL score is around

50 points; but by developing three performers who can lead 100 people each, his TLL grows to 150 points. Top leaders with over 1,000 people in multiple communities can score over 300 points on their TLL evaluations. By knowing the total score based on his numbers, a person can estimate his individual scores in character, task, and relationships and ensure that he isn't suffering from self-delusion. Every leader has room to grow because no one hits 1,000 points, although a few hit above 500 points. And this leads to Woodward's law—a law on leadership that is corollary to Sturgeon's law—which states that "90 percent of leaders are convinced they are part of Sturgeon's 10 percent." Even though only 10 percent of the people truly lead as the upper echelons in any category, the single biggest reason that most leaders do not continue the growth journey is that they believe they have already arrived. Good is truly the enemy of great. It's only when a leader grows throughout his life that he attracts other elite leaders into his community, changing the lifetime leader's role from a leader of followers to a servant of leaders. Leaders of this magnitude refuse to work for time clock punchers, dictators, or micromanagers but love responsibility and feed on visionary leadership. Imagine developing one's TLL score and becoming a servant leader who attracts other top leaders into his community, thus creating a team of leaders who drive change in any field on which they set their minds. Leadership isn't a nice add-on feature but an essential part of every world changer. As John Maxwell stated, "Everything rises and falls on leadership."

> **It's only when a leader grows throughout his life that he attracts other elite leaders into his community, changing the lifetime leader's role from a leader of followers to a servant of leaders.**

## Sam Walton: Leadership Excellence

Sam Walton's results have clearly shown that he is one of the greatest leaders of the last one hundred years. A review of his leadership thoughts and actions reveals the secrets behind the making of a legend.

Richard S. Tedlow, in the book *Giants of Enterprise*, studied the leadership of Walton: "First he learned all the rules. Then he broke all the rules which did not make sense to him which meant almost all of them. . . . Sam Walton did not become a billionaire because he was a genius (although he was without question smart, shrewd, and astute). The real reason for his success was that he had the courage of his convictions." Because Walton broke any rules that he thought foolish, it isn't surprising that he clashed with Butler Brothers, the owner of his first retail store, Ben Franklin five-and-dime stores. Butler Brothers' tight controls clashed with Walton's ability to serve his customers, causing Walton to work around the rules, searching for less expensive merchandise suppliers. He ignored most of the higher markup items Butler Brothers offered, attempting to reduce prices and satisfy his customers.

Even though Butler Brothers was unhappy with Walton's freewheeling methods, the company tolerated his independent streak and focused instead on his massive increase in sales year after year. Indeed, sales increased over 45 percent during Walton's first full year, moving up another 33 percent the following year, and then expanding yet another 25 percent the third year! This impressive business run surprised Butler Brothers, who thought they were selling a capsizing franchise to a naive rookie. Nonetheless, Walton changed the perpetual loser into one of the franchise's elite performers, amazing everyone except the indomitable Walton himself. Walton reminisced, "I was the sucker Butler Brothers sent to save him [the former owner]." By his fifth year, Walton had a compounded annual growth rate of 28 percent, making him the leading variety store owner in the entire state of Arkansas.

Walton's story, at this point, had all the makings of a fairy tale, but it didn't last. Like many elite leaders, he suffered a severe business setback, one that would have proved fatal to a lesser man's dream. Walton had a problem with the lease that he had signed back in 1945. The impetuous Walton did not ensure the lease included the standard rental renewal clause. This oversight left Walton open to the whims of the building's owner on whether to write up a new lease or find a new renter. The rental owner, seeing an opportunity to advance his son at Walton's expense, refused to renew the lease contract. A disappointed Walton was left with no options but to sell his store inventory and fixtures to the renter's son. In a flash, Walton's storybook rise—dreaming, planning, working, and leading—had collapsed. He received a mere $50,000 for five years of tireless work, a bitter pill to swallow for the Walton family. He recollected:

> It was the low point of my life. I felt sick to my stomach. I couldn't believe it was happening to me. It was really like a nightmare. I had built the best variety store in the whole region and worked hard in the community—done everything right—and now I was being kicked out of the town. It didn't seem fair. I blamed myself for getting suckered into such an awful lease, and I was furious with the landlord. Helen, just settling in with a brand-new family of four, was heartsick at the prospect of leaving Newport. But that's what we were going to do.

Walton had pulled off a business miracle, becoming the top variety retailer in Arkansas, only to be rewarded for this exceptional achievement by being run out of Newport, a dismal ending to an otherwise stellar performance. Walton could have chosen to get bitter or better, and as a leader would, he chose to get better. Through his embarrassing setback, he learned several valuable lessons. First, he formed a trusted legal team to review all of his future contracts, ensuring the written words agreed with the expectations of both parties. With the help of his son Rob and his father-in-law, both lawyers, he protected himself from his rash nature. Second, Walton didn't pass the buck, admitting full responsibility for signing the document without proper inspection. It is this characteristic, probably more than anything else, that separates leadership producers from leadership pretenders.

Leaders refuse to pass the buck or play the victim card, regardless of how alluring it is. Third, he allowed the pain of his temporary setback to fuel his fire rather than quench it. He turned this rejection into an energy so that he could bounce back and win, unlike others, who simply turn rejections into excuses for losing.

The Walton family moved to Bentonville, Arkansas, opening Walton's five-and-ten and changing its name, even though it was still under Butler Brother's umbrella. His new project would be an uphill battle, as Bentonville was only half the size of Newport and there were three variety stores competing in the small town. In addition, his new store averaged less than half the volume of his old Newport store. But he was not deterred, later writing, "It didn't matter that much because I had big plans." He immediately invested $55,000 ($5,000 more than he had received in the sale of his Newport store) banking on his ability to produce results. In less than six months, his new store had tripled its sales, proving that his leadership formula worked wherever it was applied. From 1950 to 1962, he expanded operations across the Southwest, building the largest independent variety store in operation in the entire United States while receiving little fanfare or publicity. He recalls, "That whole period—which scarcely gets any attention from people studying us—was really successful." The years before Walmart, when no one had heard the name of Sam Walton nationally, were the years where his leadership style was developed, plying his craft in near anonymity, investing over ten thousand hours in a quest for leadership mastery—a quest he more than fulfilled.

Walton, after a decade of being Butler Brothers' top performer, began to chafe under their rigid bureaucracy and mismanagement. Butler Brothers, which at the time made huge profits with its business model, seemed incapable of recognizing the impending competitive threat of discount stores to its variety store chain. But Walton, not suffering from myopia, recognized before others did that the variety store chains must adapt or die. The billionaire Butler Brothers, in a hubris-induced coma, preferred to play it safe. The company might have secured higher margins temporarily, but ultimately, its business was destroyed by not responding to the "creative destruction" inherent in the free-enterprise system.

Walton anticipated the future, realizing the days of high margins were following the dinosaur into extinction, and realized that the discount stores' more competitively priced business model would be fatal to his business. He flew to Butler Brothers's office in Chicago and proposed a partnership with them to launch a discount model. He wasn't far into his presentation when he mentioned that the margins would have to be cut from the typical 25 percent or more to around 12.5 percent or less of the sale's price. This terminated the meeting. Walton recalled, "They blew up," not willing to risk their easy profits, choosing instead to ride out the variety store model into business oblivion. Exasperated, he explained that the profits would be made up in volume and that the high margins were going away regardless, but Butler Brothers, blinded by the past, rejected the new reality along with Walton.

Not easily dismayed, Walton flew to Texas, hoping to become a franchisee of Herb Gibson, the highly successful discounter at the time. Gibson, however, rejected Walton outright, seeing him "as a bush-league variety-store merchant who possessed neither the finances nor the experience necessary to succeed in the Gibson chain." Not surprisingly, it's the revolutionary leaders with the largest of visions who must endure endless criticisms from those who profit from the past and, therefore, stand to lose the most when a revolutionary leader's vision is fulfilled. Having been rejected at every possible avenue, Walton did what all revolutionary leaders do in this situation—he proceeded with his plan anyway. In fact, 95 percent of the money used for the start-up of the original Walmart came from Walton himself, simply because no one else believed enough in his vision to invest in it.

Walton's secret philosophy, one that drove every other action, was a yearning to create a culture whose very existence was predicated on the objective of building loyal customers by offering quality merchandise at the lowest possible price. Walton's years of retailing experience had created one unshakeable conviction: He believed that by keeping the overhead cost down, piling the merchandise high, and selling the products at a low price, the customers would beat a trail to his stores. His belief would not disappoint his superhuman expectations. Walton, from the beginning, kept everyone focused on this simple formula of success, understanding that any organization that focuses on everything ultimately focuses on nothing. He knew that if the customer received the best price, everything else would work itself out. But if he ever took his eye off the ball, his competitive pace would fall off. His genius, as well as his gift to the world, was the leadership culture he created at Walmart.

Walton's own humility was key because it led to a culture of humility at Walmart. He didn't need to be "the guy;" instead of being threatened by other leaders, Walton leveraged their unique gifts for the benefit of his company and customers. For example, he wrote, "I needed somebody to run my new store, and I didn't have much money, so I did something I would do for the rest of my run in the retail business without any shame or embarrassment whatsoever: nose around other people's stores searching for good talent." He understood that one cannot win the Kentucky Derby on the back of a mule, so finding and developing leadership talent was Job One at Walmart. But even with talent, he expected each successful individual to buy into the company's ego over individual ego, sharing, "I hate to see rivalry develop within our company when it becomes a personal thing and our folks aren't working together and supporting one another. Philosophically, we have always said, 'Submerge your own ambitions and help whoever you can in the company. Work together as a team.' By working as a team, any lessons learned in one section of the company were quickly shared across regions." Walton further shared, "Communicate, communicate, communicate.... We do it in so many ways, from the Saturday morning meeting to the very simple phone call, to our satellite system. The necessity for good communication in a big company like this is so vital it can't be overstated." By developing a world-class team that worked incredibly hard, merged individual egos into a team ego, and communicated any lesson learned across the company, Walton created the foundation of a culture that refused to lose. It's hard to compete with a talented group of individuals who are playing the game as a team. Walton commented, "This is a highly competitive business, and an even more competitive company....Ever since my peewee football days, I've believed almost any kind of competition is great."

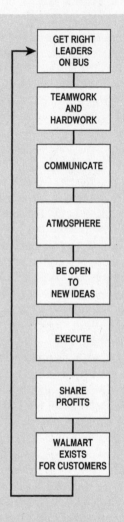

Walton's humility and intense desire to be the best drove his leadership culture to be hungry to learn, knowing that improved employees would improve customer satisfaction. Many seem to believe that the cause of Walmart's success is its superb information technology systems, forgetting that computers cannot lead a company and only report the results of leadership. Walton stated, "A computer is not—and will never be—a substitute for getting out in your stores and learning what's going on. In other words, a computer can tell you down to the dime what you've sold. But it can never tell you how much you could have sold." The computers merely communicated the satisfaction, or lack thereof, of Walmart customers. It was the leaders who made the day-to-day adjustments, ensuring that the computers showed positive results for Walmart shareholders and customers. Walton believed that the customer was king, and every move he made was geared toward satisfying him. He wrote, "Everything we've done since we started Walmart has been devoted to this idea that the customer is our boss. The controversies it has led us into have surprised me, but they've been easy to live with because we have never doubted our philosophy that the customer comes ahead of everything else." That is a simple statement, but it is certainly not easily executed, at least not by most companies.

Walton truly felt that customers wanted low prices, good quality, and courteous service; and in order to satisfy his customers, Walmart provided just that. The sales resulting from his simple formula provide irrefutable evidence that he was right. He learned from everybody. In fact, he probably visited more competitors during his career than any other retailer did. Charlie Cate, one of his store managers, recalled, "I remember him saying over and over again: go in and check our competition. Check everyone who is our competition. And don't look for bad. Look for good. If you get one good idea, that's one more than you went into the store with, and we must try to incorporate it into our company." It was this continuous learning culture, a result of Walton's humility, that drove further improvement and more customers to Walmart.

In the final analysis, what held Walmart's culture together, even after Walton's death, was his pathbreaking profit sharing plan, which allowed each of his partners to profit from the growth of Walmart. He commented, "The more you share profits with your associates—whether it's in salaries or incentives or bonuses or stock discounts—the more profit will accrue to the company. Why? Because the way management treats the associates is exactly how the associates will then treat the customers." His leadership culture followed the tried and true Golden Rule: "Do unto others as you would have them do unto you." He set the target to serve the customer, period; he created the scoreboard to measure the results; and he rewarded the entire team when they achieved success.

Many companies with more money, more resources, and better connections started in the discounting profession the same time as Walmart. In fact, in 1962, four companies with bright futures started discounting models: Kmart from the Kresge business, Woolco from the Woolworth business, and Target from the Dayton-Hudson business. All formed discounting models along with a small variety retailer from Bentonville, Arkansas. Within five years, Kmart had 250 stores and $800 million in revenue, compared to the small Arkansas firm of 19 stores and $9 million in revenue; but by creating a leadership culture, David beat Goliath in the long run. Walton reminisced, "Here's what makes me laugh today: it would have been absolutely impossible to convince anybody back then that in thirty years most all of the early discounters would be gone, that three of the four new chains would be the biggest, best-run operators in the business, that the one to fold up would be Woolco, and that the biggest, most profitable one would be the one down in Arkansas. Sometimes even I have trouble believing it."

In a true free-enterprise system, where companies must serve customers, the company that wins consistently is the one that serves the customer better, regardless of its size or connections. Walton wrote, "You start with a given: free enterprise is the engine of society; communism is pretty much down the drain and proven so; and there doesn't appear to be anything that can compare to a free society based on a market economy. Nothing can touch the system—not unless leadership and management get selfish and lazy." Paul Harvey, a celebrated radio host, provided "the rest of the story" about Walmart when he said, "What you've created here is better than communism, better than socialism could ever be, better even than capitalism. I like to call what you've got here 'enlightened consumerism,' where everybody works together as a team and the customer is finally king again." Harvey captured the marvel of Walton's success: a leadership culture whose design was predicated on satisfying the customer as its reason for existence.

Walton's story is a message for all those concerned about America and the West—a story of dreams, struggles, and eventually, impressive victories.

## CHAPTER 10

# CONFLICT RESOLUTION
## Resolved: To Develop the Art and Science of Conflict Resolution

*I know that relationship bombs and unresolved conflicts destroy a community's unity and growth.*

When a person builds a following through his character and competence, he needs to learn the art of conflict resolution in order to maintain trust. In fact, one of the most important arts of leadership, and also one of the least understood, is the art of conflict resolution. Whether one is leading a business, a church, or a charitable organization, the ability to resolve conflict is essential. If one thinks of beautiful cities, he will find that these cities have developed specific processes to purge themselves of garbage that they know will be created. The process starts with collecting and transporting garbage, until it is eventually burned in an incinerator or placed in a landfill. Every city must plan for collecting, processing, and removing garbage. In the same way, leaders must develop a plan to handle and purge conflict issues that will arise within an organization. Just as garbage is removed from a city, so must conflict be resolved in communities. Issues will come up— that is part of human nature—and resolving conflicts directly at the source will strengthen relationships through a better understanding of the expectations from all sides. This is one of the key skills of successful leaders. Gus Lee emphasized the destructiveness of not addressing conflict, writing, "Conflict aversion is the organizational bubonic plague of our times. It is cowardice wearing

> **Whether one is leading a business, a church or a charitable organization, the ability to resolve conflict is essential.**

215

a smart, politically-correct hat. The hat allows it entry into all human organizations, where it befuddles, ensnarls, and twists communication. It turns dialogue from a leadership tool into a virus to which only a precious few are immune." Cowardice in organizations must be eradicated, root and branch.

Conflict, like fire, is easier to snuff out when it's small but can become nearly impossible to handle when allowed to spread unchecked. Imagine, before going to bed, a person glances at a corner and notices a small flame flickering; hopefully, he wouldn't choose to ignore it until the next morning because he surely wouldn't have a house by then. Likewise, ignoring conflict is foolish, as a person might lose his relationships if he is unwilling to address conflict when it arises. Many times, the danger that small conflicts pose is not recognized. But just as leaving a small fire in a house unattended is unwise, not dealing with small conflicts is foolish because they can cause great destruction if left unattended. Conflict is a given in all personal relationships since human beings are imperfect. Moreover, every relationship requires nurturing to maintain the bond of friendship. There aren't any "no maintenance" relationships. How a person treats his relationships by fostering them, maintaining them, and resolving conflicts through open communication determines a leader's speed of trust. When a person doesn't have the ability to resolve conflict while issues are still small, the issues turn into raging forest fires, damaging many innocent bystanders along the way. It takes courage to address conflict. While cowards willingly sacrifice innocent bystanders, leaders address a conflict with the intent of finding a resolution, knowing that communities cannot grow with broken trust and that unresolved conflict breaks trust.

## Imperfect People Have Imperfect Relationships

Even when leaders are operating with character, conflicts still arise. Human beings are capable of so much good but remain imperfect, impetuous, and unreasonable, not to mention, overly emotional at times. In a community, love is the bond that holds relationships together when disappointments arise. Only a coward dwells on his hurts, running them over and over like instant replays in his mind, while, simultaneously avoiding the one individual capable of salving his wound. But why is conflict resolution feared? Lee explained, "We fear looking bad, even in our own minds. We fear hurt pride, repercussions from genuine discussions, being wrong, looking out of step, seeming awkward, being isolated.

Not big things. Small ones. This stops us from acting courageously and therefore wisely." Without a resolution, bitterness and resentment build up in a person; this is like drinking poison and expecting someone else to die. Refuse to get bitter and instead get braver— brave enough to sit down with the person you are in conflict with, seeking to understand why both of your expectations were not fulfilled. Improper conflict resolution can cause a small issue to ruin a long-standing friendship, usually because the offended party prefers to nurse the hurt rather than nurture the relationship. How sad for both parties, not to mention for the community, who suffer from the residual damage associated with the immature actions of one or both parties. These actions must be understood and avoided as they are major relationship bombs that throw gas onto conflict fires.

## Relationship Bombs

Relationship bombs are improper actions dropped on relationships that make simple conflict much more complex. Just as bombs in a war expand destruction to include many nonparticipants, relationship bombs expand the damage of conflict to include an entire community. There are two major types of relationship bombs—silence and violence. The first is formed by dwelling on hurts without addressing the appropriate party concerned, building pretense, hypocrisy, and animosity within a person who is harboring a poisonous brew. The second is formed by gossiping to others and being unwilling to discuss the issue with the party concerned. This typically results from the first relationship bomb since harboring poison is arduous work; eventually, the "venomous poison" will no longer be able to be contained and it will spread through gossip. Silence leads to poisoning the person who has clammed up, while violence is assassinating another's character with a loose tongue. Both are symptoms of cowardice and unaddressed conflict. Even when a person falls into a conflict with someone, it doesn't mean that he should drop a relationship bomb on the person. This is counterproductive and prevents any meaningful conflict resolution. In fact, both of these bombs must be permanently removed from a leader's arsenal of tools and techniques. They are simply not healthy, productive, or principle-centered. When a community approves relationship bombing, restorations become difficult, if not nearly impossible, and the residual damage lingers on even when an apparent resolution has been achieved, often damaging many innocent third parties. In today's relationship-bombing culture, communities that cease relationship bombing are the ones that will thrive and move ahead.

## Silence

The first factor that leads to silence is when a person fears confronting the conflict more than he fears dealing with the ongoing results of the conflict. In this situation, a person, instead of addressing the concerned individual, chooses to nurse the hurt, building bitterness and resentment. Everyone should make it a rule that if a person thinks about a hurt more than once, not being able to forgive the other party, he should address the issue promptly in a spirit of understanding, not with an attacking spirit. Too often, it seems that the offended party plays god, assigning malicious motives to the other person's actions without giving the person the benefit of the doubt. It's hard enough to determine one's own motives, let alone omnisciently know the motives of others. Refuse to play a godlike role; instead, be a friend to others when a conflict arises. By assuming the best of intentions on the part of the other party, one will find less bitterness and a more conciliatory spirit, reflecting less on the hurt and more on the time one has spent fellowshipping with the person with whom he is having the troubled relationship.

> **Everyone should make it a rule that if a person thinks about a hurt more than once, not being able to forgive the other party, he should address the issue promptly.**

The second factor that hinders conflict resolution is the near-limitless ability of human beings to deceive themselves. Self-deception allows one to place all the blame, all the responsibility, and all the need for apologies on the other party, leaving oneself only with all the hurt. Is it even possible for one side to be totally innocent, while the other side is completely to blame? In order to combat self-deception, pause before you judge, pray before you become bitter, and think about the entire situation from the vantage point of the other person. Perhaps after doing this, you will find the part of the issue where you are at fault.

Empathy, the ability to view the situation from another person's perspective, is essential in combating self-deceit. It frees a person, helping him let go of offenses by understanding a conflict from another person's viewpoint and replacing a judgmental spirit with a graceful, forgiving one. He thinks through the chain of events, asking himself, "What could I have done differently?" By making each conflict a "teachable moment," one learns many valuable lessons to apply in the future. The bigger the heart of the leader is, the quicker he is to take responsibility, seeking resolution for the benefit of the entire community. Remember, a leader always apologizes first, focuses on another person's position, and addresses issues, not with an attacking spirit, but with a truthful one.

The third factor that hinders relationship restoration is when people hold on to hurts to justify quitting on responsibilities or their communities. Many times, when a person is afraid to address changes needed on the inside, he seeks offense on the outside with no intention of seeking resolution. In other words, an unresolved internal conflict pours out of him and silent offenses are used as reasons to break off relationships. Usually, this process starts at the subconscious level, and the person creates a conflict to justify quitting, replacing the real reason for quitting—his lack of courage—with a scapegoat reason, which is his silent conflict with others. Of course, he refuses to sit down and address the conflict for fear that if it gets resolved, he will lose his justification for breaking off community relationships. People looking for an excuse to exit a group will avoid conflict resolution at all costs, or else their humpty-dumpty justifications for quitting will fall apart, never to be put back together. Leaders who understand this phenomenon resolve to love the people in their communities, refusing to be the reason another person can use to leave a community. Remember, hurting people hurt other people. However, instead of attacking back and giving them a justification to break off fellowship, apply grace and love to your relationship, empathizing with their fears of inadequacy until they understand their potential to change. This gives people time to address their internal conflicts, improving themselves and thus the community.

## Violence

The second relationship bomb—violence— is endemic to our violent modern culture. People either attack others physically or practice the more cowardly version: assassinate others' reputations through gossip. In the Bible, character assassinations are just one level removed from an actual assassination. When a conflict is not resolved, it doesn't go

> **When conflict is not resolved, it doesn't go away; it only goes underground.**

away; it only goes underground. Gossip is cowardly yet, sadly, very common. Conflict will be discussed either with the people involved to resolve the conflict or with countless others to justify one's behavior. If one's actions are just, why not simply sit down with the other party to address the issue by following the conflict resolution process? Regretfully, many communities have been ruined by gossip more than any other behavioral issue because gossip separates friends, breaks trust, and makes a resolution difficult. A popular story portrays the disastrous effects of gossip:

> The story is told of a peasant with a troubled conscience who went to a monk for advice. He said he had circulated a vile story about a friend, only to find out the story was not true. "If you want to make peace with your conscience," said the monk, "you must fill a bag with chicken down, go to every dooryard in the village, and drop in each one of them one fluffy feather."
>
> The peasant did as he was told. Then, he came back to the monk and announced he had done penance for his folly. "Not yet," replied the monk. "Take your bag to the rounds again and gather up every feather that you have dropped."
>
> "But the wind must have blown them all away," said the peasant.
>
> "Yes, my son," said the monk, "and so it is with gossip. Words are easily dropped, but no matter how hard you try, you can never get them back again."

Gossip spreads its net wide, which is why proper conflict resolution is so vital for healthy communities. Without a resolution, one or both parties will seek to justify their positions by character-assassinating the other. This hurts both parties' reputations, as well as the many innocent people who should never have to deal with the dirty laundry. Can anyone imagine dumping garbage on a neighbor's front lawn? This is what gossip, in effect, does. When someone attempts to "dump garbage" or cast aspersion on another person's character, a person's role isn't to take sides but to become the facilitator for an urgent restoration. Anyone planning on leading a large community must master conflict resolution and teach it to his community, having no tolerance for endless gossipers.

Stephen Covey explained, "One of the most important ways to manifest integrity is to be loyal to those who are not present. In doing so, we build the trust of those who are present. When you defend those who are absent, you retain the trust of those present." If someone gossips about another person, ask him, "Can I quote you on this?" Only a few, it seems, desire to be quoted. One may not have asked for a mediation role, but when a leader is drawn into a circle of gossip, he becomes part of the solution rather than part of the problem by telling a concerned individual, "Either go back to the person and address it alone, or both of us will go to the person and address the situation." Either way, one must follow through until resolution is achieved for the sake of the relationship and the rest of the community. These are the only two options since proper leadership refuses to gossip and insists on addressing and resolving conflict.

## Communication Triangulation

When dealing with a conflict, don't fall victim to communication triangulation, a vile process where people attempt to draw others into gossip from their unresolved conflicts. As Joseph Stowell writes, "The 'juicy morsels' stay with us, permanently staining our perceptions of and appreciation for those about whom we are hearing. The vicious chain of gossip continues until it finally comes up against someone willing to stop spreading information about feuding factions and start praying. Only then will the fire die down." Why would anyone willingly choose to help assassinate one of his friends by listening to gossip? Unless a person is asking an individual to help mediate a conflict and achieve a resolution, in which case, the mediator hears both sides of the story, he is simply gossiping, no matter what his claimed intentions are. Instead of falling victim to this sickness, follow the process described by Kibbie Ruth and Karen McClintock of Alban, keeping the focus on resolving conflict, not on furthering gossip or taking sides:

> While people often suggest that venting is good for the soul, it is actually not very productive. Venting to someone about a third person is simply an avoidance technique that creates what is known in counseling theory as a relationship triangle, or triangulation. Triangulation is talking about feelings, opinions, or personal issues regarding some person or group with a third party instead of with the person or group actually concerned. Relationship triangles usually involve three people who each take one of three roles: victim, persecutor, and rescuer. Once in a triangle, people change places among its three points. The only way to stop the triangulation is for each person to communicate his or her feelings, concerns, or opinions directly to the other.

221

Of course, the best communication strategy is to avoid being recruited to a triangle in the first place. However, so often, well-intentioned leaders and congregants listen to a person's concerns, feelings, or opinions and then realize they have inadvertently let themselves be co-opted, becoming involved and sometimes even taking sides. Once an individual is in a triangle, escaping may require some courage and clarity, but it is possible. A triangulated person can redirect a concerned person straight to the appropriate individual or committee—the one who is actually involved in the issues or the one who can address the concern or mend the relationship. A three-way conversation sometimes helps, but only if the third party facilitates without taking sides or having an agenda, without speaking for any of the parties, and without adding to the emotional drama.

The gossiper quickly learns that communication triangulation isn't condoned in the community and that if he refuses to go directly to the person he has gossiped about, then he will be called out by being quoted. This does two key things. First, it let's everyone know that one isn't a gossiper. Second, by protecting the party not present, one builds trust throughout the organization, as others know that he will do the same for them when needed. Through these actions, a person displays his scorn for gossipers, refusing to be drawn into a foolish losing triangulation game. Only by addressing a conflict directly can the merry-go-round of gossip and lies end. Organizations cannot thrive in a negative environment; therefore, the gossiping garbage must be cleaned out of, not cultivated within, one's community.

## Five Steps for Conflict Resolution

Now that we have avoided the "relationship bombs" that blow up even long-term relationships, let's discuss how to confront a situation and resolve it with the goal of improving the relationship with the individual with whom one is having a conflict. Over the years, I have, by reading books and studying great leaders, developed a five-step pattern for resolving conflict. Conflict will occur; whether it's addressed and resolved or left alone to keep festering is up to the leaders. I know of no other process that leaders can apply within their communities that will yield as positive a result as mastering the conflict resolution process. Conversely, I know of nothing that will destroy a community quicker than conflict aversion, or avoiding dealing with a conflict. The five-step process will only work when both parties want to resolve the conflict, which, surprisingly, isn't a given. If both parties are not sold out to the idea that the relationship is more important than the conflict, then no amount of effort from one party will resolve the issue. It takes two or more to get into a conflict, and it requires the same parties to resolve it. Relationships can bring so much joy into a person's life; on the other hand, damaged relationships can bring a great deal of heartache. Mastering the ability to re-

> **It takes two or more to get into a conflict, and it requires the same parties to resolve it.**

solve a conflict quickly will improve your relationship and leadership influence. To resolve any conflict, we must assume that both parties desire resolution and are willing to sit down in person and have a face-to-face meeting to discuss the issue. This is a major point in resolving any conflict because one cannot pick up on the unspoken cues of body language over the phone, through email, etc. If both parties do not agree to meet in person, then, most likely, one of the parties no longer values the relationship enough to expend the time and effort to resolve the conflict and restore the relationship. But when one learns to apply the five steps of conflict resolution, relationships, instead of being hurt and lost, will be strengthened through each misunderstanding.

1. Affirm the relationship.
2. Seek to understand.
3. Seek to be understood.
4. Own responsibility by apologizing.
5. Seek agreement.

The first step is to affirm the relationship before diving into the details. An example opening statement to start the process of resolution is, "I am here, even though it's uncomfortable, because I value our relationship and would rather be uncomfortable while resolving our misunderstandings than be comfortable with the misunderstandings in our relationship." If you think about it, a person must value the relationship if he is willing to sit down and talk; if he didn't, why would he sit down for a conflict resolution at all? Let the other party know how important the relationship is. If amenable to it, one can even ask for prayer before initiating the five steps. The goal of the affirmations is for both parties to validate each other as human beings in a valued relationship. When hurtful issues are addressed later, both sides should understand that the goal isn't to attack a person but to address behaviors and underlying issues. People are affirmed, issues are addressed, and behavior adjustments are made to restore, if not strengthen, the relationship. In the best-selling book *Crucial Conversations*, the authors teach on creating a safe environment where true communication flourishes by pouring all thoughts into a shared pool of meaning:

> When two or more of us enter crucial conversations, by definition we don't share the same pool. Our opinions differ. I believe one thing, you another. I have one history, you another.
>
> People who are skilled at dialogue do their best to make it safe for everyone to add their meaning to the shared pool— even if the ideas, at first glance, appear controversial, wrong, or at odds with their own beliefs.

The second step of the process is to seek to understand the other person's thinking and viewpoints. This is a critical step. The objective should be to listen intently, seeking to see the conflict from the other's perspective, not attempting to justify one's own position. One should let the other party know that he is there to listen and understand his thoughts and views. By providing the freedom for the other party to share his feelings, hurts, and thoughts, a person can expand his insights into how the conflict started and think through solutions to ensure better conduct in the future. One has to allow the other party to unburden himself, not taking the words personally, but professionally, always remembering that hurting people can hurt other people; by doing so, hopefully, one can purge the other party of any bitterness building within him. In other words, one should be curious, not furious. It's only after listening to the other party and asking questions to clarify and understand, that one should consider moving to the next step. A person isn't seeking to defend his actions here but rather to get a clear understanding of the other party's position, expressing concern over the pain caused by the conflict. Even though hurting others is not one's intention, it usually is the effect; therefore, one needs an empathetic spirit before one shares his perspective of the issues. Many times, the hurt comes from an expectation not met by one or both parties. Better communication reduces false expectations and the subsequent conflicts surrounding them. After listening, one should state back to the other person the concerns addressed, summarizing and affirming his views. Genuinely listening to another person is one of the most affirming things that one can do for another, helping both parties to resolve any misunderstandings.

**One should be curious, not furious**

The third step in the process is to seek to be understood. By this time, a person has taken the time to sit down with the other, affirmed the value of the relationship, and listened to the other's viewpoint. Only after these steps have been accomplished is a person ready to respectfully share about the issues from his perspective. Hopefully, by being affirmed and having received deposits in his love/respect tank, the other party will listen intently to one's thoughts and feelings. The goal isn't to blast the other person but to address the issues, sharing where things can be handled differently in the future. Remember, resolution, not justification, is the object. This requires both sides to be honest about the parts they played in the conflict, as it always "takes two to Tango." One must bring up the issues, but he shouldn't assign motives to the other. For example, a person might state that the other party neglected him by not calling. When he states that the other party intentionally didn't call, he leaves the realm of humanity and enters God's, as only God knows a person's motives. In fact, it's hard enough to discern one's own motives, let alone claim to know the motives of others. Share the tough issues without being dogmatic ("you always" or "you never"). Give the other party as much benefit of the doubt as possible. The Bible states, "love covers a multitude of sins" (I Peter 4:8, New Living Translation). In most cases, if the other party has been affirmed, listened to, and loved, the willingness to accept some responsibility for the conflict is increased, making resolution possible. If a person focuses on incorrect behaviors and actions, rather than on incorrect people and motives, the chances of resolution are greatly increased.

The fourth step is to own as much of the conflict as possible while still being truthful. Leaders search for teachable moments, or areas where they can improve, in every conflict resolution. The objective is for both parties to see where one's actions caused pain to the other person, leading to an apologetic spirit and a restored relationship. Why do so many people struggle with apologizing for their hurtful actions? Many people, even though they know they aren't perfect, seem unwilling to admit their imperfection by apologizing; therefore, they leave a trail of broken relationships in their wake. But every leader learns that a genuine apology creates more good will than a thousand justifications ever will.

A great example demonstrating the power of an apology was illustrated in a story from *Crucial Conversations*. The story told of an Executive VP who asked a local supervisor for a tour to learn about a new manufacturing process. Six hourly workers volunteered to work late, preparing for the anticipated tour. The supervisor, upon discovering that the VP had formed plans that were harmful to the quality of the operations, made a leadership decision to skip the tour, using the remaining hour to address his concerns with the VP's direction instead of going on the tour and avoiding the issue. Although he changed the VP's mind, saving the jobs of his employees, he forgot to inform his team, leaving them wondering what was going on. As the supervisor was escorting the VP to his car, he ran into his six disappointed employees. *Crucial Conversations* described what happened next:

> "We pulled an all-nighter, and you didn't even bother to come by! That's the last time we are busting our hump for you!"
> Time stands still. The conversation has just turned crucial. The employees who had worked so hard are obviously upset. They feel disrespected.
> But you miss the point. Why? Because now you feel disrespected. They've attacked you. So you stay stuck in the content of the conversation—thinking this has something to do with the factory tour.
> "I had to choose between the future of the company and the plant tour. I chose our future, and I'd do it again if I had to."

Both sides were now fighting for respect and were not truly communicating with one another. Instead of defending his violated respect, a person should attempt to see the other's actions as violated trust and restore the trust by apologizing. *Crucial Conversations* shared this proper response: "I'm sorry I didn't give you a call when I learned that we wouldn't be coming by. You worked all night, it would have been a wonderful chance to showcase your improvements, and I didn't even explain what happened. I apologize." Since we all know we aren't perfect, revealing this fact to others by apologizing doesn't have to be a monumental revelation. In fact, the higher a person climbs the leadership ladder, the more he has to apologize to others simply because, as a leader, he juggles many things at the same time, causing some to be dropped accidentally. When the supervisor apologized, he restored trust in the relationship, and so he was able to explain what happened without having to defend himself. Alexander Pope, the great English writer, declared, "To err is human, to forgive divine." Leaders will err, and then sincerely apologize. Leaders will also be hurt by others, but a good leader must respond with sincere forgiveness when apologies are offered. If two people genuinely value their relationship and willingly follow the five-step process for resolution, then their conflict will be resolved.

The fifth and final step in the process is to seek agreement in roles and responsibilities for partnerships in the future. Both parties have been affirmed, both sides have been heard, apologies have been made where appropriate, and now an agreement, which is designed to unite and strengthen the relationship, is confirmed. Flushing the issues out of the relationship leaves only stronger bonds of love, unity, and trust. Seeking agreement conveys the strengths of both parties in accomplishing their community's objectives, affirming again the value of the relationship to work together for the common good. The vision of their community aligns the task of each person, creating a unity in the team and generating results much easier because of the interdependence among the leaders. Agreement between two leaders is a form of a "buy in," making both leaders desire unity in the team to accomplish a mission bigger than either of their own missions. Conflict between them is now in the past, and the restored unity will lead to greater accomplishments in the future. Unity in a community creates harmony and good results; conversely, disunity in a community creates disharmony and decline. Leaders understand that conflict is a given, while resolution is a choice.

I have been personally blessed with many long-term relationships, including my relationship with Laurie, my wife of nineteen years, as well as my relationships with leaders like Chris Brady, Tim Marks, George Guzzardo, Claude Hamilton, Bill Lewis, and Dan Hawkins, who have been my friends and business partners for more than a decade. Conflicts certainly arose, but by practicing the methods of conflict resolution discussed above, not only did we resolve our issues, but we strengthened our relationships. Trust is built between conflicting parties when both know that the other values their relationship more than he values his pride of being right on all points. In fact, conflict resolution provides the best teachable moments on blind spots in one's life.

**Why should one run from conflict resolution when it is one of the best learning experiences around?**

Why should one run away from conflict resolution when it is one of the best learning experiences around? Only when pride gets out of control and people value their egos more than truth do they slide down the slippery slope of character assassination and conflict resolution procrastination. Communities that choose to follow the five steps of conflict resolution will enjoy the strength of unity, which will propel them to unusual results.

### Lewis and Tolkien: Lost Friends

What happens when two of the most prolific writers and friends allow little slights and misunderstandings to go unaddressed? Moreover, how is it possible that two men, who did so much to advance the cause of good in this world, failed to maintain a good relationship? The answer is similar to the answer G. K. Chesterton once gave to the question "What's wrong with the world?" Chesterton's essay was short and to the point: "Dear Sirs, I am. Sincerely yours, G. K. Chesterton."

No matter how deeply held a person's friendship is, the pesky little thing called self that's inside each and every person can cause trouble with even the closest of friendships.

C. S. Lewis and J. R. R. Tolkien didn't start their relationship with a conflict. Indeed, the two shared a unique friendship built on three key principles, which sharpened the iron of both: a common interest, a consistent stream of encouragement to one another, and a permission to speak truthfully in love. One can see all three principles at work in the story of their friendship. It was the magnitude of this friendship that permitted both authors to become better writers than either of them would have been on his own.

Author Colin Duriez, in an interview about Lewis and Tolkien, was asked, "You have said that Lewis and Tolkien shared three interrelated commitments—to 'romanticism, reason, and Christianity.' Can you elaborate?" This was his answer:

> The two friends were interested in the literature of the romantic period because many of the poems and stories attempted to convey the supernatural, the "otherworldly"—and thus provided a window into spiritual things. Lewis explored romantic themes like joy and longing, and Tolkien emphasized the nature of people as storytelling beings who by telling stories reflect the creative powers of God. But they both rejected an "instinctive" approach to the imagination. Many romantic writers were interested in a kind of nature mysticism. They looked within themselves and at the world around them and sought flashes of insight into "the nature of things"—illuminations of truth that could not be explained, reasoned, or sys-

tematized. But Lewis and Tolkien insisted that the reason and the imagination must be integrated. In any understanding of truth, the whole person must be involved.

In 1929, when Tolkien gave Lewis the poetic version of Beren and Lúthien called *The Lay of Leithian*, it was already apparent that Lewis was Tolkien's greatest encourager. Lewis wrote to Tolkien after reading it: "I can quite honestly say that it is ages since I have had an evening of such delight: and the personal interest of reading a friend's work had very little to do with it. . . . The two things that come out clearly are the sense of reality in the background and the mythical value: the essence of a myth being that it should have no taint of allegory to the maker yet it should suggest incipient allegories to the reader."

Lewis was careful not to offend the delicate ego of Tolkien, having learned to speak truth with love to his friend. Lewis knew that Tolkien's response to criticism was either to ignore the criticism, along with the author of it, or to start over with a complete rewrite. Lewis commented, "His standard of self-criticism was high and the mere suggestion of publication usually set him upon a revision in the course of which so many new ideas occurred to him that where his friends had hoped for the final text of an old work they actually got the first draft of a new one." Lewis learned to offer suggestions to his friend by indirect methods, desiring to help Tolkien's work without hurting his friend. After reading *The Lay of Leithian* and praising it profusely, Lewis waited nearly a year before writing fourteen pages of mock academic commentary, presented as make-believe German critics, sharing profound suggestions for Tolkien's poem in a nonoffensive manner. Many of the suggestions were implemented by Tolkien, who appreciated the feedback given as a spoof, learning through the humor without feeling attacked personally.

It was their common interest that brought them together, and it was the love for truth that deepened their relationship. But it was the respect and encouragement given to each other that made them best of friends. Friendships that have these qualities are rare and should be cultivated with tender loving care, as they have a value that's beyond any price. Ethan

Gilsdorf studied extensively the unique friendship between these two authors and wrote:

> Intellectually, they craved each other's companionship. But their relationship had emotional depth as well. They bonded over their harrowing experiences in the trenches of World War I. They shared the loss of their parents, which they had both endured as children. Sorrow over their pasts and their retreat from modernity gave them nowhere to go but their imaginations. They lost themselves in anachronistic tales and created make-believe places— engaging in what today we might disparagingly call "escapism." Of course, the realms of Lewis' Narnia and Tolkien's Middle-earth are fraught with troubles, wars, and imperfections, at least as much as our so-called real world.

The two authors made each other better, maintaining a close relationship for well over a decade despite major differences in temperaments. Lewis was socially extroverted, outgoing, and voluble, developing friends across the world with his professional achievements in books and broadcasting, which reached the pinnacle of worldly success in 1947, when he graced the cover of *Time* magazine.

Tolkien, on the other hand, was socially introverted—reserved and soft-spoken. Despite his professional competence, writing groundbreaking essays on *Beowulf* and translating many early Anglo-Saxon works, he did not achieve the same level of professional fame in his lifetime as his younger cohort. Compounding this frustration was the fact that Tolkien's peers, his professorial colleagues at Oxford, were unable or unwilling to recognize the genius of his Middle-Earth creation, ridiculing his second life of wizards, dragons, and rings and denigrating him and his work by asking, "How is your hobbit?"

Lewis's second life, on the other hand, was readily accepted, opening doors for Lewis wherever he turned. His Christian sermons were entertaining, informative, and thought-provoking, not to mention highly popular. In fact, by the 1940s, between his BBC broadcasts and his best-selling *The Screwtape Letters*, Lewis was a bona fide international figure. His first *The Chronicles of Narnia* book was released in 1950, which fueled his fame even further. Lewis easily eclipsed, at least at that time, the success of his friend Tolkien.

Lewis's schedule, along with Tolkien's unspoken but strongly felt desire for quality time, led to several unaddressed issues that began to chill their once-warm friendship. The first issue was Lewis's meteoric rise to success, forcing Lewis to divide his time among his many interests, reducing the quality and quantity of time he could spend with Tolkien. The second issue, Tolkien's twinge of jealousy, arose when he compared his monumental efforts and moderate successes with his friend's seemingly moderate efforts and monumental successes. Sadly, their rift grew bigger, although with a little more understanding and communication on Lewis's part and a willingness on Tolkien's to discuss his hurts openly, the friendship could have, and should have, thrived through the changing seasons of life.

When issues are not discussed, envy and jealousy rear their ugly heads. What makes the poison of unaddressed jealousy so damaging to friendships is that its acids are poured directly into the roots of the relationship. Tolkien, by nature, was not a jealous man; but he valued Lewis's fellowship so greatly that when fame pulled on his friend's time, a silent, subtle, but all-pervasive hurt corroded the bonds that bound them. Tolkien, the introvert, was troubled because he no longer had Lewis's undivided attention. Lewis, the extrovert, on the other hand, was overjoyed with his new celebrity status, making new friends everywhere he went. By the time Lewis had departed from Oxford, accepting a chair of literature at Cambridge, the two friends were speaking less regularly than probably either preferred. Time and distance, plus the unspoken hurts, had tempered their fruitful collaborations. Their differences in beliefs, personalities, and opinions could not cause a crack in their relationship; but Lewis's move to Cambridge, his new friends, and his subsequent marriage did. All these ripped apart the unity that had made them the best of friends. Fueling the stress, and further dividing the friendship, was Lewis's prodigious book-writing exploits. He literally completed the seven-book Narnia series in seven years—a torrid pace, writing a book every year!

Tolkien, in contrast, toiled for over seventeen years on *The Lord of the Rings*, rewriting it numerous times in the pursuit of perfection. He worked tirelessly with no applause before releasing it. Eventually, the world would learn of his remarkable gifts, just as it had learned of Lewis's previously; but sadly, it was too late to repair the frayed friendship.

*The Lord of the Rings* became the fourth best-selling book series of all time, topping Lewis's *The Chronicles of Narnia*, the fifth best-selling series. Lewis would not have been surprised, having predicted his friend's success many years before. In 1954, he wrote, "This book is like lightning from a clear sky. It represents 'the conquest of new territory.'" In a letter written to a friend, Lewis shared that the book "would inaugurate a new age."

Tolkien, however, having swallowed the poison of his own pain, began to believe that Lewis didn't like his work, writing in 1967, four years after his friend's death, "To tell the truth, [Lewis] never really liked hobbits very much." Tolkien had grossly misread his friend, as nothing could have been farther from the facts, as Lewis was enthralled by *The Lord of the Rings* series, believing in Tolkien and his fantasy fiction years before anyone else had heard of Middle-Earth. Lewis was one of the first people to recognize Tolkien's genius.

In his book, Duriez discussed a 1964 letter where Tolkien described the fraying of his friendship with Lewis: "We saw less and less of one another after he came under the dominant influence of Charles Williams"—a writer whom Tolkien perceived as a wedge between himself and Lewis—"and still less after his very strange marriage." That marriage was to Joy Gresham, which was unacceptable to Tolkien because she was divorced and an American. Although Tolkien later called Lewis "his closest friend from about 1927 to 1940," by the early 1950s, their friendship had soured.

For fourteen years, the two men were best friends, leading to two of the most prolific and productive series of works in the written history of mankind. When Lewis accepted the Chair in Medieval and Renaissance Literature at Cambridge in 1954, a position that Tolkien ironically helped him obtain, the fire of their friendship died down due to lack of oxygen, although the remaining embers smoldered for the rest of their lives. Lewis leaving Oxford was similar to Frodo leaving the Shire, choosing the adventure of the unknown in the Undying Lands rather than the peace and security of the comfortable Shire:

> "But I thought you were going to enjoy the Shire too for years and years, after all you have done," said Sam, choking on his tears.
>
> Frodo, looking at Sam, resolutely replied, "So I thought too, once. But I have been too deeply hurt, Sam."

Like Frodo, both Lewis and Tolkien were hurt, carrying their unresolved pains to their graves, apparently missing each other dearly but unwilling to resolve their issues. When Tolkien heard of Lewis's passing in 1963, he wrote to his daughter that it felt "like an axe-blow near the roots."

Reflecting on their lives, I believe there are few, if any, friendships in recorded history that have had as great an impact on both friends as Lewis and Tolkien did on each other. The two Oxford professors created a lasting legacy by loving, respecting, and encouraging one another and utilizing the gifts given to them by the Author of all gifts. Therefore, they accomplished what they set out to achieve and fulfilled their God-given purposes. The bad, however, is an equally "teachable moment." When two friends who love each other dearly do not communicate, petty jealousies and enviousness, which can poison the hearts of one or both of them, are bound to develop. There is no such thing as a "no maintenance" relationship; therefore, it is wise to constantly nurture one's friendships through words, thoughts, and deeds. In addition, when misunderstandings arise, a person must deal with them immediately and not stew on them for months. Imagine if Tolkien, when he thought about Lewis's neglect of their friendship for the second time, had sat down with Lewis in person, spoken from his heart, and resolved the conflict while it was still small. Who knows what this collaboration of geniuses would have produced!

In spite of the fact that Lewis and Tolkien drifted apart, I would say that the world is still a better place today because on a spring day in 1926, two professors met and became inseparable friends, providing the oxygen to each other that lit fires, setting the world aflame with stories of faith, hope, and redemption and their enduring legacies.

CHAPTER 11

# SYSTEMS
## Resolved: To Develop Systems Thinking

*I know that by viewing life as interconnected patterns rather than isolated events, I improve my leverage.*

## What is a System?

Systems are everywhere. Indeed, both nature and organizations operate with innumerable systems. Nature is filled with ecosystems involving air, water, plants, animals, and more in organized patterns to sustain life, while organizational systems consist of people, structures, and processes that interact to produce results.

One can take something as basic as filling a glass of water and see that it is a simple system because there is a systematic way to achieve a specific result. Filling the glass with water follows an ongoing water regulation system involving a PDCA between the person's mind, the faucet, and the glass.

First, a person creates a plan to fill a specific glass with water from a chosen faucet. Second, he initiates action by placing the glass under the faucet and turning the faucet on. Third, he checks the gap between desired water level in the glass and the current level. Fourth, as the water fills the glass, he adjusts the faucet until it is turned completely off when the desired water level is reached. If something as remedial as filling a glass with water is a system, imagine how many systems have been misidentified by leaders, who, in their attempt to improve a situation, only made it worse for their lack of a systematic mind-set. Regretfully, the more specialized our world becomes, the less systematic most people think.

Peter Senge, in his classic book *The Fifth Discipline*, gave the following description:

> Systems thinking is a discipline for seeing wholes. It is a framework for seeing interrelationships rather than things, for seeing patterns of change rather than static "snapshots."...
>
> Today, systems thinking is needed more than ever because we are becoming overwhelmed by complexity. Perhaps for the first time in history, humankind has the capacity to create far more information than anyone can absorb, to foster far greater interdependency than anyone can manage, and to accelerate change far faster than anyone's ability to keep pace...
>
> Systems thinking is the antidote to this sense of helplessness that many feel as we enter the "age of interdependence." Systems thinking is a discipline for seeing the "structures" that underlie complex situations, and for discerning high from low leverage change.

This is why systems thinking is so invaluable to a leader. In order to think systematically, though, one must learn to recognize the system and its parts, or put another way, the forest and the trees.

## Parts or Whole?

Detailed knowledge on specialized fields has helped man improve his quality of life by dividing the workload into manageable tasks, but it also has a downside. The fractionalization of knowledge, caused by specialization, has taught many to be experts in one tree, while remaining clueless on the forest that one lives in. The story of the blind men and the elephant displays the effects of fractionalized knowledge, revealing how snapshots of individual truths must be connected together to receive a larger view of truth:

Once upon a time, there lived six blind men in a village. One day, the villagers told them, "Hey, there is an elephant in the village today."

The blind men had no idea what an elephant was. They decided, "Even though we would not be able to see it, let us go and feel it anyway." All of them were guided to the elephant, and every one of them touched it.

"Hey, the elephant is a pillar," said the first man, who touched the leg. "Oh, no! It is like a rope," said the second man, who touched the tail. "Oh, no! It is like a thick branch of a tree," said the third man, who touched the trunk of the elephant. "It is like a big hand fan," said the fourth man, who touched the ear of the elephant. "It is like a huge wall," said the fifth man, who touched the belly of the elephant. "It is like a solid pipe," said the sixth man, who touched the tusk of the elephant.

They began to argue about the elephant, and every one of them insisted that he was right. It looked like they were getting agitated, each blind man wondering how the others could be so stupid and each believing he had the truth since he felt it with his own hands.

A wise man was passing by, and he saw this. He stopped and asked them, "What is the matter?" They said, "We cannot agree to what the elephant is like." Each one of them told what he thought the elephant was like.

The wise man calmly explained to them, "All of you are right and all of you are wrong. The reason each of you is telling it differently is because each one of you touched a different part of the elephant. Each of you has a partial truth. The elephant has all the features that each of you described, but isn't fully what you described unless you combine all of your answers."

Each of the blind men had touched on a truth of the elephant, but none of them had the whole truth. How many issues in life stem from people arguing from their specific experiences, insisting on their version of truth when actually, in many cases, the truth cannot be understood without a systematic mind-set? Only when individuals realize that all are parts of the system will they seek out alternative perspectives in search for the invisible but active systems archetype.

## Learning to "See" Systems

When a person watches a team of five mountain climbers scaling a one-thousand-foot cliff, he can recognize the systematic interdependence of the climbers by viewing the ropes and pulleys that attach one climber to the next. The five climbers are a system, and each action by one of them effects the actions of the rest. No climber can climb to the top if even one of them chooses to rest because the others need his help. The role of the leader, in this case, is to direct all the climbers moving in a system up the cliff. If one is tired, then they must all rest, as their efforts will be in vain, leading only to fatigue and frustration, not to the results intended. Conversely, a leader who moves too fast, leaving the other climbers in the dust, will only exhaust himself on the systematic constraints applied by the rope. The leader in this system makes a balancing act. If he allows one or more to slack, expecting the other climbers to make up for the difference, he hurts the team's performance and morale. Each climber in the system has a personal responsibility and an obligation to the team to ensure the objective is achieved.

In the same way, all organizations require personal and team responsibilities in order to achieve their goals. The ropes that connect the climbers are a visual representation of their interconnectedness, magnifying the need for teamwork within the system in order for everyone to scale to the top, but even without the physical ropes in human organizational systems, the connections are just as binding. Each person in a community needs to understand the systematic mind-set as his actions will affect others in interdependent communities. Every leader, like the cliff-climbing leader, must learn to think and see systematically, understanding how individual parts influence one another within the entity as a whole, in order to lead his team to its full potential.

Senge described the need for leaders to see and think systematically: "Structures of which we are unaware hold us prisoner. Conversely, learning to see the structures within which we operate begins a process of freeing ourselves from previously unseen forces and ultimately mastering the ability to work with them and change them."

Autostereograms are an example of hidden structures, but since a person's mind is held hostage to his two-dimensional (2-

D) paradigm, he cannot see the hidden picture without training his mind. A single-image stereogram (SIS) is designed to create the visual illusion of a three-dimensional (3-D) scene from a 2-D image in the human brain. The brain must be trained to see the 3-D view in the 2-D picture by overcoming the brain's normally automatic coordination between focusing and vergence (movement of the eyes in opposite directions). Magic Eye produces books filled with random-dot autostereograms that one can study for hours at a time. When one is first attempting to see the 3-D picture, it can be a frustrating experience; but with enough practice, he can develop the skills to routinely see past the 2-D surface into the 3-D reality.

In a similar way, one's mind can be trained to recognize the 3-D systematic order hidden beneath the apparent 2-D cause-and-effect data. Naturally, the mind defaults to the simple cause-and-effect linear 2-D thinking; but when the world's systematic architecture, 3-D, is discovered, one will never view problems the same way again. Systems are all around us, and training the brain to see them will open a new world of patterns and potential solutions for the leader. Indeed, organizational theorist Charles Kiefer described the mental training that must occur in order to recognize systems: "When this switch is thrown subconsciously, you become a systems thinker ever thereafter. Reality is automatically seen systematically as well as linearly (there are still lots of problems for which a linear perspective is perfectly adequate). Alternatives that are impossible to see linearly are surfaced by the subconscious as proposed solutions. Solutions that were outside of our 'feasible set' become part of our feasible set. 'Systemic' becomes a way of thinking (almost a way of being) and not just a problem solving methodology."

## Solving Challenges Systematically

Stephen Covey provided another classic story about thinking in systems. He shared about a fisherman going to a river to enjoy a day of fishing. Just minutes after getting there, he sees a young boy flailing his arms in the middle of the river, screaming for help. The fisherman quickly jumps into the water and saves the young boy. The boy is disheveled but otherwise fine. The fisherman starts fishing again, and fifteen minutes later, a young girl is flailing her arms, yelling for help in the middle of the river. The fisherman saves her also. At this point, he wonders what the odds are that two children would need help on the same day on the same river. Fifteen minutes later, when a third child needs to be rescued, he is certain that there is more to the picture (system) than the isolated events he is experiencing. At this point, he starts asking questions, no longer believing that the children needing to be rescued are isolated cause-and-effect events. He believes there is more to this system than meets the eye. The fisherman, in an effort to solve the cause at its roots rather than just trim the leaves of the tree, walks the trail upstream and finds a children's camp on the riverside. The fisherman soon discovers the cause of the distressed kids. A bully is tossing kids in the river every fifteen minutes until he ensures that everyone surrenders their lunch money. The fisherman, a true problem solver, takes the bully by the ear and walks him into the camp's office, solving the root cause of the problem and, thus, being able to enjoy the remaining fishing time in peace.

Although this is a simple example, how many times are issues "solved" by pulling "distressed kids" out of the river while not truly addressing the underlying systemic issues? Most people run from emergency to emergency in life, never stopping to think if the emergencies have an underlying systematic cause. The cyclical system described above included the boys and girls, the bully, the river, and the fisherman downstream. The fisherman would have had a busy day if he hadn't solved the problem at the root cause level. In the same way, one can stay busy dealing with systematic effects for an entire lifetime. For unless problems are solved at the root cause level, nothing of long-term consequence is accomplished. Think about how many lives would be improved if people stopped diving into rivers saving "distressed kids" and instead learned the underlying systems thinking to end the madness once and for all. Business leaders must recognize systems in order to eliminate customer challenges at the roots rather than just engaging in a never-ending trimming of the leaves.

> **Most people run from emergency to emergency in life, never stopping to think if the emergencies have an underlying systematic cause.**

## Building Business Systems

The best businesses design systematic solutions to their customers' needs. Building a great business requires building a system that can produce the "good fruit" of consistent results for the customer without the need for superhuman efforts. Systems guru Michael Gerber wrote in his book *The E Myth*, "It is literally impossible to produce a consistent result in a business that is created around the need for extraordinary people; you will be forced to ask the difficult questions about how to produce a result without the extraordinary ones." Gerber explained, "You will be forced to find a system that leverages ordinary people to the point where they can produce extraordinary results. To find innovative solutions to the people problems that have plagued business owners since the beginning of time. To build a business that works. You will be forced to do the work of business development, not as a replacement for people development but as its necessary correlate." The question to be asked and answered is: How does one create a "super systems dependent," not a "super people dependent," process for customer satisfaction? Gerber shared, "'How can I give my customer the results he wants systematically, rather than personally?"

The business equivalent of the biblical saying "As [a man] thinks in his heart, so is he" (Proverbs 23:7, New King James Version) is "As a business man thinks, so is his business." Thomas Watson, the founder of IBM, understood systems, creating a business model that produced results long after he retired:

> I realized that for IBM to become a great company, it would have to act like a great company long before it ever became one. From the very outset, IBM was fashioned after the template of my vision. And each and every day, we attempted to model the company after that template. At the end of each day, we asked ourselves how well we did, discovered the disparity between where we were and where we had committed ourselves to be, and, at the start of the following day, set out to make up for the difference. Every day at IBM was a day devoted to business development, not doing business. We didn't do business at IBM, we built one.

Business systems make extraordinary results an ordinary occurrence. The secret is to learn where the leverage points lie within the system. Senge explained, "The bottom line of systems thinking is leverage—seeing where actions and changes in structures can lead to significant, enduring improvements. Often, leverage follows the principle of economy of means: where the best results come not from large-scale efforts but from small well-focused actions." Few disagree with the principle of leverage, but the difficulty is in determining where energy needs to be expended to leverage results. The leader, in other words, must understand systems interactions to orchestrate duplicatable results through the power of leverage.

## Systems Thinking to Satisfy Customers

Theodore Levitt said, "Discretion is the enemy of order, standardization, and quality." Put in simpler terms, discretion is the enemy of duplication. Duplication is the goal for the best systematic process to be used across all similar operations, reducing learning curves and increasing output. The way to create a system that guards against operating discretion is to discover what works consistently and teach those best practices to everyone performing similar processes.

> **For people to duplicate, leaders must orchestrate the best practices through culture, recognition, and rewards.**

For people to duplicate, leaders must orchestrate the best practices through culture, recognition, and rewards. Gerber explained orchestration: "Orchestration is based on the absolutely quantifiable certainty that people will do only one thing predictably— be unpredictable. For your business to be predictable, your people must be. But if people aren't predictable, then what? The system must provide the predictability. To do what? To give your customer what he wants every single time. Why? Because unless your customer gets everything he wants every single time, he'll go someplace else to get it!"

In fact, if an organization is not duplicating, a person knows that the leaders are not orchestrating the "best practices" across their communities. The plan is simple: Develop the patterns and systems to satisfy the customer, teach the patterns and systems to the employees, and reap the harvest of satisfied customers through a duplicatable business system. Gerber explained, "The system becomes a tool your people use to increase their productivity to get the job done. It's your job to develop that tool and to teach your people how to use it. It's their job to use the tool you've developed and to recommend improvements based on their experience with it."

Even duplication, however, can be taken too far. If it denigrates into "just do it this way and stop thinking," then a team loses the creativity needed to continuously improve. Leaders work on the system, and the team works within the system, but both must be constantly engaged in looking for ways to improve. A great idea to improve the system can come from anyone, and many times, it comes from the person who is responsible for a certain step in the process since he spends the most time doing it.

The Japanese became famous for their system of Kaizen, recognizing and rewarding good ideas from anyone in the company who could help improve their systems. Ray Stata, former CEO of Analog Devices, said, "In the traditional hierarchical organization, the top thinks and the local acts. In a learning organization, you have to merge thinking and acting in every individual." As Lao-Tzu said, "A leader is best when people barely know he exists, when his work is done, his aim fulfilled, they will say: we did it ourselves."

**Finding the right balance between duplication, creativity, and discretion is essential for long-term systematic results.**

Finding the right balance between duplication, creativity, and discretion is essential for long-term systematic results. In today's competitive environment, if the system isn't broken, then a person must break it anyway to improve it before his competitors do this and put him out of business.

## Scoreboard and PDCA

When a person applies systems thinking to his life, many times, a seemingly small change can have a huge effect, as Donella Meadows illustrated in her book *Thinking in Systems*:

> Near Amsterdam, there is a suburb of single-family houses all built at the same time, all alike. Well, nearly alike. For unknown reasons it happened that some of the houses were built with the electric meter down in the basement. In other houses, the electric meter was installed in the front hall.
>
> These were the sort of electric meters that have a glass bubble with a small horizontal metal wheel inside. As the household uses more electricity, the wheel turns faster and a dial adds up the accumulated kilowatt-hours.
>
> During the embargo and energy crisis of the early 1970's, the Dutch began to pay close attention to their energy use. It was discovered that some of the houses in this subdivision used one-third less electricity than the other houses. No one could explain this. All houses were charged the same price for electricity, all contained similar families.
>
> The difference, it turned out, was in the position of the electric meter. The families with high electricity use were the ones with the meter in the basement, where people rarely saw it. The ones with low use had the meter in

the front hall where people passed the little wheel turning around, adding up the monthly electricity bill many times a day.

The Dutch families unconsciously used the PDCA process to improve their results, thanks to an ever-present scoreboard: the electric meter. By changing the location of the electric meters, or scoreboards, their electric bills were reduced by one-third. In studying this example through the lens of the PDCA process, one can see that the scoreboard is part of the feedback loop within the system. Notice how a small change in location produced leveraged consequences. The meter, then, becomes the check step in the process. When the families noticed the wheel in the meter turning faster, they were able to check and therefore make adjustments in their electricity use, ultimately reducing their electrical loads. Because the scoreboard was visible, adjustments were made quickly, leading to decreased electrical usages, thus conserving energy and money.

## Butterfly Effect

The butterfly effect, a part of the chaos theory, confirms the massive results that slight changes can have when applied to a leverage point in a system. The butterfly effect posits that a butterfly flapping its wings has the capacity to change the initial atmospheric conditions enough to trigger a series of changes that compound into a hurricane on the other side of the world. The same effect applies to human affairs in that subtle adjustments to initial conditions can create profound differences in results. According to the University of Bath, it was by studying weather patterns that the butterfly effect was first expounded:

> In 1960 a meteorologist named Edward Lorenz was researching into the possibilities of long-term weather prediction. He created a basic computer program using mathematical equations which could theoretically predict what the weather might be. One day he wanted to run a particular sequence again, and to save time, he started it from the middle of the sequence. After letting the sequence run, he returned to find that the sequence had evolved completely different from the original. At first he couldn't comprehend such different results but then realized that he had started the sequence with his recorded results to 3 decimal plac-

es, whereas the computer had recorded them to 6 decimal places. As this program was theoretically deterministic, we would expect a sequence very close to the original; however, this tiny difference in initial conditions had given him completely different results.

Lorenz's findings teach that slight changes running through complex systems compound over time, creating significant differences in results. For leaders who understand systems, a little extra "flapping of the wings" at key points of leverage can multiply over time, creating major changes in the long-term outcomes. Although no one can predict the results in complex systems omnisciently (as in weather forecasting), leaders know that small variances in initial conditions can produce big differences in the finished products. History is filled with examples of how little incidents impacted the destiny of civilizations. *The Great Courses* series, taught by historian J. Rufus Fears, dramatized this point:

January 10, 49 B.C.: Julius Caesar crosses the Rubicon River into Rome, igniting a civil war that leads to the birth of the world's greatest ancient civilization.

October 12, 1492: The Spanish explorer Christopher Columbus, weary after months at sea, finally drops anchor at the island of San Salvador and takes Europe's first steps into the New World.

September 11, 2001: On a calm Tuesday morning, a series of terrorist attacks on the United States of America ignites a global war on terrorism that continues to this day.

History is made and defined by landmark events such as these—moments that irrevocably changed the course of human civilization. While many of us are taught that anonymous social, political, and economic forces are the driving factors behind events of the past, acclaimed historian and award-winning Professor J. Rufus Fears believes that it's individuals, acting alone or together, who alter the course of history. These events have given us:

- Spiritual and political ideas,
- Catastrophic battles and wars,
- Scientific and technological advances,
- World leaders both influential and monstrous, and
- Cultural works of unparalleled beauty.

Without them, human history as we know it today would be shockingly unfamiliar. It's because of these events that our world will never be the same again.

## Systems Thinking to Change the World

History is one of the most complex of social systems, but it's still true that individual actions, just like a butterfly flapping its wings, can cause impactful historical changes for good or for bad. By studying systems thinking, a leader can learn the leverage points where he can create huge changes through small seemingly insignificant adjustments. As Senge described, "Tackling a difficult problem is often a matter of seeing where the high leverage lies, a change which—with minimum effort—would lead to lasting, significant improvement."

Creating change on a world-sized scale requires leadership and leverage. A person cannot lift ten thousand pounds by himself, but with the right system, a fulcrum, and a long-enough lever, the same task is easier, just as Archimedes exclaimed, "Give me a lever long enough and a fulcrum on which to place it, and I shall move the world." What is believed impossible by a non–systems thinker is known to be achievable to a leader who thinks systematically.

One of the systems gurus of the twentieth century is a man named Buckminster Fuller. When Fuller was a young man, he initially felt he had wasted his life. When he was thirty-two, his only daughter died, leaving him severely depressed. Soon afterward, alone at an ocean beach, Fuller waded farther and farther from shore, contemplating ending his life. But at the point of surrender, he realized he hadn't really given life a chance. On the brink of suicide, he resolved to spend all of his energy discovering what a single human life could achieve. In a 1972 interview, Fuller explained the power a single human life had to change the direction of the world:

> Something hit me very hard once, thinking about what one little man could do. Think of the *Queen Mary*—the whole ship goes by and then comes the rudder. And there's a tiny thing at the edge of the rudder called a trim tab. It's a miniature rudder. Just moving the little trim tab builds a low pressure that pulls the rudder around. Takes almost no effort at all. So I said that the little individual can be a trim tab. Society thinks it's going right by you, that it's left you altogether. But if you're doing dynamic things men-

tally, the fact is that you can just put your foot out like that and the whole big ship of state is going to go. So I said, call me Trim Tab.

A trim tab is a small tab placed on the main rudder that turns the rudder, which ultimately turns the big ship. The trim tab's function is to make it easier to turn the ship by helping to turn the rudder. The larger the ship, the more important the trim tab becomes because it's progressively more difficult to turn the rudder as the size of the ship increases. Senge explained why the trim tab is so appropriate for leverage in a system:

> What makes the trim tab such a marvelous metaphor for leverage is not just its effectiveness, but its nonobviousness. If you knew absolutely nothing about hydrodynamics and you saw a large oil tanker plowing through the high seas, where would you push if you wanted the tanker to turn left? You would probably go to the bow [front] and try to push left. Do you have any idea how much force it requires to turn an oil tanker going fifteen knots by pushing on its bow? The leverage lies in going to the stern and pushing the tail end of the tanker to the right, in order to turn the front to the left. This, of course, is the job of the rudder. But in what direction does the rudder turn in order to get the ship's stern to turn to the right? Why to the left, of course. . . .
>
> The trim tab—this very small device that has an enormous effect on the huge ship—does the same for the rudder. When it is turned to one side or the other, it compresses the water flowing around the rudder and creates a small pressure differential that "sucks the rudder" in the desired direction. But, if you want the rudder to turn to the left, what direction do you turn the trim tab?—to the right, naturally.
>
> The entire system—the ship, the rudder, and the trim tab—is marvelously engineered through the principle of leverage. Yet, its functioning is totally nonobvious if you do not understand the force of hydrodynamics.
>
> So, too, are the high-leverage changes in human systems nonobvious until we understand the forces at play in those systems.

One can quickly see that although purpose, vision, and work ethic are all crucial, the resolutions are not complete without the holistic understanding gained through systems thinking. Senge described the disastrous consequences of visionary leadership without a systematic mind-set:

> Such 'visionary crisis managers' often become tragic figures. Their tragedy stems from the depth and genuineness of their vision. They often are truly committed to noble aspirations. But noble aspirations are not enough to overcome systemic forces contrary to the vision. As the ecologists say, 'Nature bats last.' Systemic forces will win out over the most noble vision if we do not learn how to recognize, work with, and gently mold those forces.

A person must learn to see the "trim tabs" in his organization. He must learn to see the interconnectedness of the world around him and learn to think in systems. In doing so, he will learn how to lead his organization toward its destiny, fulfilling the purpose for which it was created.

### Ray Kroc and McDonald's

Early in 1954, a fifty-two-year-old salesman whose multimixer sales business was plummeting traveled to California, where he discovered his destiny. The salesman was none other than Ray Kroc, and his destiny was McDonald's.

Kroc needed a break, as he had already cut all extraneous expenses, laying off two of his employees, but his business continued to stumble backward. He was fighting for the life of his business. Then an order came in for an unprecedented tenth mixer from an unknown San Bernardino–based fast-food restaurant called McDonald's. Intrigued, he decided to pay one of his best customers a visit. What happened on Kroc's California boondoggle changed the course of franchising history.

In California, Kroc experienced the future of fast-food service when touring the McDonald's facility; he decided that he wanted in on the action. In his book *Grinding It Out*, he wrote, "This had to be the most amazing merchandising operation I had ever seen!" His thirty years of extensive business effort, despite his never receiving a big break, had created a hunger, an unquenchable thirst for an opportunity to do something big, making him a man on a mission for McDonald's. He knew in his gut that he was just the man needed, having the skills and the leadership to take this single McDonald's store and build it into something special.

Kroc flew back to Chicago, but he couldn't get McDonald's out of his mind. A week later, he called the owners the McDonald brothers. In John Love's book *Behind the Golden Arches*, the story is told:

> He called Dick McDonald. "Have you found a franchising agent yet?" he inquired.
>
> "No, Ray, not yet," was McDonald's response.
>
> "Well then," asked Kroc, "what about me?" Ray realized that he could sell McDonald's franchises, saying, "This will go anyplace. Anyplace!"
>
> Neal Baker, a fast-food competitor in California, said, "Ray Kroc was always traveling, and when he thought of McDonald's, he thought big. He had seen cities all over the country, and he could just picture a

McDonald's in every one of them."

Kroc recognized that the McDonald brothers had created the best fast-food system, a system birthed in the late 1940s when Dick and Maurice McDonald were searching for a way to improve profitability while reducing complexity at their drive-in restaurant. Pulling the sales receipts from their last three years of business and studying the data, the McDonald brothers realized that 80 percent of their business was hamburgers, not the complex barbecue items. This new understanding led the brothers to a revolutionary conclusion: create the first mass production assembly process for food.

Requisitioning their tennis court, the brothers drew out a prototype assembly line for hamburger production, just as Henry Ford did for automobiles. The brothers knew to place the equipment most efficiently by studying crew members in the process of assembling various foods, an idea they got from Frederik Taylor, the management guru of the early twentieth century. They eliminated the carhop and replaced him with a self-service counter. Inspired by the data, the brothers eliminated the barbecue pit completely, reducing their twenty-five-item menu down to just eleven: hamburgers, cheeseburgers, french fries, three soft drink flavors, milk shakes, milk, coffee, potato chips, and pie.

With a fully reengineered stainless-steel kitchen, capitalizing on the advantages of speed and quality in the mass production process, the McDonald brothers slashed the price of their hamburger from a competitive 30 cents to an unbelievable price of just 15 cents. They hadn't just improved their old restaurant; they had created the future of fast food. In total, the changes made to the restaurant increased sales from a healthy $200,000 to an astronomical $350,000. Love shared their strategy: "The brothers refused to let even the choice of condiments impede their fast food format. All hamburgers were prepared with ketchup, mustard, onions and two pickles. Any order deviating from that was penalized by a delay in service. That not only allowed the McDonald brothers to streamline their production techniques, but it also opened the way for preparing food in advance of the order. That was a major break from conventional food service practices, but the brothers believed it was vital to their concept of volume through speed. 'If we gave people a choice,' explained McDonald, 'there would be chaos.'" The McDonald brothers, with a twelve-man crew, had revolutionized the fast-food industry.

The McDonald brothers might have created the system, but it took a leader of Ray Kroc's ability to visualize and fulfill McDonald's potential. He knew that the McDonald's system was a winner, a franchising system that he was convinced he could sell all over the world. However, in order to go worldwide, he understood that the business needed to be packaged as more than just cheap hamburgers. Indeed, what he was offering franchisees was a complete franchising system that produced results when followed. According to Michael Gerber, "Ray Kroc created much more than just a fantastically successful business. He created the model upon which an entire generation of entrepreneurs have since built their fortunes: the franchise phenomenon....But the genius of McDonald's isn't franchising itself. The franchise has been around for more than a hundred years....The true genius of Ray Kroc's McDonald's is the Business Format Franchise." The business format franchise provided the franchisees with a turnkey system for doing business that worked for anyone who worked it.

McDonald's broke the mold for franchising because, unlike traditional franchises that sold their names and product offerings, expecting the franchisees to develop a business system to sell the merchandise, Kroc understood that his first customer, the one he needed to sell, was the franchisee. In fact, if the franchisee didn't believe the McDonald's system could produce profitable results, no one would purchase the franchise, thus no hamburgers would be sold. Kroc, then, realized that he must become a salesman for the McDonald's business system, not just hamburgers. Ultimately, his success or failure would depend on convincing hungry entrepreneurs that the McDonald's business system produced results. Gerber wrote, "At that point, Ray Kroc began to look at his business as the product, and at the franchisee as his first, last, and most important customer. For the franchisee wasn't interested in hamburgers or french fries or milkshakes; he was interested in the business. Driven by the desire to buy a business, the franchisee only wanted to know one thing: 'Does it work?'" Kroc believed the McDonald brothers had cracked the code for high-speed but low-cost fast-food service; he would complete the package by providing visionary leadership and salesmanship to make his dream a reality. He was energized for the challenge, having been in sales all his life, so he knew a winner when he saw one. Gerber concluded, "If McDonald's was to fulfill the dream he (Kroc) had for it, the franchisee would have to be willing to buy it....He wasn't competing with other hamburger businesses. He was competing with every other business opportunity."

In April of 1955, Kroc made his first move, opening the first prototype store in Des Plaines, Illinois. The prototype gave Kroc a place to test and improve his operating system. His vision drove him to create cookie-cutter concepts where anyone who followed the system could produce profitable stores. Gerber described Kroc's system: "Forced to create a business that worked in order to sell it, he also created a business that would work once it was sold—no matter who bought it. Armed with that realization, he set about the task of creating a foolproof, predictable business." Kroc's emphasis on developing a successful business format franchise was fiscally sound since his agreement with the McDonald brothers allowed for only a $950 franchising fee and a mere 1.9 percent of revenue sharing, 0.5 percent of which went to the McDonald brothers. Indeed, unless the franchisees were profitable quickly, Kroc could end up bankrupt due to his aggressive expansion plans. The Des Plaines store was crucial in the development of a duplicatable system. In Gerber's words, "How could the components of the prototype have to be constructed so that the resulting business system could be replicated over and over again? . . . The business-as-a-product would only sell if it worked. And the only way to make certain it would work in the hands of a franchisee anywhere in the world would be to build it out of perfectly predictable components that could be tested in a prototype long before ever going into mass production."

Kroc's system had perfectly predictable component parts, leading to uniform best practices across McDonald's; however, this didn't mean he was against creativity. In fact, Kroc inspired his people to constantly improve his system, leveraging his community of like-minded franchise entrepreneurs. Love elaborated:

The real secret to McDonald's successful operating system is not found in its regimen but in the way it enforces uniform procedures without stifling the entrepreneurship of franchisees....Without the freedom of franchisees and suppliers to exercise their entrepreneurial instincts, to test their own ideas on new products and procedures, and even to challenge the corporation head-on, McDonald's might still have attained its celebrated uniformity, but at a terrible price. It would lose the grassroots creativity that diverse franchisees and suppliers provide. It would, in short, lose touch with the marketplace.

Fred Turner, former CEO and the brains behind McDonald's system, said, "It's one of the superficial notions about McDonald's that no one has put into perspective. The independent-mindedness of our operators prevents regimentation. While they stick to the basics of the system, they zig and zag by making refinements and changes, and everyone benefits from their willingness to zig and zag. The system deals with setting uniform standards, but regimentation? No way!" In other words, through Kroc's leadership, McDonald's achieved the benefits of systems and the creativity of the community— a rare combination in the days of command and control management.

McDonald's unique blend of uniform systems and creativity energized the entire community, becoming one of Kroc's original contributions and his competitive advantage. The corporate-like rules were needed to maintain quality standards, while the creativity manifested itself through the leadership teams' encouragement of innovative ideas. These two seemingly conflicting principles were the backbone of McDonald's growth. Indeed, what other franchise has created so many top sellers, such as the Big Mac, Egg McMuffin, and Filet-O-Fish, that were not ideas from the corporate staff, but from the franchisee leaders?

Love shared, "Decisions at McDonald's have always been the product of individual initiative. Ideas are never homogenized by committees. New directions are the result of a continuous trial-and-error process, and new ideas spring from all corners of the system. The key ingredient in Kroc's management formula is a willingness to risk failure and to admit mistakes." McDonald's wasn't the typical top-down decision-making corporation. Instead, Kroc searched, listened, and asked for ideas from everyone, intuitively understanding that the whole team was better than any individual on the team. His leadership style encouraged people to make suggestions and test ideas.

James Kuhn, former McDonald's vice president, explained McDonald's corporate culture: "We have a public image of being slick, professional, and knowledgeable marketers who also happen to be plastic and shallow. In fact, we are a bunch of motivated people who shoot off a lot of cannons, and they don't all land on target. We've made a lot of mistakes, but it is the mistakes that make our success, because we have learned from them. We are impulsive, we try to move faster than we can, but we are also masters at cleaning up our messes."

Kroc created a win-win system, where each participant had common economic incentives and a common standard of quality, service, and cleanliness, and nearly everything else was up for discussion.

By leasing the restaurant site to the franchisee and only approving store expansion one at a time, Kroc had the necessary influence to keep maverick franchisees in line for the good of the entire store system. By late 1957, Turner was producing training films for franchisees, teaching best practices and procedures, but he soon realized this would not be enough. In 1961, McDonald's was the first fast-food franchise to launch a full-time training facility, which they called Hamburger University. Kroc said, "Our aim, of course, was to ensure repeat business based on the system's reputation rather than on the quality of a single store or operator. This would require a continuing program of educating and assisting operators and a constant review of their performance."

Nancy Fraser, a *Life* magazine reporter, visited Hamburger U., intending to write a tongue-in-cheek article on the hamburger zealots. But after attending the class, she changed her mind, saying, "I realized how dedicated you all are to Hamburger University. It didn't deserve to be put down."

All future franchisees attended the university, giving McDonald's a leg up on the competition. Eventually, seeing McDonald's incredible results, every fast-food franchise created its own training facility as well.

Kroc's vision and drive helped him see and build something big; his salesmanship helped him assemble a winning team of franchisees, corporate managers, and suppliers; his leadership helped him unite the team in a win-win fashion; and his Hamburger University assured that he captured the best principles, processes, and procedures, creating a competitive advantage for his McDonald's franchising system.

Kroc's leadership produced a business that, at his death, had grown from humble beginnings to over eight thousand stores producing nearly $9 billion in sales. These figures are dwarfed by the over thirty-two thousand outlets today, which generate nearly $24 billion in sales. Results like this are a testament to the business and organizational systems Kroc created. McDonald's was built to last by a founder who knew how to inspire others with his compelling vision and competitive drive.

Love concluded, "The history of the McDonald's System is the story of an organization that learned how to harness the power of entrepreneurs—not several but hundreds of them. It is run by decisions and policies considered to be for the common good. But the definition of common good is not set by a chief executive or by a management committee. Rather, it is the product of the interaction between all the players....In essence, the history of McDonald's is a case study on managing the entrepreneurs in a corporate setting."

Leaders can learn from Kroc's example and begin to unleash the latent creativity locked within a community's entrepreneurial-minded people. Systems thinking in no way requires one to sacrifice originality. The two are not mutually exclusive. In fact, the two go very well together. Ray Kroc proved how successful one can become by using systems thinking to recognize a brilliant business model and leverage the predictability of that model as well as the ingenuity of the franchisees in order to continuously improve upon the model and boost sales and customer satisfaction.

CHAPTER 12

# ADVERSITY QUOTIENT (AQ)
## Resolved: To Develop Adversity Quotient

*I know that AQ leads to perseverance in overcoming obstacles and setbacks.*

Everyone gets knocked down, but winners get back up. Adversity quotient (AQ) is a combination of mental and emotional intelligences, used for one to have the ability to endure the challenges of life. A person with high AQ refuses to compromise on personal and professional excellence no matter how difficult the obstacles are. In *Adversity Quotient*, author Paul Stoltz described, "Your success in life is largely determined by your AQ:

1. AQ tells you how well you withstand adversity and your ability to surmount it.
2. AQ predicts who will overcome adversity and who will be crushed.
3. AQ predicts who will exceed expectations of their performance and potential and who will fall short.
4. AQ predicts who gives up and who prevails."

Not surprisingly, AQ is one of the biggest factors lacking in people and one that is sorely needed in our progressively complacent, faithless, and purposeless generation because AQ strengthens perseverance. And perseverance is one of the traits that all abidingly successful people have. During the moment where one has given his all and results are not achieved, perseverance is critical.

Without a strong faith in his purpose, a person will make fatal shortsighted decisions, compromising his dreams and ideals for his comfort. When the scoreboard of life displays dismal outcomes, he must exert his AQ, persisting despite the current facts. It's during the gloomy times, when everything seems to be going wrong, that a person decides to quit or press on, birthing victims or victors based on the choices made. In fact, a person can implement all the other resolutions, but if he lacks AQ, he will fall when the "chicken hits the fan." But great leaders are *Rascals*, displaying unyielding perseverance in their quest for meaningful success.

## The Formula AQ = IQ × EQ × WQ

The formula for adversity quotient is AQ = IQ (intelligence quotient) × EQ (emotional quotient) × WQ (will quotient). Some may be surprised to find that intelligence comes in many forms, but one must realize that AQ is only developed by someone who can join the mind, heart, and will together as was discussed in the Introduction of this book.

Many people feel they are not smart enough to succeed, but typically, the most successful people are not the highest scorers on an IQ test. For example, Henry Ford, the automobile tycoon, although scoring off the chart in AQ, was just average in IQ. In fact, in a lawsuit between Ford and the *Chicago Tribune*, he showed that IQ was not the most important factor in a person's success. Dr. David Schwarz wrote, "The *Tribune* asked him scores of simple questions such as 'Who was Benedict Arnold?', 'When was the Revolutionary War fought?', and others, most of which Ford, who had little formal education, could not answer. Finally he became quite exasperated and said, 'I don't know the answers to those questions, but I could find a man in five minutes who does.' Henry Ford was never interested in miscellaneous information. He knew what every major executive knows: the ability to know how to get information is more important than using the mind as a garage for facts."

> **Many people feel they are not smart enough to succeed, but typically, the most successful people are not the highest scorers on an IQ test.**

The world is filled with educated derelicts, but anyone, even someone who has a below-average IQ, can develop and implement a plan for success. More importantly, every person must plan according to his strengths and weaknesses. The key is to magnify one's strengths and guard against one's weaknesses. In fact, the ability to do just that is a bonus for the average individual because people with high IQs tend to overestimate their abilities, leading them to believe they are experts in areas where they actually need help. Ford said:

None of our men are "experts." We have, most unfortunately, found it necessary to get rid of a man as soon as he thinks himself an expert because no one ever considers himself an expert if he really knows his job. A man who knows a job sees so much more to be done than he has done, that he is always pressing forward and never gives up an instant of thought to how good and how efficient he is. Thinking always ahead, thinking always of trying to do more, brings a state of mind in which nothing is impossible. The moment one gets into the "expert" state of mind a great number of things become impossible.

Ford understood that IQ isn't enough to achieve enduring success. As Henry Hazlitt once said, "Nothing is more securely lodged than the ignorance of the experts."

## EQ and Phineas Gage

The physical pathways of the senses travel through the spinal cord into the back of the brain, moving into the center limbic system (where you feel), finally moving to the front rational system (where you think). Since all senses go through the feeling limbic portion before reaching the rational brain, it's easy to respond emotionally without allowing time to rationally develop a proper response.

Phineas Gage, a railroad supervisor, was instrumental in the development of understanding the function of the brain and EQ. Gage was considered to be one of the best leaders, always punctual and reliable in his work. But tragically, in an on-the-job accident, a forty-three-inch-long tamping iron with a diameter of 1.25 inches rocketed through the frontal lobe of Gage's brain. Amazingly, Gage survived the grisly accident! It was a miracle that he lived, but others quickly realized that he wasn't the same man. Instead of exhibiting his normally high EQ, Gage now lost his temper quickly, becoming emotionally unstable at the slightest provocation. He would curse like a sailor when under stress, creating tension and chaos among his confused crew, who were used to his previous demeanor. He quickly descended from the top supervisory position to unemployed simply because of his lack of EQ. Gage, unlike us, had an excuse for his low EQ because he literally lacked the frontal lobe where reasoning and emotions combine, which made it impossible for Gage to think through his feelings. But that isn't the case with most EQ-impaired people, who simply have no excuse for not responding appropriately to the stressful situations in life.

EQ is a choice to slow down and think through issues before

reacting. It is true the senses hit the "feeling" part of the brain first, but with patience, one can train himself to allow the senses to combine with the "reasoning" mind, responding with the whole brain in a high-EQ fashion. Leaders refuse to react to an emotional stimulus, choosing instead to respond with high EQ after allowing the mind to feel and think. No one enjoys associating with low-EQ people because tension is created when behaviors are unpredictable. It's hard to be friends with someone who hugs a person one time and hits him the next. People with low EQ haven't mastered their own emotions; therefore, they cannot lead themselves, which disqualifies them from leading others. All great victories in life begin with a victory over self. If one cannot even control his own emotions, how can he influence others properly? Before reacting to stress emotionally, a person should take a deep breath, forcing the mind to remain calm until one can reflect rationally, causing one to respond to the situation rather than just react to it. This will take practice, but the results are well worth the investment. When a person lifts his EQ, it reverses the Phineas Gage effect. Gage lost his EQ when he lost a portion of his brain; a leader, on the other hand, gains EQ when he uses a certain portion of his brain. It's literally like having brain surgery, adding a portion to one's brain, since this portion is practically unused by the multitude. Developing EQ is one of the single biggest changes a person can make on his leadership journey, one that is quickly noticeable to everyone.

> **All great victories in life begin with a victory over self.**

## Will Quotient (WQ)

There are two aspects of AQ that make perseverance possible, and both are needed in order to endure the dark nights of the soul: trust (EQ) and obey (WQ). WQ is the ability to align the will to obey the laws of success, consistently doing what everyone else merely discusses. Simply put, when all is said and done, much more is said than ever done. For example, if a person trusts but doesn't obey, his success will never arrive. On the other hand, if a person obeys but doesn't trust, he will quickly become disillusioned by the slow process of growth. Results typically require longer time periods than expected, providing ample opportunity to apply AQ on one's success journey. A common saying among Christians is, "Work as if everything depends upon you, and pray as if everything depends upon God." This, in essence, describes the mix between faith and work (trusting and obeying) needed to achieve enduring success.

The trust-and-obey process applies even when people do not believe in the Creator who developed the process. In fact, Matthew 5:45 reads, "That you may be the children of your Father which is in heaven: for he makes his sun to rise on the evil and on the good, and sends rain on the just and on the unjust" (American King James Version). Therefore, the process of reaping and sowing, in this world at least, works for believers and unbelievers alike.

Consider the farmer as an example. He farms his fields on faith, trusting God to provide an increase. No farmer has a right to trust God for an increase, unless he has first obeyed the process by sowing his field. To say a person trusts when he hasn't obeyed is a logical fallacy. John Locke explained this well, declaring: "The best way to read a man's mind is through his actions." People who say they trust but do not obey are lying to themselves and, thus, to others. AQ leaders plan (IQ) their work, do (WQ) the work consistently, and trust (EQ) that if they do it long enough, they will succeed. A farmer has no right to expect a harvest until he has planned and performed the work required.

Trust is the highest EQ response to the stressful events in a person's life. The preceding chapters have covered different steps of obeying, which are important parts of any long-term success. But even if all the resolutions are implemented and obeyed, one must still trust the process, persevering through the tough times and poor results until one achieves victory.

AQ is nonnegotiable because real success isn't the destination. The real destination is who one becomes on the success journey. When a person terminates his journey, he also quits on his personal growth. Exercising AQ, in moments of trials, is what separates the winners from the wannabes in life. Planning, obeying, and trusting are equivalent to IQ, WQ, and EQ, which, when combined, form AQ. One can move ahead confidently, knowing that everything that can be done has been done, having an AQ that can endure disappointments without cracking, trusting the process to produce the results desired, even if not as quickly as he had hoped. It's always darkest before dawn, but many times, people give up just inches away from the goal line, getting heartache and disappointment instead of elation and victory as their lasting legacy. When one stops trusting the process, hope is lost, leading to the loss of the willingness and perseverance needed to endure the process. Regretfully, many talented people remain nameless in the annals of history, lacking the AQ needed to persist when the going gets tough.

Author Paul Stoltz shared a sobering story about dreams and perseverance from when his friend Eric and several of his graduating class buddies attempted to relive a class tradition during their

261

fifteenth-year reunion:

It is said that you can never go back. Likewise, their ritual could not be relived. That night, they drove the same roads they had fifteen years before—roads now populated with malls and fast-food franchises. Flagstaff was now a mountain-chic city of fifty-six thousand. The dirt clearing was now a fully-lit parking area patrolled by the National Forest Service. They were greeted by a huge trail sign, welcoming them and enumerating a long list of hikers' dos and don'ts. Yes, they brought beer. But since they were more sensible now, no one dared drink an entire six-pack. Instead, three guys drank a couple of light beers, and another guy, a recovering alcoholic, responsibly chose an alcohol-free brand. After making a fairly weak display of downing the beverages, they started their hike. They started out singing, but this time the trail seemed steeper; the song gave way to the panting of these thirty-something-year-old hikers—the hike had become a climb. Eric, still in reasonably good shape, was dismayed by how soft his friends had become. Even Bucky, the ex–running back, was struggling. It seemed like yesterday that they had bounded up this hill, half-drunk, singing at the tops of their lungs. Now they gasped and panted, and the hill had become as formidable as Mount Everest.

Halfway up, three guys reluctantly called it quits, probably sparing themselves a coronary. The rest persevered. At the top, they lay on their backs, more exhausted than exhilarated, looking at the stars, except this time, there was pain in their voices as most of them reflected on their dreams for the first time in over a decade, and each rationalized the compromises he had made along the way. The entire group was strangely quiet on the way down. How had all the others aged so much? Eric wondered. What had happened to their spirits and strength? It struck Eric as odd, if not chilling, that had he told his friend Bucky fifteen years ago that he would someday be bald, overweight, divorced, and never travel beyond the West Coast, Bucky would have punched him in the face. Tonight, Bucky was matter-of-fact, if not resigned. Eric was stunned by the power of gradual change. Fifteen years ago, had he and his buddies awoke to the malls, concrete, government regulations, receding hairlines, and pot-bellies-in-the-making, they would have been immobilized with shock. Yet when these changes occur over time, they are accepted if not completely unnoticed.

Upon returning home, Eric walked by the bathroom mirror and paused. This time, for the first time, he saw the face his friends must have seen. Although healthy and strong, he too had aged. For a moment, he saw the passage of fifteen years.

Staring into the mirror, in a moment of introspection, Eric confronted the gap between his and his friends' former elephant-sized dreams and their current antlike aspirations. He realized that the significant compromises that each had made led to the growing disparity between their old dreams and the new reality.

Without applying AQ daily, one's dreams, like Eric's and his friends', crumble into yesterday's fantasies through seemingly small, subtle compromises. AQ provides the faith for a person to persevere in his ideals, even when everything inside him is screaming to compromise for his convenience. Winners endure the pain of the process in order to achieve their dreams, while others skip the pain in the process by compromising. Although compromising temporarily alleviates the short-term pain, it

> **AQ provides the faith for a person to persevere in his ideals, even when everything inside him is screaming to compromise for his convenience.**

eventually leads to a much greater long-term pain: the pain of regret. Eric and his friends experienced the gnawing pain of regret when their adolescent dreams collided with their adult realities. They became like the proverbial frog in room-temperature water. When the water temperature is slowly raised to boiling, people are often unaware of it and are cooked by their subtle compromises.

What is this process that seems to replace hope and optimism with despair and pessimism? If hope is based on the faith that one can overcome by controlling his destiny, then despair, conversely, is the belief that fate has assigned a person to a Sisyphus-like struggle for the duration of his life. But what are the compromises that cause people to despair and, as Thoreau said, "lead lives of quiet desperation"?

## Learned Helplessness

One compromise was discovered by Dr. Martin E. P. Seligman in 1965, when he stumbled across what the American Psychological Association has called the landmark theory of the century— learned helplessness. Learned helplessness is a belief that what a person does cannot alter his outcomes, that somehow, life's cards are stacked against him. Seligman's studies created a revolution in the psychology field, displacing Skinner's hopeless behaviorism (stimulus controls response). Pavlov's original study, in which he rang the bell and provided food, showing that dogs would salivate after ringing a bell, seemed to prove that only humans responded to the stimulus provided. From this experiment, Pavlov, and later Skinner, concluded that man lives by learned behaviors only, leaving no room for thinking, responsibility, and change, and, therefore, no room for destiny. But Seligman's experiments altered the field of psychology forever with the hopeful cognitive psychology revolution (thinking determines behavior). His experiments revealed, in other words, that what we do matters.

Seligman tested three groups of dogs based on Pavlov's foundation, but with a key variation in the stimulus. Group A dogs were harnessed individually, hearing a bell tone and receiving a harmless electric shock afterward. Group A dogs could stop the shock by pressing a bar with their nose, which they quickly learned to do. Group B dogs, on the other hand, heard the bell tone and received the shock but had no ability to stop the electric shock. Lastly, Group C received no shocks at all; they merely heard the bell tone. The breakthrough occurred on the second day of testing when each of the dogs from the previous day were randomly placed in a shuttle box, a box with a low barrier down the middle. One at a time, the dogs were place in the shuttle box. Each dog heard the bell tone and received the shock, but the different responses of the three groups initiated the cognitive revolution. Both groups A and C quickly jumped the middle barrier, eliminating the discomfort of the electric shock. Group B, contrary to expectations, did not attempt to jump over the barrier; instead, the dogs merely crouched down and whimpered. Stoltz described the breakthrough theory: "What Seligman and others discovered is that these dogs had learned to be helpless, a behavior that virtually destroyed their motivation to act. Scientists have discovered that cats, fish, dogs, rats, cockroaches, mice, and people all are capable of acquiring this trait. Learned helplessness is simply internalizing the belief that what you do does not matter, sapping one's sense of control."

When a person believes that he cannot change his situation, he won't even try, becoming hopeless because he believes he is helpless. On the other hand, people can change nearly anything with the right knowledge applied consistently and persistently. Learned helplessness, because it destroys hope for change, must be exposed for the lie that it is. Leaders must rid themselves and their teams of learned helplessness as its acid is fatal to personal growth. One must learn that change is possible when a person believes that it is.

## Improper Response to Pain

Another compromise that leads to failure and despair is an improper response to the pain inherent in the process of growth. There are actually two types of pain: one comes from the inside due to the change process, the other comes from the outside due to criticisms from those unwilling to make the same changes. Hope is the only fuel capable of burning through both types of pain. Without hope, either of these two types of pain will trump one's willingness to endure, enticing one to choose to stop the pain by quitting the journey. Author Robert Grudin wrote, "One might reply that most people who surrender simply lack the ability to get very far. But it is more accurate to say that ability and intelligence, rightly understood, include a readiness to face pain, while those characteristics which we loosely term 'inadequacy' and 'ignorance' are typically associated with the avoidance of pain." When pain reaches a certain threshold, everything inside a person screams for relief, but champions, people with high AQ, persevere. Pain is overcome through continuous focus on one's purpose. Moreover, achieving greatness will require a faith that can move mountains and an AQ to endure the rising pain in the process, but with perseverance, one will eventually reach levels of success that more timid souls refuse to believe possible.

> **Pain is overcome through the continuous focus on one's purpose.**

Grudin elaborated on the outside pain given to achievers as an unjust reward for their quest for personal excellence:

> Modern society has evolved an idiomatic defense of non-achievement so subtle and elegant that it almost makes failure attractive. We can equivocate with failure by saying that we could not stand "the pressure." We can inflate mediocrity by calling cow colleges universities, by naming herds of middle-level executives vice presidents or partners, and by a thousand other sorts of venal hype. We can invert the moral standard by defending a fellow non-achiever as being too sensitive or even too good for the chosen arena. This double rejection of pain—a surrender sanctified by a euphemism—has in our time achieved institutional status. Because it includes its own anti-morality, it can be passed on with pride from generation to generation.

Other ages may have been as full of non-achievers as ours, but no other age, I believe, has developed so comprehensive a rhetoric of failure. To conclude, then: those people in quest of intellectual dignity and independence in the late twentieth century must act in a cultural context that has done its best to annul or camouflage one of the key elements in the quest, the challenge of pain. For this reason such people currently labor under a double burden: they must face the pains inherent in their task, and they must do so in a culture that has little appreciation for their suffering.

Today's achievers, then, handle not only the traditional pain associated with excellence but also the additional pain associated with the envious prattle of today's Internet age nonachievers. Champions understand that it's better to be mocked and criticized by nonachievers than become nonachievers themselves.

AQ can be developed, but only by discarding excuses, rejecting compromises, and choosing to feed one's faith, not one's fears. In order to achieve dreams, people must willingly surrender who they are to become who they dream to be. One cannot have his cake and eat it, too. AQ refuses to surrender personal responsibility (what one desires) to an impersonal environment (what is offered). Best-selling author Chris Brady articulated in his book *Rascal* what it takes to break free from the herd: "It takes character to be different. It takes character to stand apart from the masses for legitimate, purposeful reasons. It takes character to be who God called you to be without succumbing to the pressures of others and their ideas of who you should be and how you should live. For those who embody this concept and live a truly authentic life, we will assign the name of *Rascal*." People with AQ are *Rascals*, refusing to be lulled to sleep by comfort, choosing instead to follow their convictions over conveniences. *Rascals* pay the temporary price of pain for success, rather than the permanent price of regret for failure.

> **In order to achieve dreams, people must willingly surrender who they are to become who they dream to be.**

Washington, Franklin, and Edwards developed AQ and heroic virtues by consistently studying their resolutions, but where are the heroes of this type today? George Roche explained:

Heroes are a fading memory in our times, but we can still recall a little about them. We know at least what sets the hero apart is some extraordinary achievement. Whatever this feat, it is such as to be recognized at once by everyone as a good thing; and somehow, the achieving of it seems larger than life. Even by this sparse definition, the hero's deeds rebuke us. We have been struggling frantically merely to achieve the ordinary: that measure of happiness each of us is supposedly entitled to. The hero in contrast overcomes the ordinary and attains greatness, by serving some great good. His example tells us that we fail, not by aiming too high in life, but by aiming far too low. Moreover, it tells us we are mistaken in supposing that happiness is a right or an end in itself. The hero seeks not happiness but goodness, and his fulfillment lies in achieving it. His satisfaction such as it may be is thus a result: a reward if you please for doing well. This path to happiness is open to all, not just heroes, and until modern times nobody believed there was any other. To pursue happiness for its own sake was believed to be the surest way to lose it.

## Colonel Harland Sanders

Every so often, a person comes along and, through the strength of his resolves, shows an immeasurable AQ. Such a person breaks through the mass of mediocrity. In *Notes from a Friend*, Tony Robbins shared the story of Colonel Sanders, the founder of Kentucky Fried Chicken:

> Have you ever heard of a guy named Colonel Sanders? Of course you have. How did Colonel Sanders become such an unbelievable success? Was it because he was born wealthy? Was his family rich? Did they send him to a top university like Harvard? Maybe he was successful because he started his business when he was really young. Are any of these true?
>
> The answer is no. Colonel Sanders didn't begin to fulfill his dream until he was 65 years old! What drove him to finally take action? He was broke and alone. He got his first social security cheque for $105, and he got mad but instead of blaming society or just writing Congress a nasty note, he started asking himself, "What could I do that would be valuable for other people? What could I give back?" He started thinking about what he had that was valuable to others.
>
> His first answer was, "Well, I have this chicken recipe everyone seems to love! What if I sold my chicken recipe to restaurants? Could I make money doing that?" Then he immediately thought, "That's ridiculous. Selling my recipe

won't even pay the rent." And he got a new idea: "What if I not only sold them my recipe but also showed them how to cook the chicken properly? What if the chicken was so good that it increased their business? If more people come to see them and they make more chicken sales, maybe they will give me a percentage of those additional sales."

Many people have great ideas. But Colonel Sanders was different. He was a man who didn't just think of great things to do; he put them into action. He went and started knocking on doors, telling each restaurant owner his story: "I have a great chicken recipe, and I think if you use it, it'll increase your sales. And I'd like to get a percentage of that increase."

How many times do you think Colonel Sanders heard no before getting the answer he wanted? He was refused 1,009 times before he heard his first yes. He spent two years driving across America in his old, beat-up car, sleeping in the back seat in his rumpled white suit, getting up each day eager to share his idea with someone new. Often, the only food he had was a quick bite of the samples he was preparing for perspective buyers. How many people do you think would have gone for 1,009 no's—two years of no's!—and kept on going? Very few. That's why there is only one Colonel Sanders. I think most people wouldn't get past twenty no's, much less a hundred or a thousand! Yet this is sometimes what it takes to succeed.

Colonel Sanders, through his off-the-chart AQ, refused to surrender. He applied the PDCA process to his efforts over and over until he got it right, eventually founding one of the most successful franchises in the world. What if Sanders gave up after one hundred, five hundred, or even a thousand rejections? AQ is what keeps someone in life's game going when he is doing everything right but still hasn't achieved the success he deserves. If he compromises at any time during this crucial period, success will never reveal its secrets. Sanders denied himself the comfort of compromising; instead, he relentlessly pursued his purpose and vision with AQ, thus fulfilling his destiny, by never surrendering to overwhelming odds. Romans 5:3–4 says, "And not only that, but we also glory in tribulations, knowing that tribulation produces perseverance; and perseverance, character; and character, hope" (New King James Version). Anyone climbing life's mountain must build AQ. He must overcome innumerable tribulations in developing his character, hope, and perseverance, proving that nearly anything can be conquered as long as he refuses to surrender, no matter how difficult the adversity is.

## Billy Durant: Adversity Quotient

William "Billy" Durant is an icon of adversity quotient (AQ). Indeed, if a person were looking for one man to epitomize the term, he could do no better than point out Durant. Durant grew up in Flint, Michigan, and from his humble beginning, he created the world's largest company. In fact, he founded Buick, GM, Chevrolet, and Durant Motors—all of them successful car companies. He was the quintessential serial entrepreneur, founding or purchasing many companies during his lifetime. His story represents the "can do" spirit of free enterprise because one can see his hopes, challenges, and failures, along with his AQ to get up and do it again. Inspired by his dreams, humbled by his setbacks, and educated by his entrepreneurship, I have studied Durant's life extensively, believing that his life story strengthens every entrepreneur's AQ.

Starting with nothing but vision and drive, Durant foresaw the coming of the worldwide automotive ownership phenomenon. Even though he founded many of today's most successful brands, regretfully, his story doesn't have a happy ending. He died nearly penniless despite his creative genius. Nevertheless, one can learn key principles of life from both great successes and great failures since many times, the failures reveal more lessons than the successes do.

Durant started in the horse carriage business but left it behind when he recognized the potential of the automotive field. He teamed with David Buick, building Buick into a household name, selling more cars than any other manufacturer at the time. But Buick wasn't big enough for Durant, so Durant pursued his brainchild of forming a trust to hold multiple car manufacturers in one holding company, which he called General Motors (GM). By offering stocks and cash, he purchased Pontiac, Oldsmobile, and Cadillac, to name just a few of the automotive manufacturers that he integrated into GM.

On several occasions, Durant nearly bought out Henry Ford of Ford Motors' fame. He offered GM stocks in return for bringing Ford Motors into the GM trust, but Ford demanded cash, not wanting any stocks. Indeed, not once but twice, the price at which Ford agreed to sell Ford Motors to

GM had been set. Durant missed the deadline both times, once by less than a day, changing the course of automotive history as Ford went on to build the Model T. The true king of the automobile industry, the true visionary that predicted the automobile's meteoric future, was not Henry Ford but Billy Durant, regardless of how history has been rewritten. Can one even imagine the history of automobiles had Durant raised the money in time to bring Ford Motors into the GM conglomerate?

As is normally the case with huge leaders, Durant's drive surpassed his financing. Early in the second decade of the twentieth century, during an economic downturn, the car market stalled, tightening cash flows throughout GM's divisions. Durant subsequently ran out of money, having used all of his and his friends' money reserves. This forced him to sell his GM stocks to a banking syndicate. The bankers were all too happy to take GM from Durant at a bargain basement price. For the majority of people (those without AQ), a setback of this magnitude would have knocked them out, but Durant's legendary AQ carried him forward, undaunted by his "failure."

Moving quickly, he partnered with a little-known (at the time) racer and mechanic named Louis Chevrolet. With Durant's business savvy, Chevrolet zoomed to the top of its class, selling cars so quickly that it became one of the top manufacturers, even surpassing most of the GM brands. Meanwhile, at GM, the nonvisionary group of bankers was managing the company into the ground, so averse to risk that little to no innovation was occurring. The GM stock was plummeting as Chevrolet's stock was rising, revealing that the bankers were no match for the perseverance and drive of Durant. The bankers might have had money, but they were no match for Durant's daring strategy fostered by his high AQ. Simply put, Durant wasn't afraid of failure, while the bankers were deathly afraid to lose any of their precious capital. Parlaying his success at Chevrolet, Durant started swapping single shares of the high-value Chevrolet stock for multiple shares of the low-value GM stock with the intention of building enough stock ownership to wrest control of GM from the bankers and bring GM back into his orbit.

In 1916, Durant achieved his goal. At a now-legendary

moment, Durant walked into the GM board meeting and announced that he was now the majority shareholder of GM stock. One can only imagine the shock and dismay on the bankers' faces when they realized that Durant had outwitted the money powers through his entrepreneurship and AQ. Durant announced to the board that he intended to merge GM and Chevrolet. In other words, it was Chevrolet that purchased GM, not the other way around. Durant's AQ is a testament to the power of an aligned ant and elephant vision, as he rebounded from a humiliating defeat to achieve an astounding victory. He had refused to stay down and surrender his vision for GM, regardless of the odds against him, thanks to one of the most amazing AQs in American business history.

In addition to his incredible AQ, Durant had an understanding that talented people were essential to the success of GM. With his magnetic vision, he drew strong leaders into the GM community. Nearly all the top automotive men of the time either worked for GM or, like Ford, nearly did. In fact, Walter Chrysler, later the founder of Chrysler Motors, worked for Durant for many years as the head man of Buick Motors, being paid over $100,000 per year to do so. Durant's strong AQ attracted other strong leaders into the automotive field, helping GM prosper. Charles Kettering and Alfred Sloan are a couple of the other top names who worked with Durant.

Durant's successful takeover of GM, however, did not go unnoticed by the Wall Street bankers. They weren't happy that an upstart businessman had outfoxed them for control of GM, and they waited patiently for an opportunity to settle the score. With his business booming, Durant needed to raise more money for expansion. Eventually, John Raskob and his DuPont family friends purchased large chunks of GM stocks, making them one of the largest investors behind Durant. But if selling millions of vehicles and expanding his company across the globe was Durant's major objective, the Eastern Establishment bankers and businesses had another goal in mind. Knowing Durant's loyalty to his business partners, the Eastern Establishment, the same partners who had helped him fund Chevrolet and the GM takeover, began a covert operation to reduce the GM stock price by selling shares. Even though GM was profitable, the stock price began to tumble as the market was manipulated against the GM shares. Durant, always loyal to his friends, purchased millions of dollars of GM stocks with his own money. He didn't need any more stocks, but out of loyalty to his friends, he invested and invested in an effort to stabilize the stock price and to protect his friends, whose life savings were invested. The Wall Street crowd, knowing Durant's loyalty, calmly drove the stock price down until Durant ran out of personal funds. With over $10 million of his own money invested (a huge sum even in today's inflated dollars), Durant was at the brink of bankruptcy. Forced finally to concede defeat, he had no remaining options but to sell out his business empire, this time to a syndicate consisting of J. P. Morgan, the DuPont family, John Raskob, and other Wall Street bankers for nickels on the dollar. Durant, for the second time in his life, had lost his beloved GM.

Durant's second business failure wasn't a failure of business strategies but a failure to conceive of the level of animosity against him. His AQ and intense desire to win generated jealousy and envy from the Eastern Establishment. At this point, most people would have surrendered their dreams, choosing to become bitter at the injustices suffered, but Durant was not like most people.

Durant, instead of wallowing in misery or having a pity party, had his AQ lead him to start his third automobile manufacturer, known simply as Durant Motors. He had now created his third successful brand in less than twenty-five years. But as fate would have it, in 1929, he lost his remaining millions in the stock market crash that led to America's Great Depression. Durant was now penniless and companyless (but not hopeless, thanks to his AQ) at an age when most were thinking about retirement.

Durant certainly wasn't perfect. An honest evaluation would conclude that he would have benefitted from a more financially conservative friend to help him with "reality checks" once in a while. For example, had Durant had a brother who played a role similar to that Bud Walton played in Sam Walton's life, he may have still progressed without gambling everything on each move he made. With that said, I would venture to contend that no one can discount the strength of Durant's AQ, which helped him overcome any setback he faced in his life. Perhaps he should have played it safe after going from millionaire to broke three times in his life, but that just wasn't the way he played the game.

In his late seventies, with his AQ still intact, Durant began working in two new fields. While America was in the middle of World War II, he saw a bright future for fast-food restaurants and bowling alleys. The automobile industry had changed the American landscape, creating thriving suburbs outside the cities. Durant believed that intersections and highways would be dotted with restaurants to feed the motorists. It's hard to comprehend the level of entrepreneurial spirit and AQ inside Durant, who recognized the upcoming fast-food revolution over a decade before Ray Kroc of McDonald's fame did. Indeed, it was only Durant's failing health and eventual death in the mid-1940s that was able to overcome his inspiring AQ and prevent it from helping him succeed in his last comeback attempt.

There are many lessons to be learned from Durant's life. First, he didn't have the perfect upbringing, as his dad left his mother when he was young and his mom had to raise him on a minimal budget. Durant knew that if he was going to make his dreams a reality, it would be with his own leadership and AQ, not with gifts from a rich family. Not only was he up to the task, but the challenge fueled his AQ and enthusiasm, urging him to do something great, which ultimately led him to create what became the largest car company in the world for nearly a century. Durant also understood that it isn't where a person starts in life but how far he goes that counts. It didn't matter that he had to borrow money from a local Flint bank to get started in the horse carriage industry, it didn't matter that he had to ditch the horse carriage business when automobiles were invented, and it didn't matter that he failed as long as his AQ didn't fail him. It's AQ, not ease, that determines how far one goes in his quest for success. Billy Durant's life teaches a person that AQ is more important than his current resources in reaching for his dreams.

Second, Durant possessed keen foresight and saw a bright future for automobiles. His visionary mind saw it earlier than others did as he dropped his carriage business to put all his energies into cars. As early as 1910, long before most people had a car, he spoke of every household owning an automobile and espoused the vision of roads crisscrossing America. But the dream alone wasn't enough; it was his

superhuman level of AQ that made his dream of superhigh-
ways connecting big cities become a reality, providing better
travel for all Americans. Durant's is the story of a young man
whose never-failing AQ helped him accomplish greatness, not
once, not twice, but three separate times in his life. With his
dream, struggle, victory stories, he symbolized the American
Dream for an entire generation. In a superb tribute to Durant, Clarence Young wrote:

> In the creation of the Mass Production Age, Du-
> rant was not only the presiding genius; he was, in-
> deed, the Titan—and, as was the fate of the original
> Titans, he was destroyed by the Olympians whom he
> had created.
>
> It is almost poignant now to tell the beads of carp-
> ing criticism reiterated against Durant: He lacked or
> ignored technical mastery....he was a good promoter,
> but no administrator....He had no organization....He
> could not delegate authority....He made poor choices
> of executives....He was a promoter, a gambler....He
> was wrong in believing in himself....
>
> It is completely true that W. C. Durant had a
> weakness: He was human. His humanity included
> love and trust of his associates—the not-always-cor-
> rect assumption that they were as honorable as he.
> He gave a degree and quality of loyalty to "his peo-
> ple" beyond any measurement; he expected the same
> magnitude of loyalty from them.
>
> He surrendered the control of General Motors
> in 1910 to preserve the company for its investors. In
> 1920, his loyalty to his company and its stockholders
> drove him to spend more money than he had preserv-
> ing the value of the company's name, reputation, and
> stock. As for his feckless choice of executives, he hired
> and developed Charles W. Nash, Charles F. Ketter-
> ing, Alfred P. Sloan (also Walter Chrysler and almost
> Henry Ford), and a few thousand others.
>
> What was Durant? . . . A small-town boy from a
> broken home who had no advantages at all except
> his own character. With a borrowed $2000 he built
> up the largest carriage company in the world. With a

debt-ridden, faltering motor company, he created the world's largest corporation, providing millions of jobs all over the world in the past 65 years [over a 100 years now].

Although small in stature, W. C. Durant was larger than life in every aspect of his thought, spirit, and practice. He was, indeed, so much larger in concept that he made the lesser men who surrounded him uncomfortable—he was unpredictable as an elemental force of nature.

Durant was an original genius who escapes classification and definition. He had an almost-godlike presence. He had the creativity to translate his vision into reality, not only for himself but for his fellow men. He was compassionate, gentle, charming, delightful, considerate, brilliant, generous, ingenious, and infinitely loyal.

Mass production—the greatest servant ever tamed for mankind to use—was just an idea when Durant grasped it. He, more than any other man, implemented this great multiplier of goods for mankind. He was, indeed, what Dickens called the "Founder of the Feast"—and we are still eating at his bountiful table, although we have forgotten his name.

## CHAPTER 13

# LEGACY
## Resolved: To Reverse the Current of Decline in My Field of Mastery

*I know that a true legacy leaves the world a better place than I found it.*

The reader has now reached the last resolution, the one that ties all the others together, capping off the symphony of success. People will not remember a person for what he has, but they will always remember what he gives. With our Western civilization falling into decline, leaving a leadership legacy has become more crucial today than ever before.

### The Decline of Civilizations

Why do civilizations rise, decline, and fall? Civilizations as diverse as the Sumerians, Egyptians, Persians, Greeks, Romans, and Chinese all declined, eventually falling under their own weight. Is decline the natural condition of life, with growth being a temporary leadership anomaly in the march of history? Arnold Toynbee, an English historian, authored *A Study of History*, a multivolume classic on the history of world civilizations, in which he details the rise and decline of twenty-three civilizations. Despite detecting uniform patterns of disintegration in each civilization, Toynbee insisted that leaders have a moral responsibility to end the cycle of decline. Schmandt and Ward, in Cambridge Press, wrote:

> Toynbee reserved the terms "challenge and response" for major threats and actions that impacted the well-being of the entire population. "Challenge" threatened the very survival of the existing system. "Response" would range from

inaction to major change in the living conditions of individuals as well as the group. It could embody new technology, social organization, and economic activities, or a combination of various factors. "Response" was never predictable, and its outcome would only be known over time. This was the risk humans took—resulting in success or failure.

Toynbee's historical analysis focused on the spiritual, economic, and political challenges in civilizations, believing that leadership "creative minorities" responded to the challenges in order to sustain a civilization's progress. Conversely, however, a civilization declines when its leaders do not respond creatively to the challenges they face. Indeed, the growth or decline of civilizations, according to Toynbee, is not based on historical determinism but on leadership capabilities present in society. Unlike the deterministic Oswald Spengler, who, in the book *The Decline of the West*, treated civilizations as unalterable machines following predictable cycles of decline, Toynbee viewed them as networks of social relationships susceptible to leadership decisions, both wise and unwise, which determine their fates. When leaders in a civilization stop responding creatively, the civilization sinks under nationalism, militarism, and the tyranny of a despotic minority. After decades of research, Toynbee proclaimed, "Civilizations die from suicide, not by murder."

Why does it seem that life is a never-ending struggle against powerful forces conspiring to cause decline in every field? Indeed, it requires little effort for things to deteriorate but rigorous discipline for them to consistently improve. Leaders must overcome the degenerative tendencies inherent in all human communities, for decline is the natural state of any civilization, while growth is a leadership anomaly.

However, even the most successful leadership examples will not last forever. Regardless of how strong a leadership team, an organization, or a civilization appears to be, in due time, it will fall. The goal of a leader is to create a culture (current) of progress that can extend the life of his organization for as long as possible. Eventually, when leadership is lacking for a few successive generations, all progress reverses itself. Even so, this is not intended to depress potential leaders; instead, it's intended to help leaders identify the forces working against all human progress in order to overcome them. These forces of decline can be conquered and have sometimes been overcome for centuries at a time.

What are these forces of decline, and how can one identify and overcome them? Imagine a pool with five water jets streaming below the surface in the same direction. Each jet has its own regressive current, but when all five are working together, they form a current or system of decline. For leaders, this is not new, as one rarely comes to the poolside without the current already flowing toward a decline. In fact, it's the challenge of all leadership teams to align together and run against the current of decline. Countering the current of decline is a tough job; that is why leadership is so needed in every generation because it's up to the leaders to create progress.

As a systems engineer, I have studied many leadership teams, organizations, and cultures searching for underlying patterns in the companies. Through extensive historical reading, I began to see similar failure modes or laws of decline at work in communities. With appreciation to thinkers as varied as Frédéric Bastiat, Albert Jay Nock, Theodore Sturgeon, and Isaac Newton, I developed a systems model that explains why civilizations, nations, and communities fail—the five laws of decline (FLD). The laws explain the patterns of disintegration observed repeatedly throughout mankind's history. Each of the above authors provided clues, helping me piece together the pool analogy and the five laws of decline. The laws systematically flow against all progress, similar to gravity working to ground all flying objects or entropy working from order to disorder. Leadership in organizations and communities is the only known way to reverse the decline, but in order for it to last long, it must be applied generationally, that is, maintaining progress against the declining forces when the leadership baton is passed from one generation to the next. Identifying the systematic forces working against progress helps leaders design systems to overcome the regressive effects of the five laws.

## The Five Laws of Decline

**1. Sturgeon's law.** The first law was discussed previously in the leadership chapter. Theodore Sturgeon, in developing his law, stated, "90 percent of science fiction writing is crud, but then again, so is 90 percent of anything." This law applies to nearly everything, but it's meaning to leadership is that 10 percent of any typical group are leaders and 90 percent are followers. Only 10 percent of the people who say they are running in the pool are actually running; most are simply bobbing in the water. The 90 percent are just along for the ride, coasting with the current, or worse yet, running in the wrong direction. The goal is to mentor the 10 percent to have the courage to run against the declining current and help reverse it. Leaders cannot beat Sturgeon's law, but they can create a culture that attracts the 10 percent who choose to lead, rewarding performance, not politics. Communities explode when the 10 percent of leaders fill the leadership spots responsible for creating the current of progress. Alexander the Great understood this thousands of years ago when he declared, "An army of sheep led by a lion is better than an army of lions led by a sheep." Communities decline when the 90 percent sheep are given leadership spots since they are incapable of reversing the current of decline.

**2. Bastiat's law.** Frédéric Bastiat, a French economist, taught the fatal tendency existing in man's heart to satisfy his wants with the least possible effort. This is Bastiat's law: Since men are naturally inclined to avoid pain, which labor is itself, it follows that they will resort to plunder whenever it is easier than work. Much of history is a record of man's plundering of his fellow man. Bastiat wrote:

> Man can live and satisfy his wants only by ceaseless labor; by the ceaseless application of his faculties to natural resources. This process is the origin of property. But it is also true that a man may live and satisfy his wants by seizing and consuming the products of the labor of others. This process is the origin of plunder. Now since man is naturally inclined to avoid pain—and since labor is pain in itself—it follows that men will resort to plunder whenever plunder is easier than work. History shows this quite clearly. And under these conditions, neither religion nor morality can stop it. When, then, does plunder stop? It stops when it becomes more painful and more dangerous than labor. It is evident, then, that the proper purpose of law is to use the power of its collective force to stop this fatal tendency to plunder instead of to work. All the measures of the law should protect property and punish plunder.

Every organization must ensure that people carry their own weight rather than riding off the backs of others' labors. This law is why creating a scoreboard to accurately identify performers from non-performers is essential for any thriving organization. Sadly, bureaucratic companies and governments violate this law repeatedly because it's hard to separate performers from political exploiters in an environment with no quantifiable scoreboard. Why would someone work hard when he is assured a job either way? Bastiat's law is the fatal flaw in communistic theories, since the 90 percent will do as little as possible if given an opportunity, while the 10 percent will be driven to despair because they aren't rewarded for their productive efforts. The only proven way to combat Bastiat's law is to develop, score, and reward performance.

**3. Gresham's law.** Thomas Gresham, an English financier, developed his law originally to be applied to monetary policy. He stated "that when government compulsorily overvalues one money and undervalues another, the undervalued money will leave the country or disappear into hoards, while the overvalued money will flood into circulation." For example, throughout history, when inflated paper money flows into the marketplace, real gold and silver coins are removed from the marketplace. No one willingly pays for goods and services with real money when paper is made a legal currency by government fiat. Real money remains out of circulation until the paper fraud runs its course. The same principle applies to other areas: bad education drives out good education, bad leadership drives out good leadership, and poor character drives out good character, to name just a few. It occurs in companies when political managers are promoted ahead of productive leaders. When the poor behaviors are rewarded, the company is quickly filled with others exhibiting the same nonproductive activities. Leaders, on the other hand, are driven out of the company, not willing to play the political games of a declining company. In other words, if the 10 percent leaders are not rewarded for running in the pool to create a winning current, they will quickly hop out of the pool, leaving only the 90 percent "bobbers." Gresham's law points out that the "bobbers" drive out the leaders when "bobbers" seize control of the company. Getting the right people on the bus and in the right seats is the only way to ensure the 90 percent do not infiltrate and eventually take over the company. What is rewarded will increase; conversely, what isn't rewarded will decrease.

**4. Law of diminishing returns (LDR).** This law, one of the more famous in economic history, is defined as "a law affirming that to continue after a certain level of performance has been reached will result in a decline in effectiveness." In other words, when a certain point of production is reached, the returns begin to decrease and continue to decrease as further production proceeds, assuming all other variables are held constant. For example, a garden produces tomatoes, and by adding a pound of fertilizer, production of tomatoes goes up. Adding another pound of fertilizer increases tomato production even further, but at some point, adding even more no longer increases tomato production and even decreases production as too much fertilizer burns the plants. The LDR affects the quality of anything when attempts are made to produce benefits on a large scale. Mass music, education, and tourism, for example, have decreased in quality with the corresponding increase in quantity. Author Wendy McElroy wrote, "Consider the everyday experience of vacationing at a location that has not yet been 'discovered' by floods of tourists. When tourists begin to flock to the location, the return to everyone abruptly decreases. Both the many and the few no longer receive real benefit. In accommodating popular demands, the vacation site (and all other experiences in life) fall prey to the law of diminishing returns." The LDR, according to Albert Jay Nock, explains America's educational disaster: "Socrates chatting with a single protagonist meant one thing, and well did he know it. Socrates lecturing to a class of fifty would mean something woefully different, so he organized no classes and did no lecturing. Jerusalem was a university town, and in a university every day is field-day for the law of diminishing returns. Jesus stayed away from Jerusalem, and talked with fishermen here and there, who seem to have pretty well got what he was driving at; some better than others, apparently, but on the whole pretty well. And so we have it that unorganized Christianity was one thing, while organized Christianity has consistently been another." In other words, the more people attempted to receive the benefits of education, and the bigger the educational system became, the less education actually took place.

**5. Law of inertia.** Newton's first law states: "Every body remains in a state of rest or uniform motion (constant velocity), unless it is acted upon by an external unbalanced force." In layman's terms, an object at rest tends to stay at rest, and an object in motion tends to stay in motion unless acted upon by another force. Inertia works in the pool when the current carries people in the direction of the flowing water. When a leader must reverse directions in the pool, he has to work to not only move in the new direction but also overcome the inertia of the current still moving in the former direction. Likewise, the longer the current is allowed to flow in the declining direction, the more difficult it is to reverse because one must overcome the built-up inertia. Creating a current in a stagnant pool is tough enough, but it is even tougher to reverse a current of decline, which is what most leadership assignments demand. Think of leaders who have been in a culture of decline, who, even when they decide to turn around the unhealthy culture, must struggle against the poor habits, processes, and attitudes in the existing culture. Big company turnarounds are so rare because the task is so huge. Stopping the inertia of the old culture, which fights change, burns through the leaders' energy.

A good way to illustrate this is to take a group of people and have them run in one direction in a pool. When the current is flowing briskly, have them change directions. The group will be carried by the current even though they are working hard to run in the opposite direction. Leaders must overcome cultural inertia if they plan on turning around an organization.

When a person studies the five laws of decline (FLD), he quickly sees the system of decline working against all progress, revealing why all organizations and civilizations eventually fall. Regretfully, in due time, Sturgeon's law will eventually place a "90 percent nonleader" into the top position. This person will allow the wrong people on the bus, initiating the process of decline as power, plunder, and politics work their destructive forces within the declining organization or civilization. In fact, if a "10 percent leader" doesn't appear quickly and reverse the culture before it's too late, the current will pick up speed and ultimately destroy the organization or civilization that had once prospered.

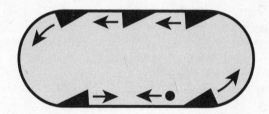

There is a solution, however. Leaders can overcome the FLD by implementing the thirteen resolutions in their lives and organizations. The question is: How long can they maintain progress in the pool amid the jets flowing against them? Indeed, the progress will last only as long as leaders are forged in the discipline of study and will run with the current of progress, resisting the jets pushing for decline.

## A Leadership Legacy

What is a true legacy? A person's true legacy, one that will stand the test of time, is living the thirteen resolutions and sharing them with the next generation. The objective is to provide an environment, a culture, for others to "school" themselves and build the leaders of tomorrow. Leaders who build the thirteen resolutions into their lives are able to model the standard of excellence from which newer leaders can learn. This helps every leader gain strength and confidence for his life's mountain climb. Successful people, the legacy builders, refuse to place people on mountaintops; instead, they build bridges at every chasm on the mountain trail, helping the next generation advance. Legacy builders, through their tireless efforts to overcome the FLD, provide a positive current and teach how to maintain it by modeling the thirteen resolutions to others. In reality, the biggest gift a generation can give to the next generation is a leadership legacy. A leader's example and teachable moments used in mentoring the next generation on how to maintain, if not increase, the positive growth current are more valuable than any of the temporary perks of money, fame, or power.

A positive growth current is more valuable than money, fame, or power because all of these will dissipate over time in the streaming jets of the FLD. For example, how much of Napoleon's wealth, fame, or power has endured after his demise? In fact, money, fame, and power deter the process of personal growth by fooling people into believing that they have already arrived at the destination when the truth is, they haven't even begun the journey. This reveals yet again that success is the journey, not the destination. When leaders do not leave a proper legacy, the next-generation leaders suffer most, struggling to maintain the positive current as the FLD gradually overcomes it.

Our Western forefathers provided a proper legacy by leaving an environment of liberty, allowing people the opportunity to develop resolutions in their lives. This legacy must be forwarded to others by recreating the positive current before it's too late. If a person has learned financial principles that have made a difference in his life, then he should document and share them with as many people as possible. Likewise, if a person has learned friendship principles that have helped him build long-term relationships, then he should capture and share them, imparting his legacy to others. Any area where one learns and applies truth, producing fruit in his life, is a platform for leaving a legacy to others. Since legacies endure longer than people do because of the positive inertia in the pool current, tomorrow's leaders are provided time to learn, gaining needed ex-

**Any area where one learns and applies truth, producing fruit in his life, is a platform for leaving a legacy to others.**

perience before filling the gap left by the previous leaders. The goal of a legacy is to maintain or increase the forward progress and battle the persistent entropy of the FLD. Legacies are lifetime gifts, offered with no strings attached and the objective of making a difference in others' lives. A legacy, then, is passing the baton of the resolutions to the next generation of leaders.

## Three Types of Liberty

The Founding Fathers and Mothers were men and women of resolve, who lived the principles discussed in this book, making mistakes but learning from them in the process. Because they lived their resolutions, they freed themselves from the day-to-day grind of working in order to eat. They focused instead on their purpose, working to fulfill it and leaving in their wake a legacy of liberty for the future generations. Washington, Franklin, and Edwards responded to the challenges of their time by helping reverse the current of decline in their day. Each of them contributed greatly to the liberties that America and the West as a whole have enjoyed for two centuries.

However, the current has reversed again. Leadership, and thus liberty, is declining in the West. Where are today's Washingtons, Franklins, and Edwardses to answer the call of leadership? The three freedoms needed for leadership and society to be restored are the following:

1. Spiritual liberty
2. Political liberty
3. Economic liberty

It's not a coincidence that political and economic freedoms resulted from improved spiritual freedoms since they stand or fall together. Spiritual liberty was fought for and won in the West several hundred years ago, beginning with the Reformation. Spiritual autonomy means that no one can force a person to believe against his conscience. Each person must stand or fall based on his own beliefs and actions before the Almighty God. Free dialogue and discussion are encouraged, while tyranny and force are not part of freedom. Everyone has the responsibility to learn what spiritual freedom means in his life. As Tim Marks has said, "Know why you believe what you believe."

Since man is free before God, a corollary that follows is that man is free before his fellow man, bound only by the rule of law.

The rule of law describes a society in which law is king; everyone, whether rich or poor, follows the laws of the land, which follow the laws of God and human nature. Where law rules, oppression and dictatorship cannot satisfy their every whim; but when tyrants rule, the rule of law is quickly destroyed. The United States Constitution was an attempt to bind the government to follow the rule of law, hindering governmental oppression and arbitrary violence against the citizens.

Lastly, liberty means economic freedom—the freedom to buy and sell without needless regulations and interventions from governments. The freest people in the world lived in Western Christendom from the end of the eighteenth century until the beginning of the twentieth century. For nearly 150 years Western man was allowed the spiritual, political, and economic freedom to flourish. It's not surprising that the greatest increase in prosperity occurred during this era. However, liberty is waning, thanks to the ever-present five laws of decline. For liberty to reign again, a group of men and women must relearn the power of resolutions, applying them into their lives and reversing the currents of decline, not only for their own liberty, but also for the enhancement of the next generation's freedoms.

Autonomy is the liberty to choose responsible actions, while license is absolute freedom that leads to chaos because license isn't tempered with responsibility. Liberty, then, is not license. The rules of the road serve as an everyday-life example of the difference between liberty and license. Although people have the liberty to go anywhere they choose, they do not have the license to drive on any side of the road or switch back and forth freely on a whim. The liberty-loving driver is responsible for following the rules of the road, regardless of whether a police officer is watching because he knows that his being responsible provides freedom for all to enjoy the roads. For without this responsibility, by demanding license rather than liberty, chaos will ensue. Cars would crash into one another since not everyone is following the rules of the road. The irony for those who demand freedom for license is that when it's granted, all people lose their liberty to drive the road, becoming too fearful of reckless drivers demanding license. In the same way, society must be designed under the rule of law, self-evident rules of society that have worked for many millennia. Ordered freedom lifts a society upward, while disordered license destroys everyone's freedom, creating a situation where force must be used to end chaos. Viktor Frankl described it thus: "Freedom is only part of the story and half the truth . . . That is why I recommend that the

Statue of Liberty on the East Coast be supplanted by a Statue of Responsibility on the West Coast." For a society to be free, then, it must also be responsible for creating leaders—thus the need for the thirteen resolutions.

By reviewing the pool analogy again, a person can see that the difference between leaders and followers in the pool is the responsibility accepted for the direction of the current. Followers, naturally, move with the current, regardless of whether the current is flowing in the proper direction for leadership growth. Leaders are different; they are *Rascals*, as Chris Brady teaches, and know that following a current of decline, no matter how easy, is just wrong. Leaders follow an inner compass, determining which direction the current should be flowing and making a stand against the current and the crowd if necessary (and, typically, it is necessary). Standing against the current is a brave act, moving against the current is the beginning of leadership, and forming a team of people willing to move against the current is what top leaders do. Only a few leadership teams run against the current, encouraging others to do the same, literally reversing the current of decline and creating a current of progress. This is the pinnacle of leadership, which is reached by only a select few. As the old saying goes, "Any dead fish can float downstream, but it takes a live one to swim against the current." It takes leadership at the uppermost echelons to reverse the current of decline. Learning to reverse the current and sharing the leadership principles needed to do so with potential future leaders is the only way to continue to progress against the currents of generational decline. This is a true legacy worth leaving to posterity.

As we near the end of this book, I wish to share a few of my personal observations. First, leadership is not for the weak of heart because every leader must make decisions that will not endear himself to all parties. But decide he must if he plans on leading. Second, being a leader in today's selfish and cynical environment causes anyone who lives the thirteen resolutions and hopes for a better tomorrow to be portrayed as out-of-touch at best and manipulative at worst. This is the tragic irony as the West denies the principles of character, honor, and purpose, yet it is dying for lack of them. C. S. Lewis concluded, "Such is the tragi-comedy of our

> **Standing against the current is a brave act, moving against the current is the beginning of leadership, and forming a team of people willing to move against the current is what top leaders do.**

situation—we continue to clamor for those very qualities we are rendering impossible. You can hardly open a periodical without coming across the statement that what our civilization needs is more 'drive', or dynamism, or self-sacrifice, or 'creativity'. In a sort of ghastly simplicity we remove the organ and demand the function. We make men without chests and expect of them virtue and enterprise. We laugh at honor and are shocked to find traitors in our midst. We castrate and bid the geldings be fruitful." Leaders must arise to reverse the current in the pool, turning Lewis's tragicomedy into a drama between the forces producing progress and the forces producing decline within a society.

In his 1920 poem "The Second Coming," W. B. Yeats conveyed the hopelessness pervading the twentieth century, a hopelessness even more prevalent today:

> *Things fall apart; the centre cannot hold;*
> *Mere anarchy is loosed upon the world,*
> *The blood-dimmed tide is loosed, and everywhere*
> *The ceremony of innocence is drowned;*
> *The best lack all conviction, while the worst*
> *Are full of passionate intensity.*

Yeats's words describe the effects of the five laws of decline unleashed upon a faithless, leaderless world. If, as Yeats wrote, "the best lack all convictions," then the worst are the only ones remaining in the pool willing to run. But the worst are running with the current of decline, making the West's defeat seemingly inevitable.

Without "challenge and response" leadership, all civilizations will fall into decline. In fact, Edward Gibbon, in his classic *The Decline and Fall of the Roman Empire*, defined five attributes that marked the Roman Empire at the time of its fall over 1,500 years ago:

1. A mounting love of show and luxury (affluence)
2. A widening gap between the very rich and the very poor
3. An obsession with sex
4. Freakishness in the arts, masquerading as originality
5. An increased desire to live off the state

Even a perfunctory examination of the modern West would reveal it is suffering from a cultural decline similar to that of the Roman Empire. Indeed, a solid argument could be made that the modern West has surpassed Rome in many of its negative influences. The parallels are not coincidental since the degenerative effects of the five laws of decline span across time and space, destroying the economic, political, and moral or spiritual foundations of any leaderless society. Confirming this assessment, Harvard historian Niall Ferguson, in his book *Civilization: The West and the Rest*, wrote, "For it is only by identifying the causes of Western ascendancy that we can hope to estimate with any degree of accuracy the imminence of our fall. My conclusion is that we are already living through the twilight of Western predominance . . . because we ourselves have lost faith in our own civilization." Sadly, when the West progressively rejected faith in God, it was only a matter of time before it lost its faith in everything.

Even with the dismal currents created from modern man's poisonous brew of beliefs, the current of decline can still be reversed. For the last eighteen years, I have communicated to millions of people across North America through a leadership and personal development training community now called LIFE. I have witnessed numerous downtrodden and depressed people turned around through the power of faith, hope, love, and leadership. In truth, there simply are no hopeless situations, only hopeless people in situations. As a Christian leader, I refuse to lose hope for the future, I refuse to succumb to the demonic despair around me, and lastly, I refuse to surrender my role in sharing the good news with others. If a leader's role is to "school his soul" and forge the thirteen resolutions into his being, leaving a legacy and reversing the currents for the next generation, then what the West needs is a leadership revolution, creating thousands of leaders who will reverse the currents of decline. To borrow Toynbee's words, the challenge has been identified and the response has been proposed, but what the West lacks is morally courageous leaders who will stand in the gap. Indeed, the Western civilization hasn't been murdered; rather, having lost faith in her guiding principles, she is committing suicide. With the signs of decay, decline, and demoralization increasing daily, the intelligentsia has been sounding an ignored alarm for nearly a century. I have resolved to respond to the distress call, dedicating my life to reversing the current of decline. Will you help me?

## Colonial New England Fiat Money

Murray Rothbard, the late dean of the Austrian School of economics, wrote a book titled *A History of Money and Banking in the United States*, an insightful read on government and money. In the book, there are many examples of monetary schemes that have failed over the years. Each of Rothbard's monetary examples displays a similar lack of systematic understanding on the part of society's political leaders. Author Henry Hazlitt explained:

> The art of economics consists in looking not merely at the immediate but at the longer effects of any act or policy; it consists in tracing the consequences of that policy not merely for one group but for all groups. Nine-tenths of the economic fallacies that are working such dreadful harm in the world today are the result of ignoring this lesson. These fallacies all stem from one of two central fallacies, or both: that of looking only at the immediate consequences of an act or proposal, and that of looking at the consequences only for a particular group to the neglect of other groups.

When governments attempt to solve society's problems by only looking at the short-term effects, instead of the long-term effects, the proposed fix becomes a tax imposed by those who are above on those who are below through the politicians' ignorance of economic laws. A person, by studying systems thinking and the five laws of decline, can identify these improper measures, aiming to teach governmental leaders the corrosive effects of wrong policies on society.

It's not well-known, but apart from the medieval Chinese, Colonial Massachusetts was the first government to issue fiat paper money. Fiat money is money that is not backed by gold or any other valuable item. The paper magically transforms itself into something that has value simply because a government says so, by fiat. Indeed, the Colonial Americans were the reigning experts on fraudulent paper money issues backed by nothing more than the misplaced trust the colonists had in their state governments.

This dismal monetary history began with a failed plundering expedition in the French colony of Quebec. The Massachusetts government had grown accustomed to victorious raids in Quebec, typically paying the colonial recruits out of the proceeds lifted from the defeated French. But in 1690, the New England colonials were defeated, causing a small problem for Massachusetts and a huge problem for the West because of the poor precedence set by the decisions made that day.

The soldiers arrived back in Boston, ill-tempered and demanding their salaries regardless of the failed outcome of the raid. Hosting discontented soldiers, who had weapons and the will to use them, was not an enjoyable experience for the Boston citizens. After their attempt to raise the funds to pay the soldiers through local merchants were rejected, the government leaders struck upon an idea that still echoes today. The Massachusetts State government concluded that printing £7,000 of paper notes to pay the soldiers was safer than not paying them while they were in the city. Concerned that the public would not accept the paper, the government made several pledges in an attempt to alleviate the public's suspicion. It pledged, first, that it would redeem the paper notes with gold or silver from tax revenues collected over the next couple of years and, second, that no more notes would be issued. Not surprisingly, both pledges were disregarded as fast as government politicians could say, "Free money." It took less than four months for more notes to be issued, ignoring the pledge altogether because of the government's greed for free funds. By February of 1691, another £40,000 of unbacked paper notes was issued to make up for a shortage of government funds, and the politicians proclaimed boldly, and falsely, that this would be the last issue of notes.

The five laws of decline went unrestrained and started crushing progress, causing the negative flow to hinder growth in the colonies. The first law of decline that came into effect was Sturgeon's law. It was at work as most of the colonial politicians had no idea what a poor precedent they were setting in their attempt to satisfy the unhappy soldiers. Any time a vote is taken, the 90 percent looking for an easy way out regardless of the long-term consequences will vote for short-term ease over the long-term principles every time. In this case, they voted to print paper money backed by nothing to pay the soldiers and hoped the issue would go away. Additionally, Sturgeon's law led to Bastiat's law since people would do the least amount of work and effort to produce the results they desired. When politicians learned that they could access money simply by printing it without the pain of asking for more tax dollars or the pain of cutting back programs, a nirvana on earth was proclaimed by local politicians. Bastiat's law created the illusion that people could have their cake and eat it, too. Not surprisingly, the politicians, feeling the Midas touch, dipped into the well again and again, multiplying the fiat money nearly seven times in just one year.

Massachusetts had stumbled across the SFN (something for nothing) formula, and notwithstanding the number of their pledges to stop issuing notes, the local politicians were like kids running loose in a candy store. Government-induced fiat paper inflation was born and bred upon the shores of America. The increasing supply of paper money, along with the citizens' increasing lack of confidence in the local politicians' inflationary intentions, led to a 40 percent depreciation of the paper money when compared with gold and silver specie. Like all governments caught with their hands in the cookie jar, Massachusetts used force to make the "greedy," "traitorous" merchants take paper on par with specie. This simply caused Gresham's law to kick in, driving real money underground while everyone bought and sold using paper (just paper, like *Monopoly* money) in the New England economy. The citizens learned quickly: Why should anyone use real specie when paper money was worth 40 percent less and other citizens were forced, by law, to take it on par with gold and silver coins (specie)? The corresponding shortage of coins drove more of the immoral behavior, which caused the inflation in the first place. Over £240,000 of paper money had been issued by 1711, and by that same time, specie had all but disappeared. The shortage of gold and silver didn't cause the need for paper money; instead, the paper money enacted Gresham's law, which caused the predictable shortage of coinage from the bad money driving out the good.

The British Crown finally intervened to halt the mad rush into insolvency caused by the SFN paper-induced fever suffered by the local New England governmental leaders.

However, before the British closed the money presses, the money printed between 1744 and 1748 had already ballooned to a shocking amount! Paper money expanded from £300,000 to £2.5 million! The depreciation of Massachusetts' money was to such an extent that silver had risen to over sixty shillings an ounce, over ten times the price that it sold for before the paper mania. Gresham's law drove out not only the real money in silver and gold but also the honest politicians, who would have nothing to do with the immoral printing of fiat money. Bad politicians with dishonorable motives and ignorant politicians with a hunger for power drove out the good politicians with honorable motives.

Next, the law of diminishing returns kicked in, as the more fiat money the government produced, the less effect it seemed to have because citizens realized the fraud, forcing the paper money to be heavily discounted compared to gold and silver. Fiat money, like a drug continually used by an addict, requires larger and larger "doses" in order for its effect to be felt mainly because of the law of diminishing returns.

The final law, the law of inertia, made it nearly impossible to stop the fraud once it had begun in Massachusetts. Politicians knew they could resort to fiat money when emergencies arose, thinking fiat money was more palatable politically than legitimate financial measures (taxation or reduced spending) in stemming the monetary decline. The five-laws-of-decline current flowed strongly in Colonial America, interrupted only by the intervention of the British Empire.

In the Revolutionary War, when the colonials squared off against the British, the colonials no longer had the restraining influence of the British, so the Continental Congress produced millions of dollars of fiat money, called Continentals. The five laws bankrupted the Continental Congress and Colonial America. Remember the famous saying "Not worth a Continental?" That phrase was the result of the Continental Congress's inflationary policies. Even though the colonials won the war, they could not service their debt, leading to the Constitutional Convention, which was in part an attempt to discover a way out of the financial morass.

One of the first items discussed and approved in the new United States Constitution was the barring of states and the federal government from ever printing fiat paper money again. (It didn't last, but that's another five-laws-of-decline story.) The vote for no paper money was unanimous. And it was said by many states that had this door not been shut, they would have left the Constitutional Convention, for so great were the painful lessons of fiat money and the colonials' resulting fear.

The founders of America stood against the five laws of decline. They built a culture that taught the value of character, work ethic, and freedom from government intervention to pursue happiness and chase one's dreams. The Constitution was designed to ensure that men and women could achieve based on their willingness to work and dream. The founding leaders built a community of like-minded people from all nations who were willing to stand against the currents of decline. The founders' legacy is measured through the generations that have lived free upon these shores.

In her poem "The New Colossus," which is displayed in the museum at the base of the Statue of Liberty, Emma Lazarus wrote:

> Not like the brazen giant of Greek fame,
> With conquering limbs astride from land to land;
> Here at our sea-washed, sunset gates shall stand
> A mighty woman with a torch, whose flame
> Is the imprisoned lightning, and her name
> Mother of Exiles. From her beacon-hand
> Glows world-wide welcome; her mild eyes command
> The air-bridged harbor that twin cities frame,
> "Keep, ancient lands, your storied pomp!" cries she
> With silent lips. "Give me your tired, your poor,
> Your huddled masses yearning to breathe free,
> The wretched refuse of your teeming shore,
> Send these, the homeless, tempest-tossed to me,
> I lift my lamp beside the golden door!"

The "tired...huddled masses" were people sick of running against the currents of decline, longing for an opportunity to reach for their dreams in a free environment. This is what the founders provided to men and women of all nationalities. Although their ideals were not lived out perfectly, the millions of people who immigrated to America hoping to enjoy the freedom available in the land of opportunity, are a testament to the founders' work.

America's Founding Fathers reversed the current of decline that was forming through tyranny, mercantilism, and fiat money and provided a progressive current for the next generation. They ensured free trade across state borders, no personal income taxes, separation of powers, an independent judicial system, and the Bill of Rights to spiritual and economic freedoms needed to pursue one's dreams.

However, in America and the West today, many of these principles are being disregarded. Total taxation in most Western countries is now greater than the taxation load that was placed on the serfs in the Middle Ages. The current isn't progressing forward anymore; rather, it's declining faster every year. Sadly, many citizens, instead of demanding freedom, are seeking government protection, security, and even exploitation of others, selling their birthrights for a pot of porridge. What the West desperately needs is a group of leaders—similar to Washington, Franklin, and Edwards—who refuse to surrender their freedoms and are willing to stand in the pool against the current of decline. Once their feet are firmly planted, they must dare to run against the current until it reverses once again, bringing the Western nations back from the precipice of imminent destruction. This feat was accomplished in the past, and it must be attempted again. Reversing any current of decline is tough work against immeasurable odds that demands the disciplined application of the thirteen resolutions, but when the fate of the West is at stake, courageous leaders cannot afford to play it safe. Action must be taken.

# George Washington's Rules of Civility and Decent Behavior in Company and Conversation

1. Every action done in company ought to be with some sign of respect to those that are present.
2. When in company, put not your hands to any part of the body not usually discovered.
3. Show nothing to your friend that may affright him.
4. In the presence of others, sing not to yourself with a humming voice, nor drum with your fingers or feet.
5. If you cough, sneeze, sigh, or yawn, do it not loud but privately, and speak not in your yawning, but put your handkerchief or hand before your face and turn aside.
6. Sleep not when others speak; sit not when others stand; speak not when you should hold your peace; walk not on when others stop.
7. Put not off your clothes in the presence of others, nor go out your chamber half dress'd.
8. At play and at fire, it's good manners to give place to the last comer, and affect not to speak louder than ordinary.
9. Spit not into the fire, nor stoop low before it; neither put your hands into the flames to warm them, nor set your feet upon the fire, especially if there be meat before it.
10. When you sit down, keep your feet firm and even; without putting one on the other or crossing them.
11. Shift not yourself in the sight of others, nor gnaw your nails.
12. Shake not the head, feet, or legs; roll not the eyes; lift not one eyebrow higher than the other, wry not the mouth, and bedew no man's face with your spittle by [approaching too near] him [when] you speak.

13.   Kill no vermin, or fleas, lice, ticks, etc. in the sight of others; if you see any filth or thick spittle put your foot dexterously upon it; if it be upon the clothes of your companions, put it off privately, and if it be upon your own clothes, return thanks to him who puts it off behavior or saluting, ought also to be observed in taking of place and sitting down for ceremonies without bounds are troublesome.

14.   Turn not your back to others, especially in speaking; jog not the table or desk on which another reads or writes; lean not upon anyone.

15.   Keep your nails clean and short, also your hands and teeth clean, yet without showing any great concern for them.

16.   Do not puff up the cheeks, loll not out the tongue with the hands, or beard, thrust out the lips, or bite them, or keep the lips too open or too close.

17.   Be no flatterer, neither play with any that delight not to be played withal.

18.   Read no letter, books, or papers in company, but when there is a necessity for the doing of it, you must ask leave; come not near the books or writings of another so as to read them unless desired, or give your opinion of them unasked,- also look not nigh when another is writing a letter.

19.   Let your countenance be pleasant but in serious matters somewhat grave.

20.   The gestures of the body must be suited to the discourse you are upon.

21.   Reproach none for the infirmities of nature, nor delight to put them that have in mind of thereof.

22.   Show not yourself glad at the misfortune of another though he were your enemy.

23.   When you see a crime punished, you may be inwardly pleased; but [damaged manuscript] show pity to the suffering offender.

24.   [damaged manuscript]

25.   Superfluous compliments and all affectation of ceremonies are to be avoided, yet where due they are not to be neglected.

26.   In putting off your hat to persons of distinction, as noblemen, justices, churchmen, etc., make a reverence, bowing more or less according to the custom of the better bred, and

quality of the persons; among your equals expect not always that they should begin with you first; but to pull off the hat when there is no need is affectation, in the manner of saluting and resaluting in word keep to the most usual custom.

27. 'Tis ill manners to bed one more eminent than yourself be covered, as well as not to do it to whom it is due. Likewise he that makes too much haste to put on his hat does not well, yet he ought to put it on at the first, or at most the second time of being asked; now what is herein spoken, of qualification in behavior or saluting ought to be taking place and sitting down for ceremonies without bounds are troublesome.

28. If any one come to speak to you while you are [are] sitting, stand up, though he be your inferior, and when you present seats, let it be to everyone according to his degree.

29. When you meet with one of greater quality than yourself, stop, and retire, especially if it be at a door or any straight place, to give way for him to pass.

30. In walking the highest place in most countries hand; therefore place yourself on the left of him whom you desire to honor: but if three walk together the middle place is the most honorable; the wall is usually given to the most worthy if two walk together.

31. If anyone far surpasses others, either in age, estate, or merits [and] would give place to a meaner than himself, the same ought not to accept it, [save he offer] it above once or twice.

32. To one that is your equal, or not much inferior, you are to give the chief place in your lodging, and he to whom it is offered ought at the first to refuse it, but at the second to accept though not without acknowledging his own unworthiness.

33. They that are in dignity or in office have in all places precedency, but whilst they are young, they ought to respect those that are their equals in birth or other qualities, though they have no public charge.

34. It is good manners to prefer them to whom we speak before ourselves, especially if they be above us, with whom in no sort we ought to begin.

35. Let your discourse with men of business be short and com-

prehensive.

36. Artificers and persons of low degree ought not to use many ceremonies to lords or others of high degree, but respect and highly honor them, and those of high degree ought to treat them with affability and courtesy, without arrogance.

37. In speaking to men of quality, do not lean nor look them full in the face, nor approach too near them at left. Keep a full pace from them.

38. In visiting the sick, do not presently play the physician if you be not knowing therein.

39. In writing or speaking, give to every person his due title according to his degree and the custom of the place.

40. Strive not with your superior in argument, but always submit your argument to others with modesty.

41. Undertake not to teach your equal in the art himself professes; it [manuscript damaged] of arrogance.

42. [damaged manuscript]; and same with a clown and a prince.

43. Do not express joy before one sick in pain, for that contrary passion will aggravate his misery.

44. When a man does all he can, though it succeed not well, blame not him that did it.

45. Being to advise or reprehend any one, consider whether it ought to be in public or in private, and presently or at some other time, in what terms to do it; and in reproving show no signs of choler but do it with all sweetness and mildness.

46. Take all admonitions thankfully in what time or place soever given, but afterwards not being culpable, take a time and place convenient to let him know it that gave them.

47. Mock not nor jest at anything of importance. Break no jests that are sharp, biting,- and if you deliver any thing witty and pleasant, abstain from laughing thereat yourself.

48. Where in [wherein] you reprove another be unblameable yourself, -for example is more prevalent than precepts.

49. Use no reproachful language against any one; neither curse nor revile.

50. Be not hasty to believe flying reports to the disparagement of any.

51. Wear not your clothes foul, or ripped, or dusty, but see they be brushed once every day at least and take heed that you

approach not to any uncleanness.

52. In your apparel, be modest and endeavor to accommodate nature, rather than to procure admiration; keep to the fashion of your equals, such as are civil and orderly with respect to time and places.

53. Run not in the streets, neither go too slowly, nor with mouth open; go not shaking of arms, nor upon the toes, nor in a dancing [damaged manuscript].

54. Play not the peacock, looking every where about you, to see if you be well decked, if your shoes fit well, if your stockings sit neatly and clothes handsomely.

55. Eat not in the streets, nor in your house, out of season.

56. Associate yourself with men of good quality if you esteem your own reputation; for 'tis better to be alone than in bad company.

57. In walking up and down in a house, only with one in company if he be greater than yourself, at the first give him the right hand and stop not till he does and be not the first that turns, and when you do turn let it be with your face towards him; if he be a man of great quality walk not with him cheek by jowl but somewhat behind him but yet in such a manner that he may easily speak to you.

58. Let your conversation be without malice or envy, for 'tis a sign of a tractable and commendable nature, and in all causes of passion permit reason to govern.

59. Never express anything unbecoming, nor act against the rules before your inferiors.

60. Be not immodest in urging your friends to discover a secret.

61. Utter not base and frivolous things among grave and learned men, nor very difficult questions or subjects among the ignorant, or things hard to be believed; stuff not your discourse with sentences among your betters nor equals.

62. Speak not of doleful things in a time of mirth or at the table; speak not of melancholy things or death and wounds, and if others mention them, change if you can the discourse; tell not your dream, but to your intimate.

63. A man ought not to value himself of his achievements or rare qualities [damaged manuscript] virtue or kindred.

64. Break not a jest where none take pleasure in mirth; laugh

not alone, nor at all without occasion; deride no man's misfortune though there seem to be some cause.

65. Speak not injurious words neither in jest nor earnest; scoff at none although they give occasion.

66. Be not froward but friendly and courteous, the first to salute, hear, and answer; and be not pensive when it's a time to converse.

67. Detract not from others, neither be excessive in commanding.

68. Go not thither, where you know not whether you shall be welcome or not; give not advice [without] being asked, and when desired do it briefly.

69. If two contend together take not the part of either unconstrained, and be not obstinate in your own opinion; in things indifferent be of the major side.

70. Reprehend not the imperfections of others, for that belongs to parents, masters, and superiors.

71. Gaze not on the marks or blemishes of others and ask not how they came. What you may speak in secret to your friend, deliver not before others.

72. Speak not in an unknown tongue in company but in your own language and that as those of quality do and not as the vulgar; sublime matters treat seriously.

73. Think before you speak; pronounce not imperfectly, nor bring out your words too hastily, but orderly and distinctly.

74. When another speaks, be attentive yourself; and disturb not the audience. If any hesitate in his words, help him not nor prompt him without desired; interrupt him not, nor answer him till his speech has ended.

75. In the midst of discourse [damaged manuscript] but if you perceive any stop because of [damaged manuscript]; to proceed: If a person of quality comes in while you're conversing, it's handsome to repeat what was said before.

76. While you are talking, point not with your finger at him of whom you discourse, nor approach too near him to whom you talk especially to his face.

77. Treat with men at fit times about business and whisper not in the company of others.

78. Make no comparisons and if any of the company be com-

mended for any brave act of virtue, commend not another for the same.

79. Be not apt to relate news if you know not the truth thereof. In discoursing of things you have heard, name not your author always; a secret discover not.

80. Be not tedious in discourse or in reading unless you find the company pleased therewith.

81. Be not curious to know the affairs of others, neither approach those that speak in private.

82. Undertake not what you cannot perform but be careful to keep your promise.

83. When you deliver a matter do it without passion and with discretion, however mean the person be you do it to.

84. When your superiors talk to anybody neither speak nor laugh.

85. In company of those of higher quality than yourself, speak not 'til you are asked a question, then stand upright, put off your hat and answer in few words.

86. In disputes, be not so desirous to overcome as not to give liberty to one to deliver his opinion and submit to the judgment of the major part, specially if they are judges of the dispute.

87. [damaged manuscript] as becomes a man grave, settled, and attentive [damaged manuscript] [predict not at every turn what others say.

88. Be not diverse in discourse; make not many digressions; nor repeat often the same manner of discourse.

89. Speak not evil of the absent, for it is unjust.

90. Being set at meat scratch not, neither spit, cough, or blow your nose except there's a necessity for it.

91. Make no show of taking great delight in your the table; neither find great delight in your victuals; feed not with greediness; eat your bread with a knife; lean not on the table; neither find fault with what you eat.

92. Take no salt or cut bread with your knife greasy.

93. Entertaining anyone at table it is decent to present him with meat; undertake not to help others desired by the master.

94. If you soak bread in the sauce, let it be no more than what you put in your mouth at a time and blow not your broth at table; let it stay till it cools of itself.

95. Put not your meat to your mouth with your knife in your

hand; neither spit forth the stones of any fruit pie upon a dish nor cast anything under the table.

96. It's unbecoming to heap much to one's meat keep your fingers clean; when foul wipe them on a corner of your table napkin.

97. Put not another bite into your mouth till the former be swallow; let not your morsels be too big.

98. Drink not nor talk with your mouth full; neither gaze about you while you are a drinking.

99. Drink not too leisurely nor yet too hastily. Before and after drinking wipe your lips; breathe not then or ever with too great a noise, for it is an evil.

100. Cleanse not your teeth with the tablecloth, napkin, fork, or knife; but if others do it, let it be done without a peep to them.

101. Rinse not your mouth in the presence of others.

102. It is out of use to call upon the company often to eat; nor need you drink to others every time you drink.

103. In company of your betters be not [damaged manuscript] than they are; lay not your arm but [damaged manuscript].

104. It belongs to the chiefest in company to unfold his napkin and fall to meat first; but he ought then to begin in time and to dispatch with dexterity that the slowest may have time allowed him.

105. Be not angry at table whatever happens and if you have reason to be so, show it not but on a cheerful countenance especially if there be strangers, for good humor makes one dish of meat and whey.

106. Set not yourself at the upper of the table but if it be your due, or that the master of the house will have it so, contend not, lest you should trouble the company.

107. If others talk at table be attentive but talk not with meat in your mouth.

108. When you speak of God or his Attributes, let it be seriously; reverence, honor and obey your natural parents although they be poor.

109. Let your recreations be manful not sinful.

110. Labor to keep alive in your breast that little spark of celestial fire called conscience.

# George Washington's
# Partial List of Maxims

1. A slender acquaintance with the world must convince every man that actions, not words, are the true criterion of the attachment of friends.
2. Associate with men of good quality if you esteem your own reputation, for it is better to be alone than in bad company.
3. Be courteous to all, but intimate with few, and let those few be well tried before you give them your confidence.
4. Discipline is the soul of an army. It makes small numbers formidable, procures success to the weak and esteem to all.
5. Experience teaches us that it is much easier to prevent an enemy from posting themselves than it is to dislodge them after they have got possession.
6. Few men have virtue to withstand the highest bidder.
7. True friendship is a plant of slow growth and must undergo and withstand the shocks of adversity before it is entitled to the appellation.
8. Happiness and moral duty are inseparably connected.
9. I hope I shall possess firmness and virtue enough to maintain what I consider the most enviable of all titles, the character of an honest man.
10. It is better to be alone than in bad company.
11. It is better to offer no excuse than a bad one.
12. It is impossible to rightly govern a nation without God and the Bible.
13. It will be found an unjust and unwise jealousy to deprive a man of his natural liberty upon the supposition he may abuse it.
14. Labor to keep alive in your breast that little spark of celestial fire called conscience.
15. Lenience will operate with greater force, in some instances, than rigor. It is therefore my first wish to have all of my

conduct distinguished by it.

16. Let us raise a standard to which the wise and honest can repair; the rest is in the hands of God.

17. Let us with caution indulge the supposition that morality can be maintained without religion. Reason and experience both forbid us to expect that national morality can prevail in exclusion of religious principle.

18. Let your heart feel for the afflictions and distress of everyone, and let your hand give in proportion to your purse.

19. My observation is that whenever one person is found adequate to the discharge of a duty . . . it is worse executed by two persons, and scarcely done at all if three or more are employed therein.

20. Liberty, when it begins to take root, is a plant of rapid growth.

21. The foolish and wicked practice of profane cursing and swearing is a vice so mean and low that every person of sense and character detests and despises it.

22. To be prepared for war is one of the most effective means of preserving peace.

23. Truth will ultimately prevail where there is pain to bring it to light.

24. We should not look back unless it is to derive useful lessons from past errors, and for the purpose of profiting by dearly bought experience.

25. Worry is the interest paid by those who borrow trouble.

26. Nothing is a greater stranger to my breast, or a sin that my soul more abhors, than that black and detestable one, ingratitude.

27. I shall not be deprived . . . of a comfort in the worst event, if I retain a consciousness of having acted to the best of my judgment.

28. There is a Destiny which has the control of our actions, not to be resisted by the strongest efforts of Human Nature.

29. It is with pleasure I receive reproof, when reproof is due, because no person can be readier to accuse me than I am to acknowledge an error, when I am guilty of one, nor more desirous of atoning for a crime, when I am sensible of having committed it.

30. I shall make it the most agreeable part of my duty to study merit and reward the brave and deserving.

31. I hold the maxim no less applicable to public than to private affairs that honesty is the best policy.

32.  To contract new debts is not the way to pay old ones.
33.  Three things prompt men to a regular discharge of their duty in time of action: natural bravery, hope of reward, and fear of punishment.
34.  Ninety-nine percent of the failures come from people who have the habit of making excuses.
35.  The administration of justice is the firmest pillar of government.

## APPENDIX C

# Ben Franklin's Thirteen Virtues

1. Temperance. Eat not to dullness; drink not to elevation.
2. Silence. Speak not but what may benefit others or yourself; avoid trifling conversation.
3. Order. Let all your things have their places; let each part of your business have its time.
4. Resolution. Resolve to perform what you ought; perform without fail what you resolve.
5. Frugality. Make no expense but to do good to others or yourself; i.e., waste nothing.
6. Industry. Lose no time; be always employ'd in something useful; cut off all unnecessary actions.
7. Sincerity. Use no hurtful deceit; think innocently and justly, and, if you speak, speak accordingly.
8. Justice. Wrong none by doing injuries, or omitting the benefits that are your duty.
9. Moderation. Avoid extremes; forbear resenting injuries so much as you think they deserve.
10. Cleanliness. Tolerate no uncleanliness in body, clothes, or habitation.
11. Tranquility. Be not disturbed at trifles, or at accidents common or unavoidable.
12. Chastity. Rarely use venery but for health or offspring, never to dullness, weakness, or the injury of your own or another's peace or reputation.
13. Humility. Imitate Jesus and Socrates.

# Jonathan Edwards's Seventy Resolutions

Being sensible that I am unable to do anything without God's help, I do humbly entreat Him by his grace to enable me to keep these resolutions, so far as they are agreeable to His will, for Christ's sake.

1.  Resolved, that I will do whatsoever I think to be most to God's glory, and my own good, profit and pleasure, in the whole of my duration, without any consideration of the time, whether now, or never so many myriad's of ages hence. Resolved to do whatever I think to be my duty and most for the good and advantage of mankind in general. Resolved to do this, whatever difficulties I meet with, how many and how great soever.
2.  Resolved, to be continually endeavoring to find out some new invention and contrivance to promote the aforementioned things.
3.  Resolved, if ever I shall fall and grow dull, so as to neglect to keep any part of these Resolutions, to repent of all I can remember, when I come to myself again.
4.  Resolved, never to do any manner of thing, whether in soul or body, less or more, but what tends to the glory of God; nor be, nor suffer it, if I can avoid it.
5.  Resolved, never to lose one moment of time; but improve it the most profitable way I possibly can.
6.  Resolved, to live with all my might, while I do live.
7.  Resolved, never to do anything, which I should be afraid to do, if it were the last hour of my life.
8.  Resolved, to act, in all respects, both speaking and doing, as if nobody had been so vile as I, and as if I had committed the same sins, or had the same infirmities or failings as others; and that I will let the knowledge of their failings promote nothing but shame in myself, and prove only an

occasion of my confessing my own sins and misery to God.

9.     Resolved, to think much on all occasions of my own dying, and of the common circumstances which attend death.

10.     Resolved, when I feel pain, to think of the pains of martyrdom, and of hell.

11.     Resolved, when I think of any theorem in divinity to be solved, immediately to do what I can towards solving it, if circumstances don't hinder.

12.     Resolved, if I take delight in it as a gratification of pride, or vanity, or on any such account, immediately to throw it by.

13.     Resolved, to be endeavoring to find out fit objects of charity and liberality.

14.     Resolved, never to do anything out of revenge.

15.     Resolved, never to suffer the least motions of anger to irrational beings.

16.     Resolved, never to speak evil of anyone, so that it shall tend to his dishonor, more or less, upon no account except for some real good.

17.     Resolved, that I will live so as I shall wish I had done when I come to die.

18.     Resolved, to live so at all times, as I think is best in my devout frames, and when I have clearest notions of things of the gospel, and another world.

19.     Resolved, never to do anything, which I should be afraid to do, if I expected it would not be above an hour, before I should hear the last trump.

20.     Resolved, to maintain the strictest temperance in eating and drinking.

21.     Resolved, never to do anything, which if I should see in another, I should count a just occasion to despise him for, or to think any way the more meanly of him.

22.     Resolved, to endeavor to obtain for myself as much happiness, in the other world, as I possibly can, with all the power; might, vigor, and vehemence, yea violence, I am capable of, or can bring myself to exert, in any way that can be thought of.

23.     Resolved, frequently to take some deliberate action, which seems most unlikely to be done, for the glory of God, and trace it back to the original intention, designs and ends of it; and if I find it not to be for God's glory, to repute it as a breach of the 4th Resolution.

24.     Resolved, whenever I do any conspicuously evil action, to trace it back, till I come to the original cause; and then both

carefully endeavor to do so no more, and to fight and pray with all my might against the original of it.

25. Resolved, to examine carefully, and constantly, what that one thing in me is, which causes me in the least to doubt of the love of God; and to direct all my forces against it.

26. Resolved, to cast away such things, as I find do abate my assurance.

27. Resolved, never willfully to omit anything, except the omission be for the glory of God; and frequently to examine my omissions.

28. Resolved, to study the Scriptures so steadily, constantly and frequently, as that I may find, and plainly perceive myself to grow in the knowledge of the same.

29. Resolved, never to count that a prayer, nor to let that pass as a prayer, nor that as a petition of a prayer, which is so made, that I cannot hope that God will answer it; nor that as a confession, which I cannot hope God will accept.

30. Resolved, to strive to my utmost every week to be brought higher in religion, and to a higher exercise of grace, than I was the week before.

31. Resolved, never to say anything at all against anybody, but when it is perfectly agreeable to the highest degree of Christian honor, and of love to mankind, agreeable to the lowest humility, and sense of my own faults and failings, and agreeable to the golden rule; often, when I have said anything against anyone, to bring it to, and try it strictly by the test of this Resolution.

32. Resolved, to be strictly and firmly faithful to my trust, that that in Prov. 20:6, "A faithful man who can find?" may not be partly fulfilled in me.

33. Resolved, always to do what I can towards making, maintaining, establishing and preserving peace, when it can be without over-balancing detriment in other respects. Dec.26, 1722.

34. Resolved, in narration's never to speak anything but the pure and simple verity.

35. Resolved, whenever I so much question whether I have done my duty, as that my quiet and calm is thereby disturbed, to set it down, and also how the question was resolved. Dec. 18, 1722.

36. Resolved, never to speak evil of any, except I have some particular good call for it. Dec. 19, 1722.

37. Resolved, to inquire every night, as I am going to bed,

wherein I have been negligent, what sin I have committed,
and wherein I have denied myself: also at the end of every
week, month and year. Dec.22, and 26, 1722.

38. Resolved, never to speak anything that is ridiculous,
sportive, or matter of laughter on the Lord's Day. Sabbath
evening, Dec. 23, 1722.

39. Resolved, never to do anything that I so much question the
lawfulness of, as that I intend, at the same time, to consider
and examine afterwards, whether it be lawful or no; except
I as much question the lawfulness of the omission.

40. Resolved, to inquire every night, before I go to bed, whether
I have acted in the best way I possibly could, with respect to
eating and drinking. Jan. 7, 1723.

41. Resolved, to ask myself at the end of every day, week,
month and year, wherein I could possibly in any respect
have done better. Jan. 11, 1723.

42. Resolved, frequently to renew the dedication of myself to
God, which was made at my baptism; which I solemnly
renewed, when I was received into the communion of the
church; and which I have solemnly re-made this twelfth day
of January, 1723.

43. Resolved, never henceforward, till I die, to act as if I were
any way my own, but entirely and altogether God's, agreeable to what is to be found in. Saturday, Jan.12, 1723.

44. Resolved, that no other end but religion, shall have any
influence at all on any of my actions; and that no action
shall be, in the least circumstance, any otherwise than the
religious end will carry it. Jan.12, 1723.

45. Resolved, never to allow any pleasure or grief, joy or sorrow,
nor any affection at all, nor any degree of affection, nor any
circumstance relating to it, but what helps religion. Jan.12,
and 13, 1723.

46. Resolved, never to allow the least measure of any fretting
uneasiness at my father or mother. Resolved to suffer no
effects of it, so much as in the least alteration of speech,
or motion of my eye: and to be especially careful of it, with
respect to any of our family.

47. Resolved, to endeavor to my utmost to deny whatever is
not most agreeable to a good, and universally sweet and be-
nevolent, quiet, peaceable, contented, easy, compassionate,
generous, humble, meek, modest, submissive, obliging, diligent and industrious, charitable, even, patient, moderate,
forgiving, sincere temper; and to do at all times what such

a temper would lead me to. Examine strictly every week, whether I have done so. Sabbath morning. May 5, 1723.

48. Resolved, constantly, with the utmost niceness and diligence, and the strictest scrutiny, to be looking into the state of my soul, that I may know whether I have truly an interest in Christ or no; that when I come to die, I may not have any negligence respecting this to repent of. May 26, 1723.

49. Resolved, that this never shall be, if I can help it.

50. Resolved, I will act so as I think I shall judge would have been best, and most prudent, when I come into the future world. July 5, 1723.

51. Resolved, that I will act so, in every respect, as I think I shall wish I had done, if I should at last be damned. July 8, 1723.

52. I frequently hear persons in old age say how they would live, if they were to live their lives over again: Resolved that I will live just so as I can think I shall wish I had done, supposing I live to old age. July 8, 1723.

53. Resolved, to improve every opportunity, when I am in the best and happiest frame of mind, to cast and venture my soul on the Lord Jesus Christ, to trust and confide in him, and consecrate myself wholly to him; that from this I may have assurance of my safety, knowing that I confide in my Redeemer. July 8, 1723.

54. Whenever I hear anything spoken in conversation of any person, if I think it would be praiseworthy in me, Resolved, to endeavor to imitate it. July 8, 1723.

55. Resolved, to endeavor to my utmost to act as I can think I should do, if I had already seen the happiness of heaven, and hell torments. July 8, 1723.

56. Resolved, never to give over, nor in the least to slacken my fight with my corruptions, however unsuccessful I may be.

57. Resolved, when I fear misfortunes and adversities, to examine whether I have done my duty, and resolve to do it; and let it be just as providence orders it, I will as far as I can, be concerned about nothing but my duty and my sin. June 9, and July 13, 1723.

58. Resolved, not only to refrain from an air of dislike, fretfulness, and anger in conversation, but to exhibit an air of love, cheerfulness and benignity. May 27, and July 13, 1723.

59. Resolved, when I am most conscious of provocations to ill nature and anger, that I will strive most to feel and act good-naturedly; yea, at such times, to manifest good nature,

though I think that in other respects it would be disadvantageous, and so as would be imprudent at other times. May 12, July 2, and July 13, 1723.

60. Resolved, whenever my feelings begin to appear in the least out of order, when I am conscious of the least uneasiness within, or the least irregularity without, I will then subject myself to the strictest examination. July 4, and 13, 1723.

61. Resolved, that I will not give way to that listlessness which I find unbends and relaxes my mind from being fully and fixedly set on religion, whatever excuse I may have for it-that what my listlessness inclines me to do, is best to be done, etc. May 21, and July 13, 1723.

62. Resolved, never to do anything but duty; and then according to Eph. 6:6-8, do it willingly and cheerfully as unto the Lord, and not to man; "knowing that whatever good thing any man doth, the same shall he receive of the Lord." June 25 and July 13, 1723.

63. On the supposition, that there never was to be but one individual in the world, at any one time, who was properly a complete Christian, in all respects of a right stamp, having Christianity always shining in its true luster, and appearing excellent and lovely, from whatever part and under whatever character viewed: Resolved, to act just as I would do, if I strove with all my might to be that one, who should live in my time. Jan.14, and July 3, 1723.

64. Resolved, when I find those "groanings which cannot be uttered" (Rom. 8:26), of which the Apostle speaks, and those "breakings of soul for the longing it hath," of which the Psalmist speaks, Psalm 119:20, that I will promote them to the utmost of my power, and that I will not be wear', of earnestly endeavoring to vent my desires, nor of the repetitions of such earnestness. July 23, and August 10, 1723.

65. Resolved, very much to exercise myself in this all my life long, viz. with the greatest openness I am capable of, to declare my ways to God, and lay open my soul to him: all my sins, temptations, difficulties, sorrows, fears, hopes, desires, and every thing, and every circumstance; according to Dr. Manton's 27th Sermon on Psalm 119. July 26, and Aug. 10, 1723.

66. Resolved, that I will endeavor always to keep a benign aspect, and air of acting and speaking in all places, and in all companies, except it should so happen that duty requires otherwise.

67. Resolved, after afflictions, to inquire, what I am the better for them, what good I have got by them, and what I might have got by them.

68. Resolved, to confess frankly to myself all that which I find in myself, either infirmity or sin; and, if it be what concerns religion, also to confess the whole case to God, and implore needed help. July 23, and August 10, 1723.

69. Resolved, always to do that, which I shall wish I had done when I see others do it. Aug. 11, 1723.

70. Let there be something of benevolence, in all that I speak. Aug. 17, 1723.

# Bibliography

## Introduction

Black, Jim. *When Nations Die.* Tyndale House Publishers, 1995.

Brady, Christopher and Orrin Woodward. *Launching a Leadership Revolution: Mastering the Five Levels of Influence.* New York: Business Plus, 2005.

Brukhiser, Richard. *Founding Father: Rediscovering George Washington.* New York: Free Press, 1997.

Covey, Steven R. *The 7 Habits of Highly Effective People.* New York: Free Press, 2004.

Franklin, Benjamin. *Benjamin Franklin's Autobiography.* New York: EP Dutton & Co., 1913.

Isaacson, Walter. *Benjamin Franklin: An American Life.* Simon Schuster, 2003.

Jones, Martin Lloyd. *Spiritual Depression: Its Causes and Its Cures.* Grand Rapids: Wm. B. Eerdmans Publishing Company, 1965.

Kersten, Katherine. "George Washington's Character." *Star Tribune.* March 6, 1996.

Lee, Major General. *George Washington! A Funeral Oration on His Death.* London: 1800.

Marsden, George M. *Jonathan Edwards: A Life.* New Haven: Yale University Press, 2003.

McGiffert, A. C. Jr. *Jonathan Edwards.* New York: 1932.

Nichols, Stephen. "The Resolutions of Jonathan Edwards." *Table Talk Magazine*, 2009.

Ortega y Gasset, José. *The Revolt of the Masses*. New York: W. W. Norton & Company, Inc., 1960.

Roepke, Wilhelm. *Human Economy*. ISI Books, 1998.

Senge, Peter. *The Fifth Discipline*. New York: Doubleday Currency, 1990.

Smith, Richard Norton. *Patriarch: George Washington and the New American Nation*. New York: Houghton Mifflin Company, 1993.

Stewart, Randall. *American Literature and Christian Doctrine*. Louisiana: Louisiana Press, 1958.

## Chapter 1

Allen, Woody. http://thinkexist.com. 2011.

Collins, Jim. *Good to Great*. New York: Harper Business, 2001.

Covey, Steven R. *First Things First*. New York: Free Press, 1996.

Elliot, Jay and William L. Simon. *The Steve Jobs Way*. New York: Harper, 2001.

Emmerson, Ralph Waldo. *Essays*. 1841.

Gladwell, Malcom. *Outliers*. New York: Little, Brown and Company, 2008.

Gray, E. N. *The Common Denominator of Success*. E-Book, 1940.

Munroe, Myles. *Power of Vision*. Kensington, PA: Whitaker House, 2003.

Nietzsche, Friedrich. *Thus Spoke Zarathustra: A Book for All and None*. Germany: Ernst Schmeitzner, 1883.

Perkhurst, Charles. http://httpthinkexist.com. 2011.

Pink, Daniel H. *Drive*. New York: Riverhead Books, 2009.

Russell, Bertrand. "A Free Man's Worship." 1903.

Senge, Peter. *The Fifth Discipline*. New York: Doubleday Currency, 1990.

Smith, Hyrum W. *10 Natural Laws of Successful Time and Life Management*. New York: Warner Books, 1994.

Warren, Rick. *The Purpose Driven Life*. Grand Rapids: Zondervan, 2002.

Williamson, Marianne. "Our Deepest Fear." *A Return to Love*. New York: Harper Perennial, 1993.

Wyatt, Ian. "Top 5 Priorities: The Story of Ivy Lee and Bethlehem Steel." January 24, 2001. http://www.marksanborn.com.

### John Wooden

Carty, Jay. *Coach Wooden's Pyramid of Success*. New York: Gospel Light Publishers, 2005.

Wooden, John and Don Yaeger. *A Game Plan for Life: The Power of Mentoring*. New York: Bloomsbury USA, 2009.

Wooden, John and Steve Jamison. *Wooden*. New York: McGraw-Hill, 1999.

Wooden, John and Steve Jamison. *Wooden on Leadership*. New York: McGraw-Hill, 2005.

### Chapter 2

Bastiat, Frédéric. *The Law*. Kessinger Publishing, 2004.

Canfield, Jack. *The Success Principles.* New York: Harper Collins, 2005.

Colson, Chuck. "The Wages of Secularism." *Christianity Today.* June 10, 2002.

Connolly, Cyril. "C.S. Lewis in the Unquiet Grave," 1944.

Csorba, Les. *Trust.* Nashville, Tennessee: Thomas Nelson, Inc., 2006.

Covey, Stephen M. R. *The Speed of Trust.* New York: Free Press, 2006.

Kramnick, Isaac, ed. *The Portable Edmund Burke.* Penguin Book, 1999.

Lee, Gus. *Courage.* San Francisco: Jossey-Bass Publishing, 2006.

Lewis, C. S. *Mere Christianity.* San Francisco: Harper Publishing, 2001.

Luther, Martin. *Biblical Studies Ministries International.* http://www.bsmi.org.

Niemoller, Martin. "Speech to the Confessing Church in Frankfurt." January 6, 1946.

Plato. *Georgia's Project.* Gutenberg.

Sanborn, Mark. "Failure of Leadership." November 9, 2009. http://www.marksanborn.com.

Scott, Walter. "Marmion." 1808. http://www.online-literature.com.

"Time Theft." *Mission Outreach.* January 1986.

Wooden, John and Steve Jamison. *Wooden.* New York: McGraw-Hill, 1999.

### *Ludwig von Mises*

Heilbroner, Robert. *The World after Communism*. Dissent, 1990.

Hitler, Adolf. http://thinkexist.com.

Holsmann, Jorg. *Last Knight of Liberalism*. Auburn, Alabama: Ludwig von Mises Institute, 2007.

Keynes, John Maynard. http://thinkexist.com.

Lenin, V. I. http://thinkexist.com.

Mises, Ludwig von. *Human Action*. Auburn, Alabama: Ludwig von Mises Institute, 2007.

Rothbard, Murray Newton. *Biography of Ludwig von Mises*. Auburn, Alabama: Ludwig von Mises Institute, 2007.

Virgil. http://thinkexist.com


### Chapter 3

Canfield, Jack. *Success Principles*. New York: Harper Collins, 2005.

Ford, Henry II. http://www.quotationsbook.com.

"Reframe Your Thinking to Change Your Attitude." 2008. http://www.creators.com.

Swindoll, Charles. http://thinkexist.com.

Ziglar, Zig. *See You at the Top*. Pelican Publishing, 1982.

### *Roger Bannister*

Bannister, Roger. "Guardian News." 2004.

Bascomb, Neal. *The Perfect Mile.* Boston: Houghton Mifflin Harcourt, 2005.


**Chapter 4**

Bristol, Claude. *The Magic of Believing.* New York: Pocket Books, 1991.

Bonaparte, Napoleon. http://thinkexist.com.

Brooke, Richard Bliss. *Mach II with Your Hair on Fire: The Art of Vision and Self Motivation.* Couer d' Aleno, Idaho: High Performance People LLC, 2000.

Calonius, Erik. *Ten Steps Ahead.* New York: Penguin, 2011.

Canfield, Jack. *Success Principles.* New York: Harper Collins, 2005.

Einstein, Albert. http://thinkexist.com.

Maltz, Maxwell. *Pshycho-Cybernetics.* New York: Pocket Books, 1964.

Ponscente, Vince. *Ant and the Elephant.* Mechanicsburg, Pennsylvannia: Executive Books, 2004.

Thoreau, Henry David. http://thinkexist.com.

Wilson, Timothy. *Strangers to Ourselves.* Boston: Belknap Press, 2004.

*Will Smith*

Smith, Will. "Accerlatime." *YouTube.* Accessed January 14, 2010. http://youtube.com.

Smith, Will. "Inner Challenge." *YouTube.* Accessed October 23, 2009. http://youtube.com.

Smith, Will. "Success Video." *YouTube.* Accessed April 5,

2010. http://youtube.com.

Smith, Will. "Will Smith's Secret to Success: Working Hard." http://www.People.com. December 3, 2007.


## Chapter 5

Colvin, Geoff. *Talent Is Overrated: What Really Separates World-Class Performers from Everybody Else.* New York: Portfolio, 2008.

Gladwell, Malcom. *Outliers.* New York: Little, Brown and Company, 2008.

Grudin, Robert. *The Grace of Great Things: Creativity and Innovation.* Mariner Bros., 1991.

Lincoln, Abraham. http://thinkexist.com.

Link, Henry. *The Rediscovery of Man.* MacMillon Co., 1939.

Roche, George Charles. *A World without Heroes.* Hillsdale College Press, 1989.

Smith, Will. "Secrets to Success." *YouTube.* Accessed June 8, 2009. http://youtube.com.

Stoltz, Paul G. *Adversity Quotient.* New York: John Wiley & Sons Inc., 1997.

### *Lou Holtz*

Holtz, Lou. *Wins, Losses, and Lessons.* New York: Harper Collins, 2006.


## Chapter 6

Anderson, Hans Christian. *The Emperor's New Clothes.*

1837.

Collins, Jim. *Good to Great.* New York: Harper Business, 2000.

Dell, Michael. *Direct from Dell.* New York: Warner Books, 1999.

Gates, Bill. *Business @ the Speed of Thought.* New York: Warner Books, 1999.

Holtz, Lou. *Wins, Losses, and Lessons.* New York: Harper Collins, 2006.

### Sam Walton

Walton, Sam and John Huey. *Sam Walton: Made in America.* New York: Double Day, 1992.


## Chapter 7

"Fable of the Pots." http://www.aesopsfables.org.

Hareyan, Armen. "American's Circle of Friends Sinking." *EMax Health.* June 23, 2006. http://www.emax-health.com.

"Isolation in America." Editorial. *Christianity Today.* November 14, 2006. http://www.christianitytoday.com.

Putnam, Robert D. *Bowling Alone: The Collapse and Revival of American Community.* New York: Simon & Schuster, 2000.

Smith, Fred. *You and Your Network.* Mechanicsburg, Pennsylvania: Executive Books, 1984.

### J. R. R. Tolkien and C. S. Lewis

Armstrong, Chris. "J.R.R. Tolkien and C.S. Lewis: A Legendary Friendship." *Christian History*. August 8, 2008. http://www.christianhistory.net.

Duriez, Colin. *Tolkien and C. S. Lewis: The Gift of Friendship*. New Jersey: Hidden Spring, 2003.

Gidsdorf, Ethan. "J.R.R. Tolkien and C.S. Lewis: A Literary Friendship and Rivalry." *Literary Traveler*. http://www.literarytraveler.com.

Tolkien, J. R. R. *The Return of the King: Being the Third Part of the Lord of the Rings*. Boston: Houghton Mifflin, 2001.


## Chapter 8

Marchex Sales Inc. *Money101.com—Money*. http://money101.com.

Word Press. *Own the Dollar: Don't Let the Dollar Own You*. 2012. http://ownthedollar.com.

### *Ben Franklin*

Franklin, Benjamin. *Benjamin Franklin's Autobiography*. New York: EP Dutton & Co., 1913.

Frasca, Ralph. *Benjamin Franklin's Printing Network: Disseminating Virtue in Early America*. Columbia: University of Missouri, 2006.


## Chapter 9

Brady, Christopher and Orrin Woodward. *Launching a Leadership Revolution: Mastering the Five Levels of Influence*. New York: Business Plus, 2005.

Collins, Jim. *Good to Great*. New York: Harper Business, 2001.

Covey, Steven R. *The 7 Habits of Highly Effective People.* New York: Free Press, 2004.

Emerson, Ralph Waldo. http://thinkexist.com.

Gerber, Michael E. *The E Myth Revisited*. New York: Harper Audio, 1995.

Johnson, Spencer. *Who Moved My Cheese?: An Amazing Way to Deal with Change in Your Work and in Your Life*. New York: Putnam, 1998.

Schein, Edgar and Bill Breen. *The Future of Management.* Boston: Harvard Business Press, 2007.

Walton, Sam and John Huey. *Sam Walton: Made in America*. New York: Double Day, 1992.

### Sam Walton

Tedlow, Richard S. *Giants of Enterprise: Seven Business Innovators and the Empires They Built*. New York: Harper-Business, 2001.

Walton, Sam and John Huey. *Sam Walton: Made in America*. New York: Double Day, 1992.

## Chapter 10

Covey, Steven R. *The 7 Habits of Highly Effective People.* New York: Free Press, 2004.

Lee, Gus and Diane Elliot-Lee. *Courage.* San Francisco: Jossey-Bass, 2006.

Patterson, Kerry, Joseph Grenny, and Al Switzler. *Crucial Conversations*. New York: McGraw-Hill, 2012.

### J.R.R. Tolkien and C. S. Lewis

Armstrong, Chris. "J.R.R. Tolkien and C.S. Lewis: A Legendary Friendship." *Christian History*. August 8, 2008. http://www.christianhistory.net.

Duriez, Colin. *Tolkien and C. S. Lewis: The Gift of Friendship*. New Jersey: Hidden Spring, 2003.

Gidsdorf, Ethan. "J.R.R. Tolkien and C.S. Lewis: A Literary Friendship and Rivalry." *Literary Traveler*. http://wwww.literarytraveler.com.

Tolkien, J. R. R. *The Return of the King: Being the Third Part of the Lord of the Rings*. Boston: Houghton Mifflin, 2001.


## Chapter 11

"Chaos Theory." *Crystalinks Home Page*. http://www.crystalinks.com/chaos.html.

Gabriel, Linda. "The Power of Trim Tabs—How Small Changes Create Big Results." *Thought Medicine*. July 2010. http://www.thoughtmedicine.com.

Gerber, Michael E. *The E Myth*. Cambridge, Massachusetts: Ballinger Publishing Company, 1986.

Meadows, Donella H. and Diana Wright. *Thinking in Systems: A Primer*. White River Junction VT: Chelsea Green Pub., 2008. Print.

Senge, Peter. *The Fifth Discipline*. New York: Doubleday Currency, 1990.

### *Ray Kroc*

Einstein, Albert. http://thinkexist.com.

Kroc, Ray and Robert Anderson. *Grinding It Out: The Making of McDonald's*. New York: St. Martin's Press, 1977.

Love, John F. *McDonald's: Behind the Arches*. New York: Bantam, 1995.

Tedlow, Richard S. *Giants of Enterprise*. New York: Harper Collins, 2001.


**Chapter 12**

Bradberry, Travis and Jean Greaves. *The Emotional Intelligence Quickbook: Everything You Need to Know*. San Diego CA: Talentsmart, 2003.

Brady, Chris. *Rascal: Making a Difference by Becoming an Original Character.* Flint, Michigan: Obstaclés Press, Inc., 2010.

Grudin, Robert. *Grace of Great Things: Creativity and Innovation*. Mariner Bros., 1991.

Locke, John. http://thinkexist.com.

Robbins, Tony. *Notes from a Friend*. Fireside, 1995.

*Billy Durant*

Gustin, Lawrence R. *Billy Durant: Creator of General Motors*. Ann Arbor: University of Michigan, 2008.

Madsen, Axel. *The Deal Maker: How William C. Durant Made General Motors*. Wiley, 2001.

Weisenberger, Bernard. *Dream Maker: William Durant Founder of General Motors*. Little, Brown and Co., 1979.


**Chapter 13**

Bastiat, Frédéric. *The Law*. Irvington-on-Hudson, NY: Foundation for Economic Education, 1950.

Lewis, C. S. *The Abolition of Man*. New York: Macmillan, 1947.

Hazlitt, Henry. *Economics in One Lesson*. New York: Arlington House, 1979.

Nock, Albert Jay. *Memoirs of a Superfluous Man*. Chicago: Regnery, 1964.

Nock, Albert Jay. *Our Enemy, the State: Albert Jay Nock's Classic Critique Distinguishing "Government" from "the State."* Delavan WI: Hallberg Pub., 1983.

McElroy, Wendy. "Nock on Education." http://www.wendymcelroy. com.

Schaffer, Francis. *How Should We Then Live?* Wheaton IL: Crossway Books, 2005.

Spengler, Oswald, Helmut Werner, Arthur Helps, and Charles Francis Atkinson. *The Decline of the West*. New York: Vintage, 2006.

"Sturgeon's Law." http://www.tvtropes.org.

Toynbee, Arnold and D. C. Somervell. *A Study of History*. New York: Oxford UP, 1947.

Yeats, W. B. "Second Coming." 1920.

### Colonial New England Fiat Money

Rothbard, Murray Newton. *A History of Money and Banking in the United States: The Colonial Era to World War II*. Auburn AL: Ludwig von Mises Institute, 2002

Shafer, Susan and Emma Lazarus. *Emma Lazarus's The New Colossus: A Play Adaptation*. Pelham, NY: Benchmark Education, 2007.

# LIFE
## SUBSCRIPTIONS

# LIFE SERIES

Our lives are lived out in the eight categories of Faith, Family, Finances, Fitness, Following, Freedom, Friendship, and Fun. The LIFE series of 4 monthly CDs and a book is specifically designed to bring you life transforming information in each of these categories. Whether you are interested in one or two of these areas, or all eight, you will be delighted with timeless truths and effective strategies for living a life of excellence, brought to you in an entertaining, intelligent, well informed, and insightful manner. It has been said that it may be your life, but it's not yours to waste. Subscribe to the LIFE series today and learn how to make yours count!

**The LIFE series** – dedicated to helping people grow in each of the 8 F categories - Faith, Family, Finances, Fitness, Following, Freedom, Friendship, and Fun. 4 CDs and a book shipped each month.
$50.00 plus S&H     Pricing valid for both USD and CAD

# LLR SERIES

Everyone will be called upon to lead at some point in his or her life, and often, at many points. The issue is whether or not people will be ready when called. The LLR series is based upon the *NY Times, Wall Street Journal, USA Today,* and *Money Magazine* best seller *Launching a Leadership Revolution*, written by Chris Brady and Orrin Woodward, in which leadership is taught in a way that applies to everyone. Whether you are seeking corporate or business advancement, community influence, church impact, or better stewardship and effectiveness in your home, the principles and specifics taught in the LLR series will equip you with what you need.

The subscriber will receive 4 CDs and a leadership book each month. Topics covered will include finances, leadership, public speaking, attitude, goal setting, mentoring, game planning, accountability and tracking of progress, levels of motivation, levels of influence, and leaving a personal legacy.

Subscribe to the LLR series and begin applying these LIFE transforming truths to your life today!

**The LLR (Launching a Leadership Revolution) series** – dedicated to helping people grow in their leadership ability. 4 CDs and a book shipped each month. $50.00 plus S&H    Pricing valid for both USD and CAD

## Don't Miss Out on the 3 for FREE Program!

As a customer or Member subscribes to any one or more of the packages, that person is given the further incentive to attract other customers who subscribe as well. Once that customer or Member signs up three or more customers on equivalent or greater dollar value subscriptions, the customer or Member will get his or her next month's subscription FREE!

# AGO SERIES

Whether you have walked with Christ your entire life or just begun the journey, we welcome you to experience the love, joy, understanding and purpose that only Christ can offer. This series is designed to touch and nourish the hearts of all faith levels as our top speakers, along with special guest speakers, help you enhance your understanding of God's plan for your life, your marriage, your children, and your character, while gaining valuable support and guidance needed by all Christians. Nurture your soul, strengthen your faith, and find answers on the go or quietly at home with the AGO series.

**The AGO (All Grace Outreach) series** – dedicated to helping people grow spiritually. 1 CD and a book shipped each month.
$25.00 plus S&H
Pricing valid for both USD and CAD

# EDGE SERIES

Designed especially for those on the younger side of life, it is a hard-core, no frills approach to learning the things that will make for a successful life.

Eliminate the noise around you about who you are and who you should become. Instead, figure it out for yourself in a mighty way with life-changing information from people who would do just about anything to have learned these truths much, much sooner in life! It may have taken them a lifetime to discover these truths, but what they learned can be yours now on a monthly basis.

**Edge series** – dedicated to helping young people grow.
1 CD shipped each month.
$10.00 plus S&H
Pricing valid for both USD and CAD